SABAN'S

MIGHTY MORPHIN POWER RANGERS™

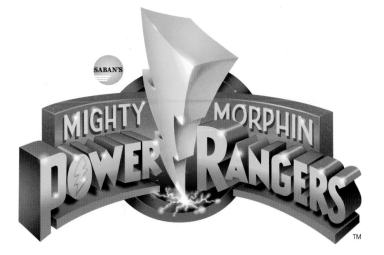

HIGGINS • PRASETYA • BAYLISS • DI NICUOLO
HERMS • LAFUENTE • BAIAMONTE
FERRIER • BACHAN • FARRELL

VOLUME FIVE

BOOM! STUDIOS

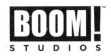

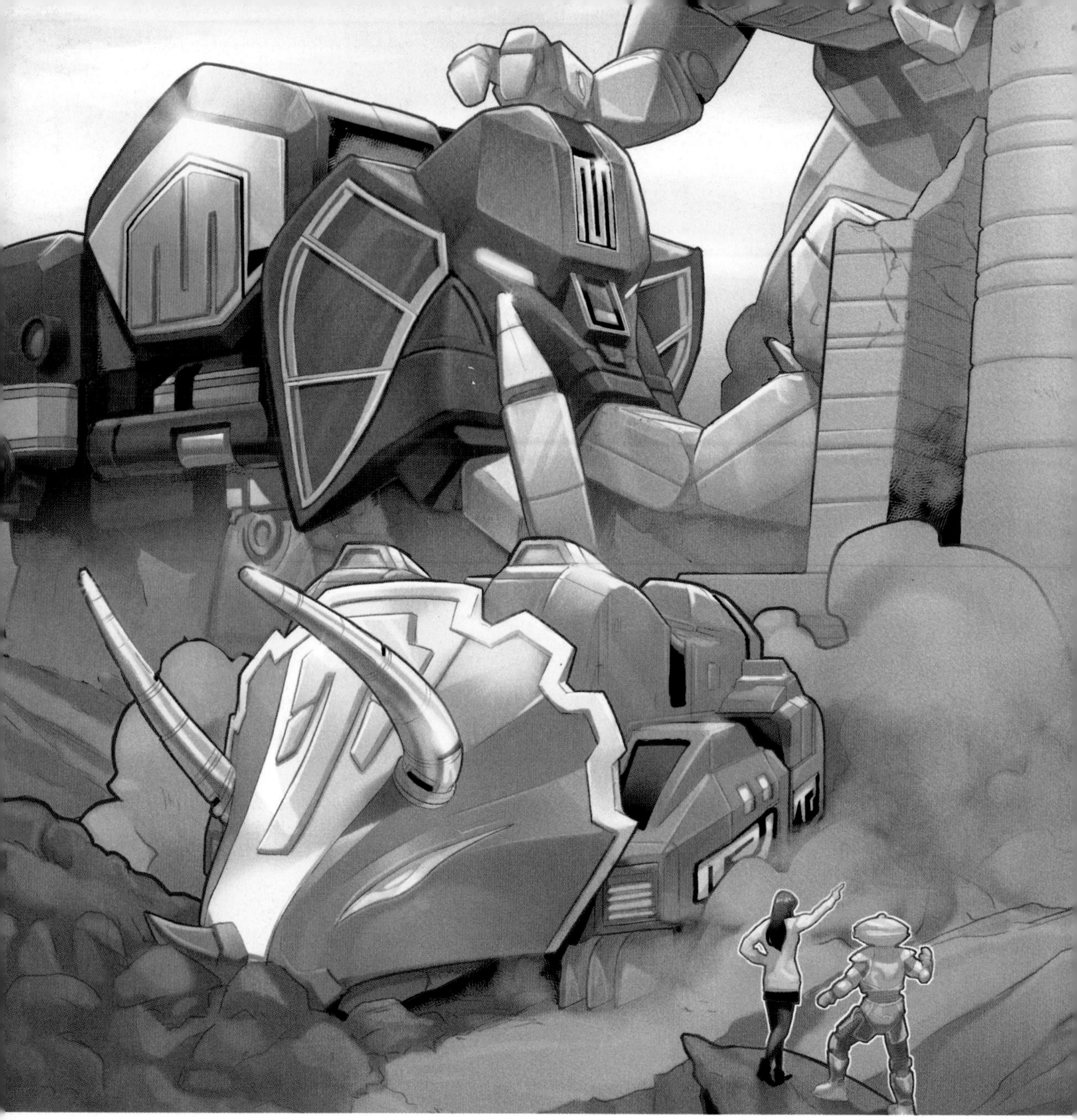

SPECIAL THANKS TO
BRIAN CASENTINI, MELISSA FLORES, EDGAR PASTEN, PAUL STRICKLAND, JASON BISCHOFF AND EVERYONE AT **SABAN BRANDS**.

Ross Richie CEO & Founder
Matt Gagnon Editor-In-Chief
Filip Sablik President of Publishing & Marketing
Stephen Christy President of Development
Lance Kreiter VP of Licensing & Merchandising
Phil Barbaro VP of Finance
Arune Singh VP of Marketing
Bryce Carlson Managing Editor
Scott Newman Production Design Manager
Kate Henning Operations Manager
Sierra Hahn Senior Editor
Dafna Pleban Editor, Talent Development
Shannon Watters Editor
Eric Harburn Editor
Whitney Leopard Editor
Cameron Chittock Editor
Chris Rosa Associate Editor
Matthew Levine Associate Editor
Sophie Philips-Roberts Assistant Editor
Amanda LaFranco Executive Assistant
Katalina Holland Editorial Administrative Assistant
Jillian Crab Production Designer
Michelle Ankley Production Designer
Kara Leopard Production Designer
Marie Krupina Production Designer
Grace Park Production Design Assistant
Chelsea Roberts Production Design Assistant
Elizabeth Loughridge Accounting Coordinator
Stephanie Hocutt Social Media Coordinator
José Meza Event Coordinator
Holly Aitchison Operations Coordinator
Megan Christopher Operations Assistant
Rodrigo Hernandez Mailroom Assistant
Morgan Perry Direct Market Representative
Cat O'Grady Marketing Assistant
Liz Almendarez Accounting Administrative Assistant
Cornelia Tzana Administrative Assistant

MIGHTY MORPHIN POWER RANGERS Volume Five, April 2018. Published by BOOM! Studios, a division of Boom Entertainment, Inc.

For information regarding the CPSIA on this printed material, call: (203) 595-3636 and provide reference #RICH – 779493.

BOOM! Studios, 5670 Wilshire Boulevard, Suite 400, Los Angeles, CA 90036-5679. Printed in USA. First Printing.

ISBN: 978-1-68415-137-0, eISBN: 978-1-61398-876-3

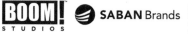

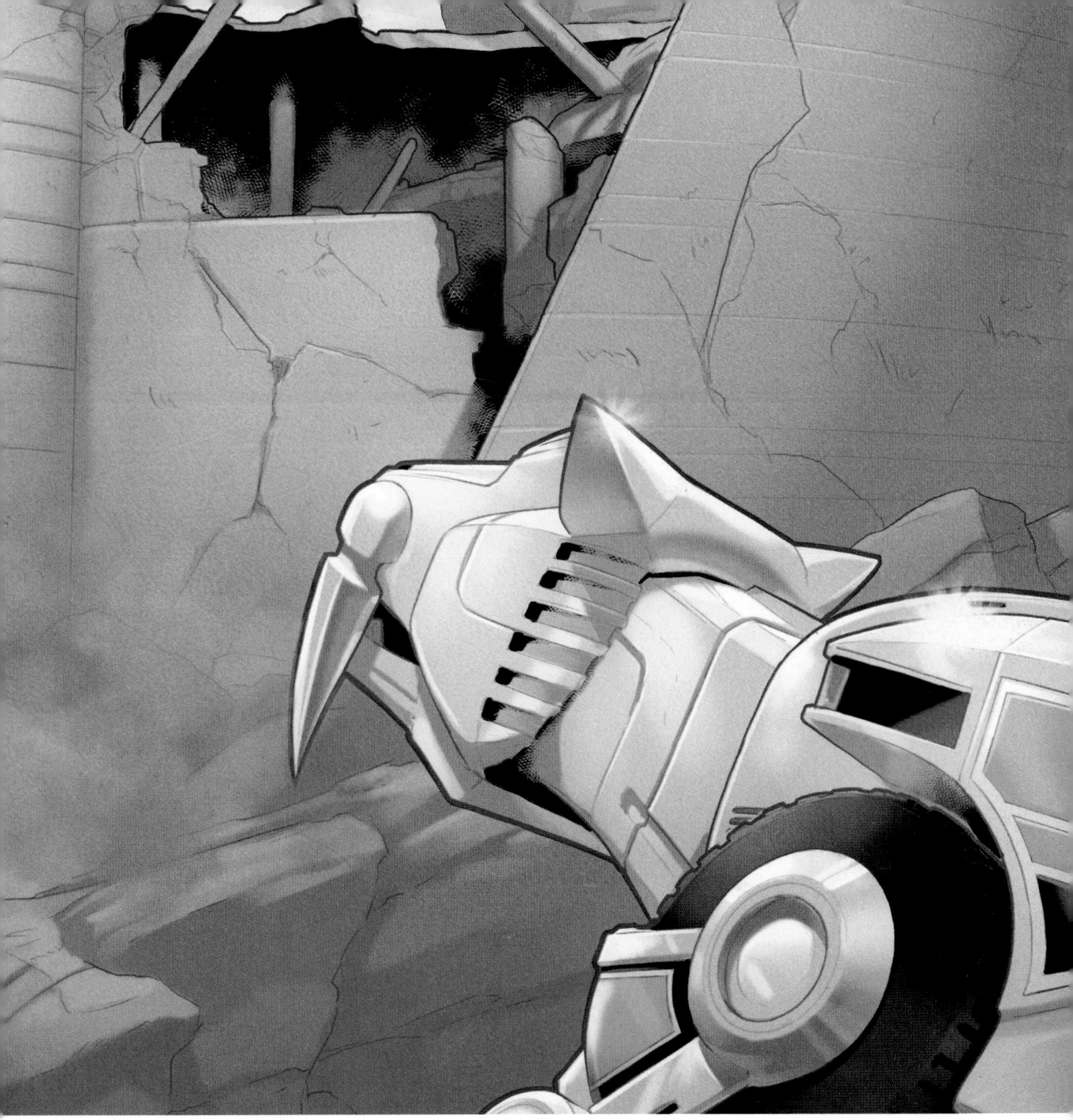

WRITTEN BY
KYLE HIGGINS

ILLUSTRATED BY
HENDRY PRASETYA CHAPTERS 17-19
WITH ASSISTANCE BY **DANIEL BAYLISS**
DANIELE DI NICUOLO CHAPTER 20

COLORS BY
MATT HERMS CHAPTERS 17-19
WITH ASSISTANCE BY **SIGI IRONMONGER**
JOANA LAFUENTE CHAPTERS 18-19
WALTER BAIAMONTE CHAPTER 20

LETTERS BY
ED DUKESHIRE

COVER BY
JAMAL CAMPBELL

DESIGNER
JILLIAN CRAB

ASSISTANT EDITOR
MICHAEL MOCCIO

ASSOCIATE EDITORS
ALEX GALER
MATTHEW LEVINE

EDITOR
DAFNA PLEBAN

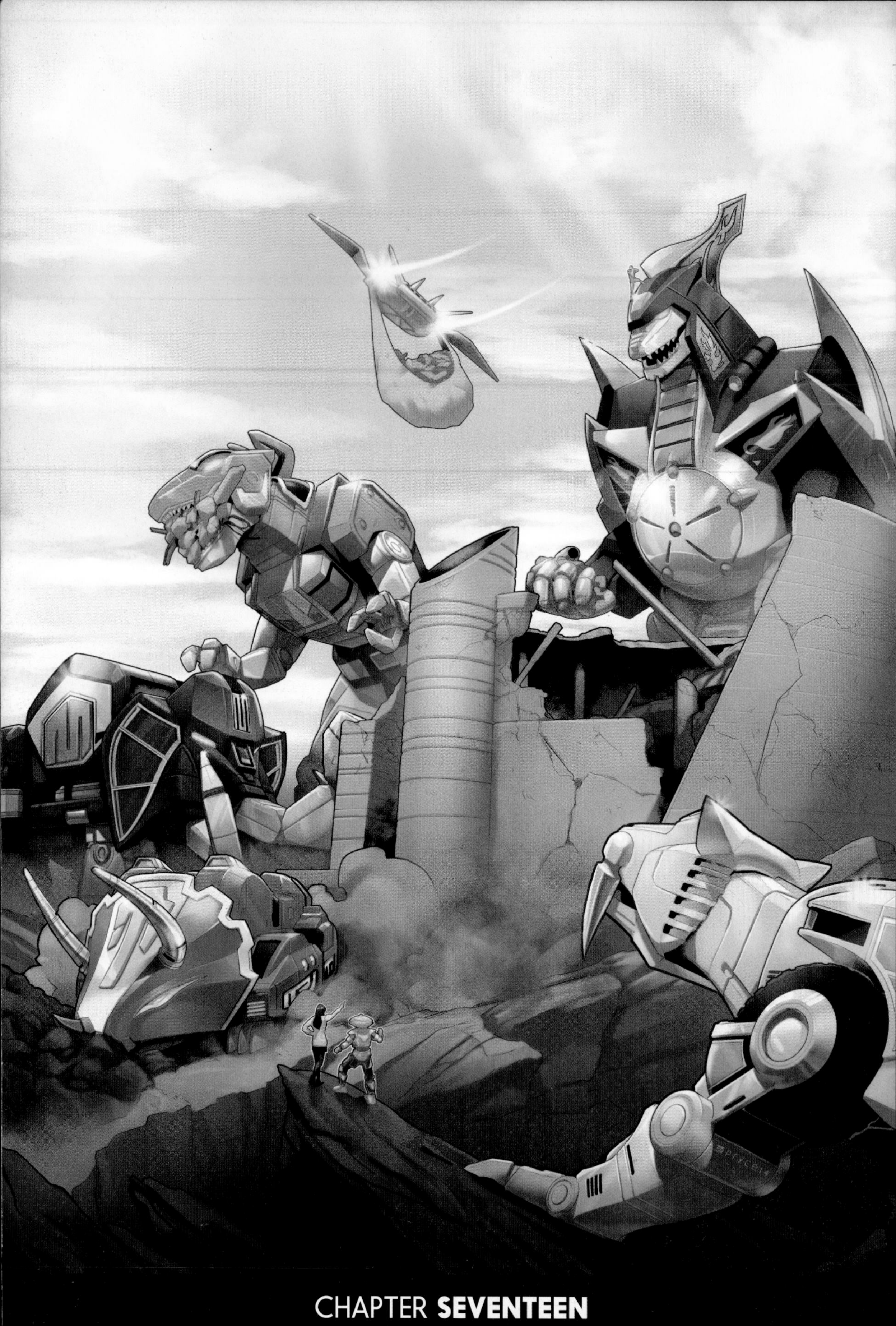

CHAPTER **SEVENTEEN**

JAMAL CAMPBELL | ISSUE SEVENTEEN COVER

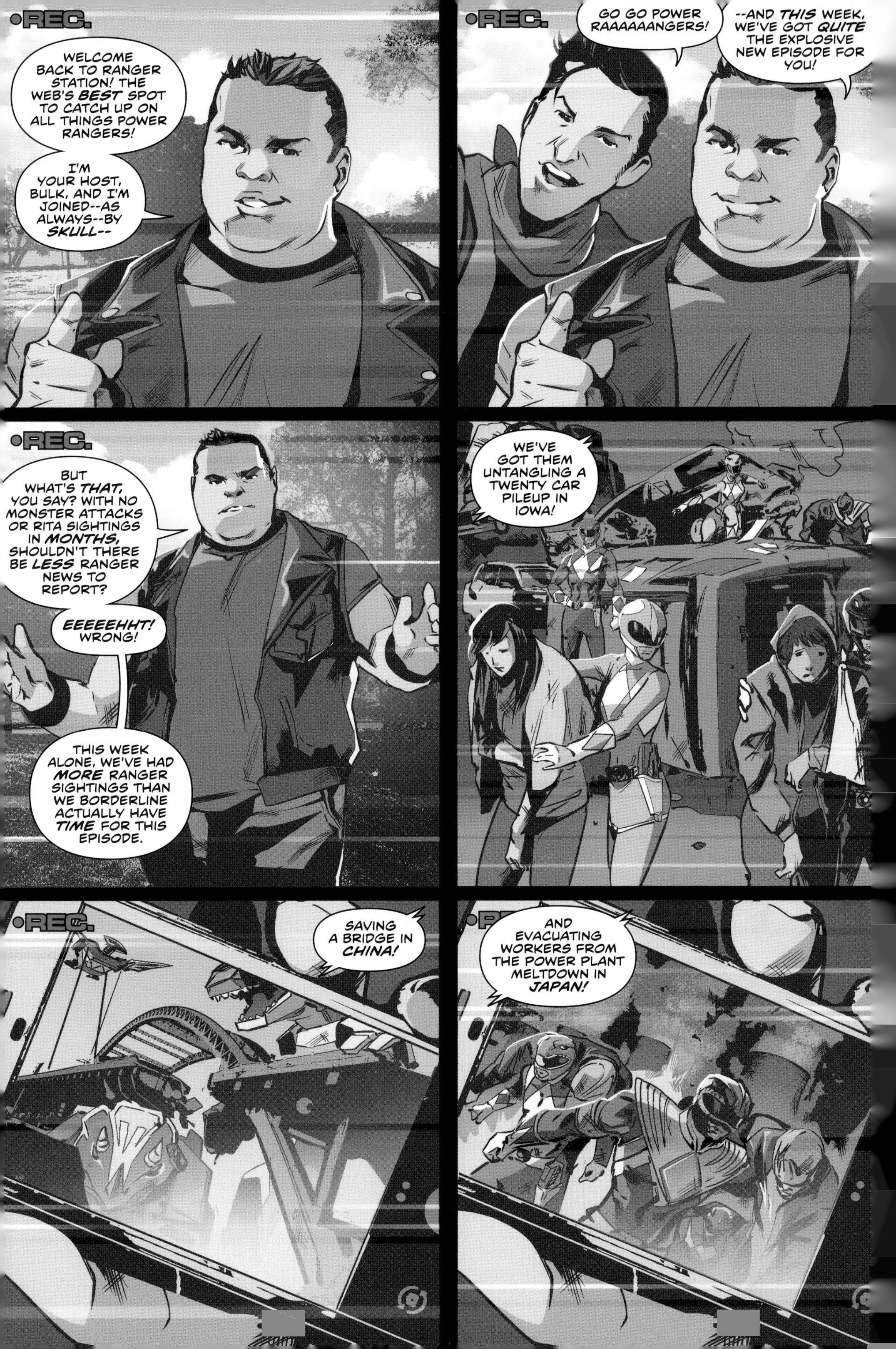
•REC.
WELCOME BACK TO RANGER STATION! THE WEB'S BEST SPOT TO CATCH UP ON ALL THINGS POWER RANGERS!
I'M YOUR HOST, BULK, AND I'M JOINED--AS ALWAYS--BY SKULL--
•REC.
GO GO POWER RAAAAAAANGERS!
--AND THIS WEEK, WE'VE GOT QUITE THE EXPLOSIVE NEW EPISODE FOR YOU!
•REC.
BUT WHAT'S THAT, YOU SAY? WITH NO MONSTER ATTACKS OR RITA SIGHTINGS IN MONTHS, SHOULDN'T THERE BE LESS RANGER NEWS TO REPORT?
EEEEEHHT! WRONG!
THIS WEEK ALONE, WE'VE HAD MORE RANGER SIGHTINGS THAN WE BORDERLINE ACTUALLY HAVE TIME FOR THIS EPISODE.
WE'VE GOT THEM UNTANGLING A TWENTY CAR PILEUP IN IOWA!
•REC.
SAVING A BRIDGE IN CHINA!
AND EVACUATING WORKERS FROM THE POWER PLANT MELTDOWN IN JAPAN!

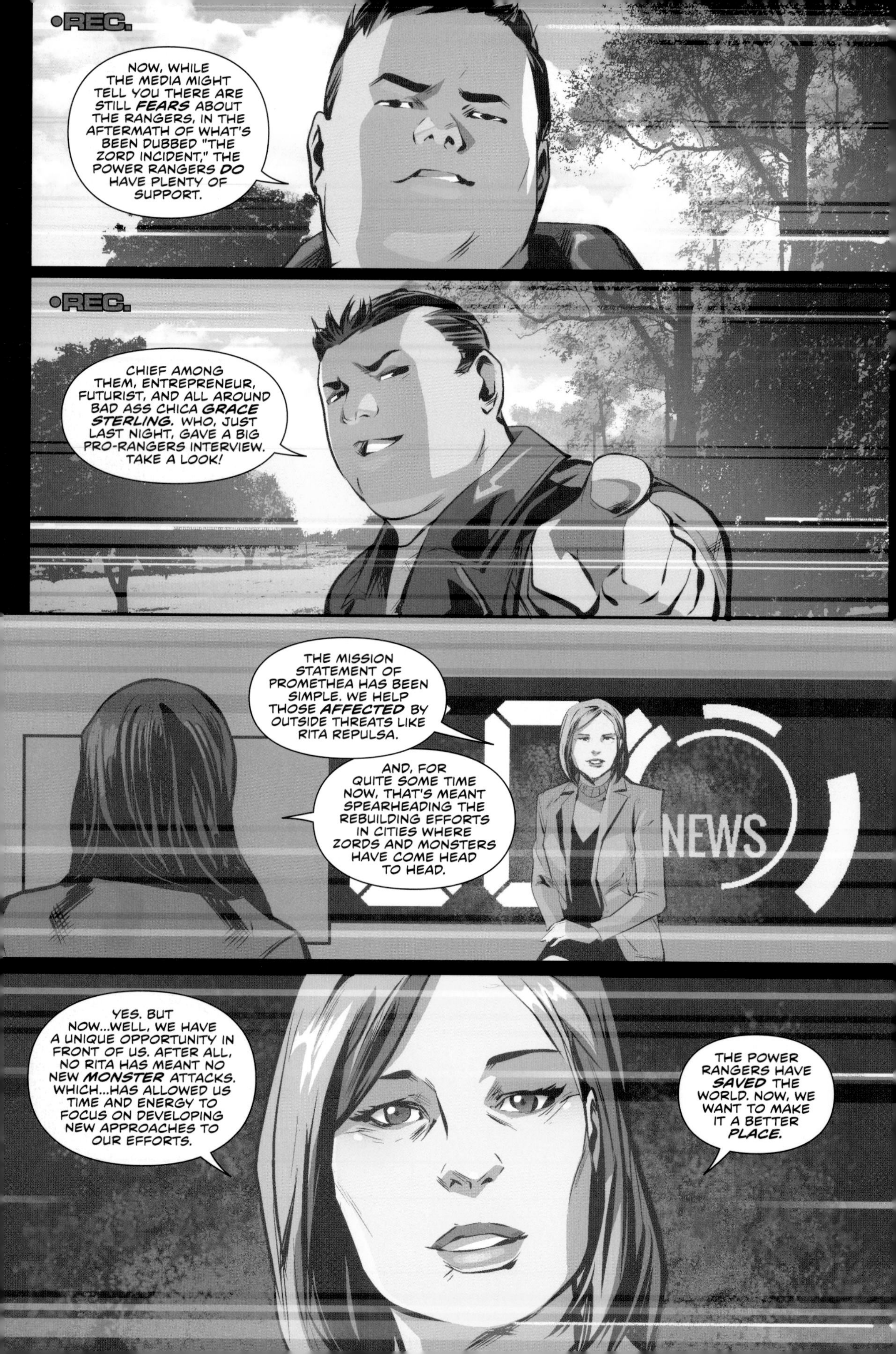

REC.
NOW, WHILE THE MEDIA MIGHT TELL YOU THERE ARE STILL FEARS ABOUT THE RANGERS, IN THE AFTERMATH OF WHAT'S BEEN DUBBED "THE ZORD INCIDENT," THE POWER RANGERS DO HAVE PLENTY OF SUPPORT.
REC.
CHIEF AMONG THEM, ENTREPRENEUR, FUTURIST, AND ALL AROUND BAD ASS CHICA GRACE STERLING. WHO, JUST LAST NIGHT, GAVE A BIG PRO-RANGERS INTERVIEW. TAKE A LOOK!
THE MISSION STATEMENT OF PROMETHEA HAS BEEN SIMPLE. WE HELP THOSE AFFECTED BY OUTSIDE THREATS LIKE RITA REPULSA.
AND, FOR QUITE SOME TIME NOW, THAT'S MEANT SPEARHEADING THE REBUILDING EFFORTS IN CITIES WHERE ZORDS AND MONSTERS HAVE COME HEAD TO HEAD.
NEWS
YES. BUT NOW...WELL, WE HAVE A UNIQUE OPPORTUNITY IN FRONT OF US. AFTER ALL, NO RITA HAS MEANT NO NEW MONSTER ATTACKS. WHICH...HAS ALLOWED US TIME AND ENERGY TO FOCUS ON DEVELOPING NEW APPROACHES TO OUR EFFORTS.
THE POWER RANGERS HAVE SAVED THE WORLD. NOW, WE WANT TO MAKE IT A BETTER PLACE.

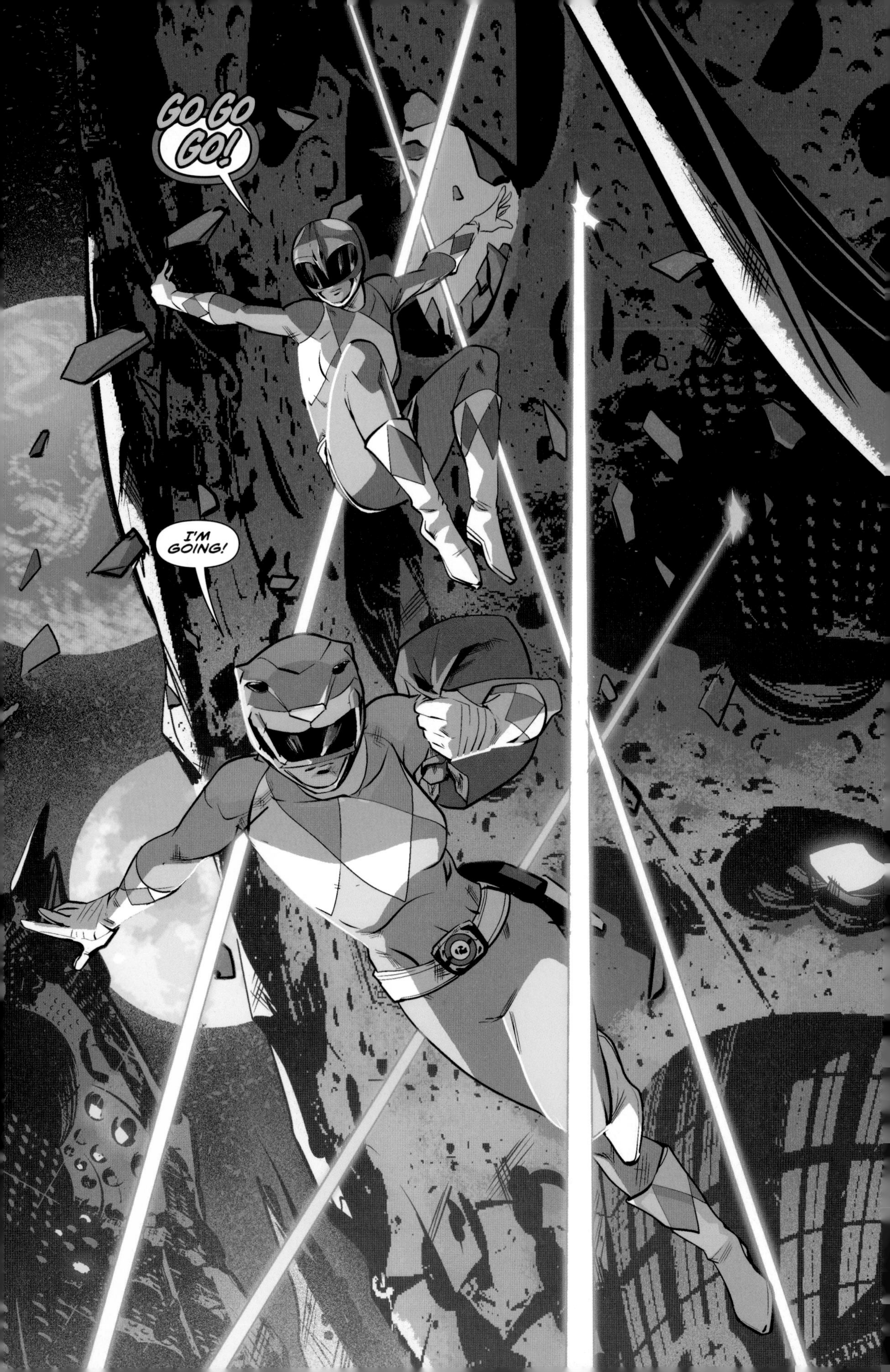
GO GO GO!
I'M GOING!

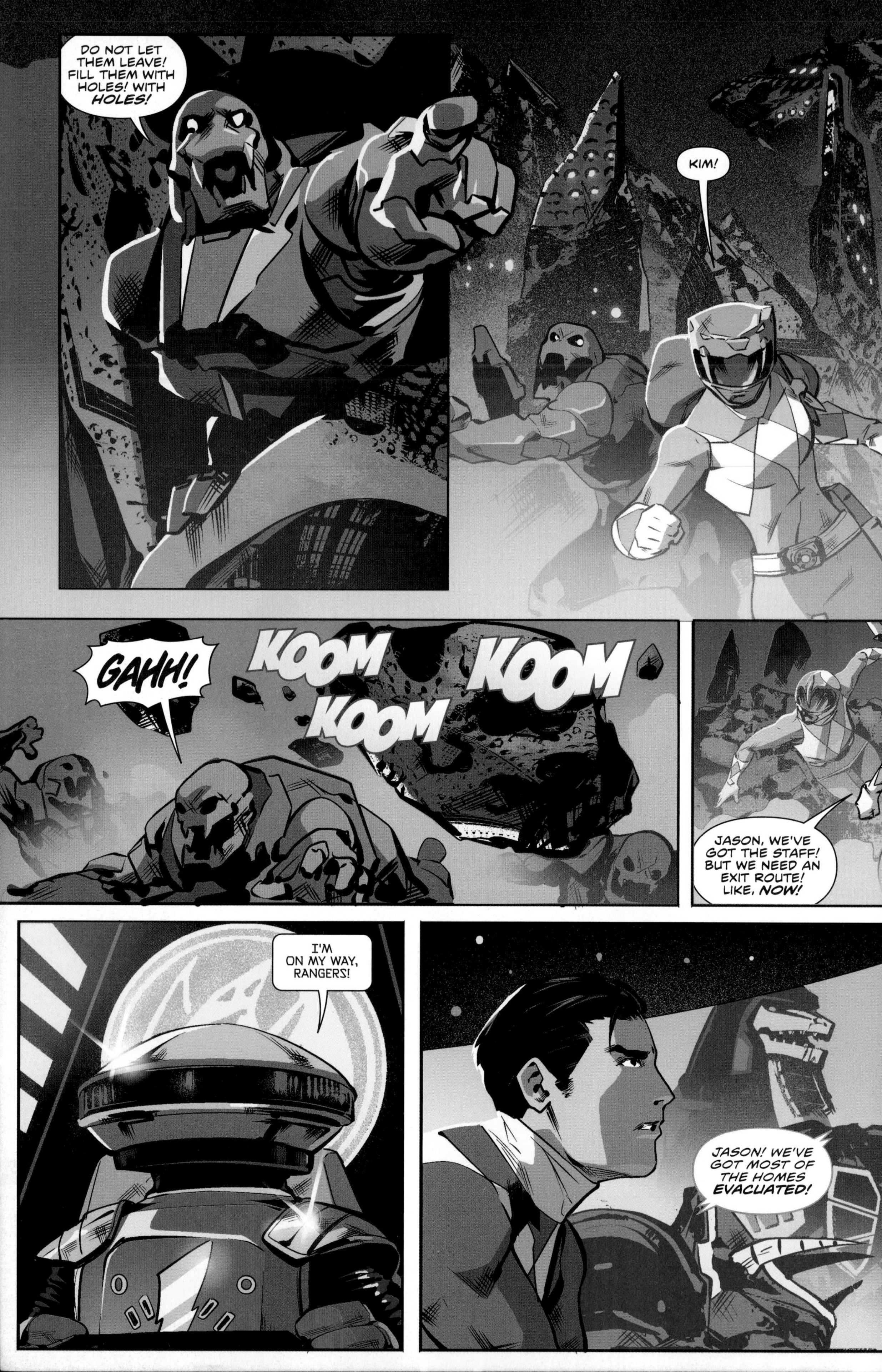
DO NOT LET THEM LEAVE! FILL THEM WITH HOLES! WITH HOLES!
KIM!
GAHH!
KOOM
KOOM
KOOM
JASON, WE'VE GOT THE STAFF! BUT WE NEED AN EXIT ROUTE! LIKE, NOW!
I'M ON MY WAY, RANGERS!
JASON! WE'VE GOT MOST OF THE HOMES EVACUATED!

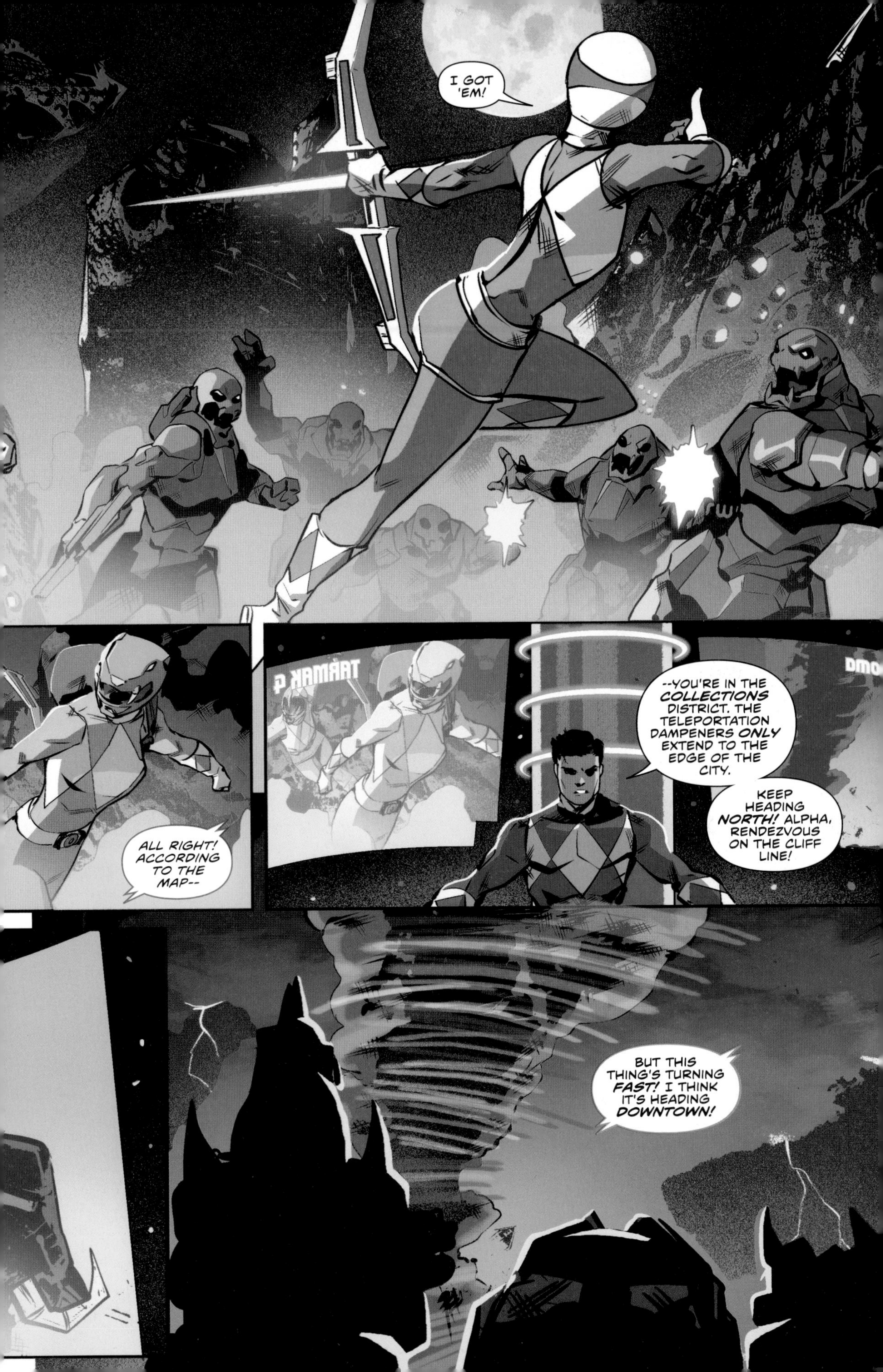
I GOT 'EM!
ALL RIGHT! ACCORDING TO THE MAP--
--YOU'RE IN THE COLLECTIONS DISTRICT. THE TELEPORTATION DAMPENERS ONLY EXTEND TO THE EDGE OF THE CITY.
KEEP HEADING NORTH! ALPHA, RENDEZVOUS ON THE CLIFF LINE!
BUT THIS THING'S TURNING FAST! I THINK IT'S HEADING DOWNTOWN!

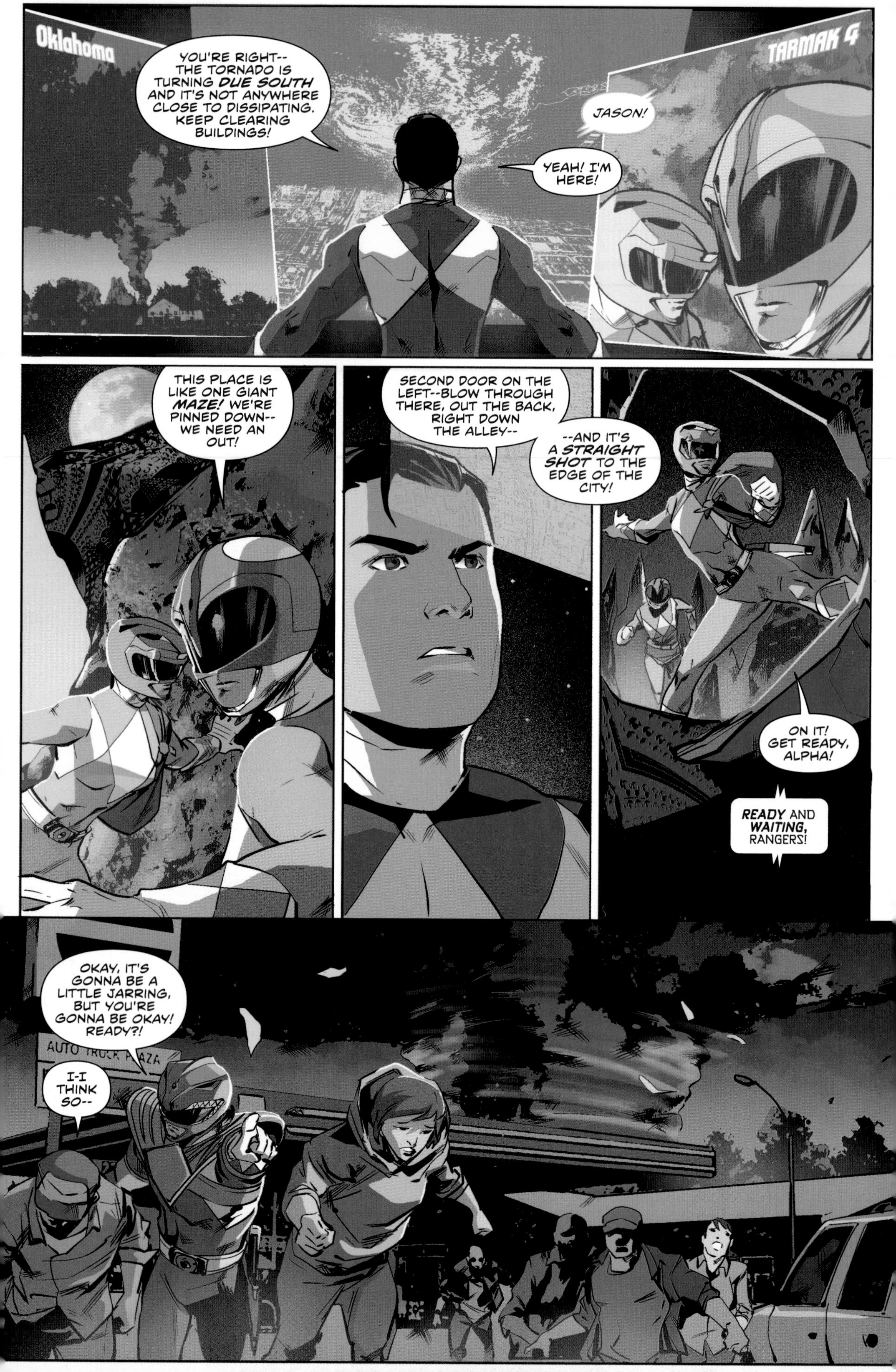
Oklahoma
TARMAK 4
YOU'RE RIGHT-- THE TORNADO IS TURNING DUE SOUTH AND IT'S NOT ANYWHERE CLOSE TO DISSIPATING. KEEP CLEARING BUILDINGS!
JASON!
YEAH! I'M HERE!
THIS PLACE IS LIKE ONE GIANT MAZE! WE'RE PINNED DOWN-- WE NEED AN OUT!
SECOND DOOR ON THE LEFT--BLOW THROUGH THERE, OUT THE BACK, RIGHT DOWN THE ALLEY--
--AND IT'S A STRAIGHT SHOT TO THE EDGE OF THE CITY!
ON IT! GET READY, ALPHA!
READY AND WAITING, RANGERS!
OKAY, IT'S GONNA BE A LITTLE JARRING, BUT YOU'RE GONNA BE OKAY! READY?!
I-I THINK SO--

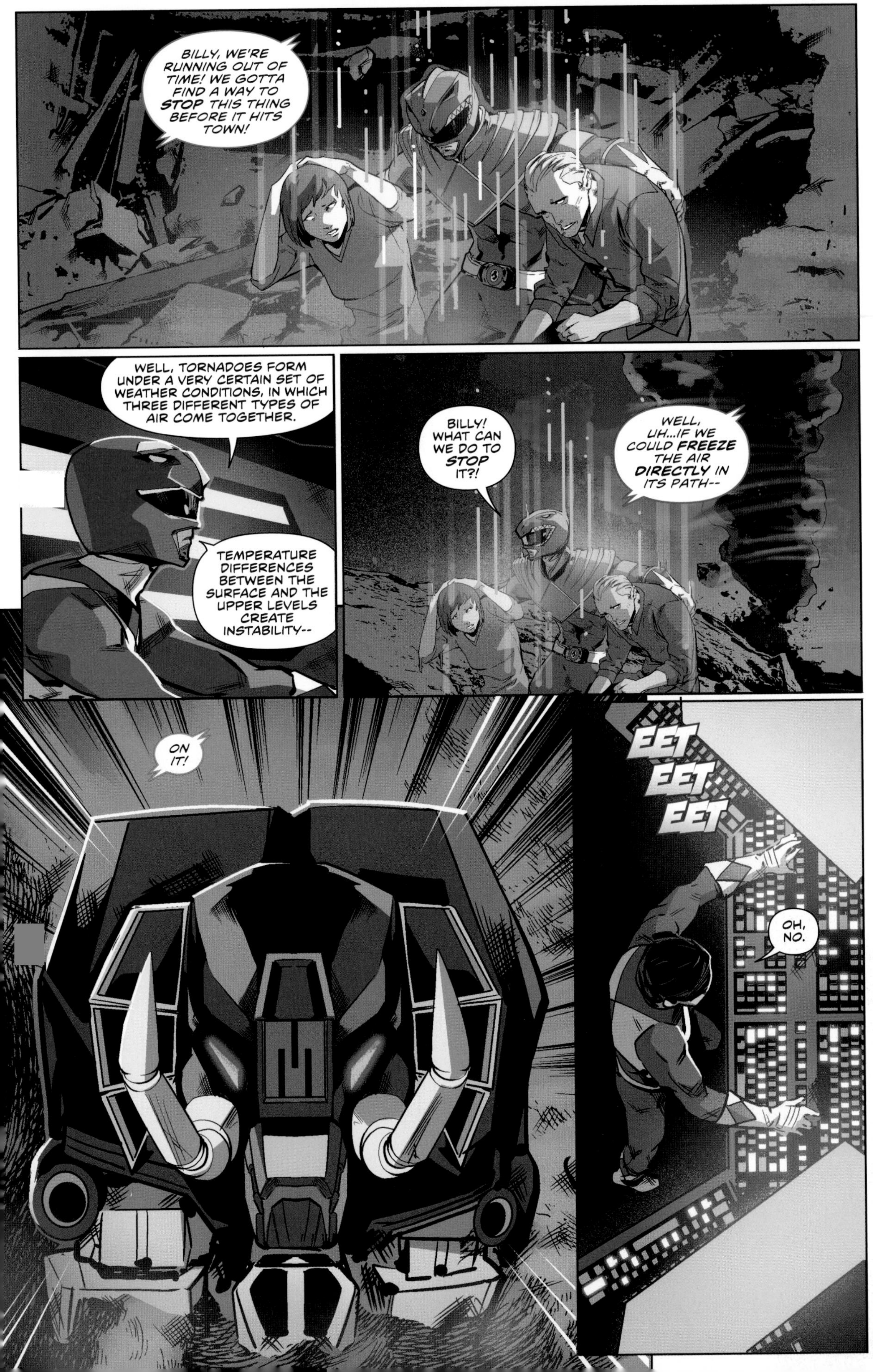
BILLY, WE'RE RUNNING OUT OF TIME! WE GOTTA FIND A WAY TO STOP THIS THING BEFORE IT HITS TOWN!
WELL, TORNADOES FORM UNDER A VERY CERTAIN SET OF WEATHER CONDITIONS, IN WHICH THREE DIFFERENT TYPES OF AIR COME TOGETHER.
TEMPERATURE DIFFERENCES BETWEEN THE SURFACE AND THE UPPER LEVELS CREATE INSTABILITY--
BILLY! WHAT CAN WE DO TO STOP IT?!
WELL, UH...IF WE COULD FREEZE THE AIR DIRECTLY IN ITS PATH--
ON IT!
EET EET EET
OH, NO.

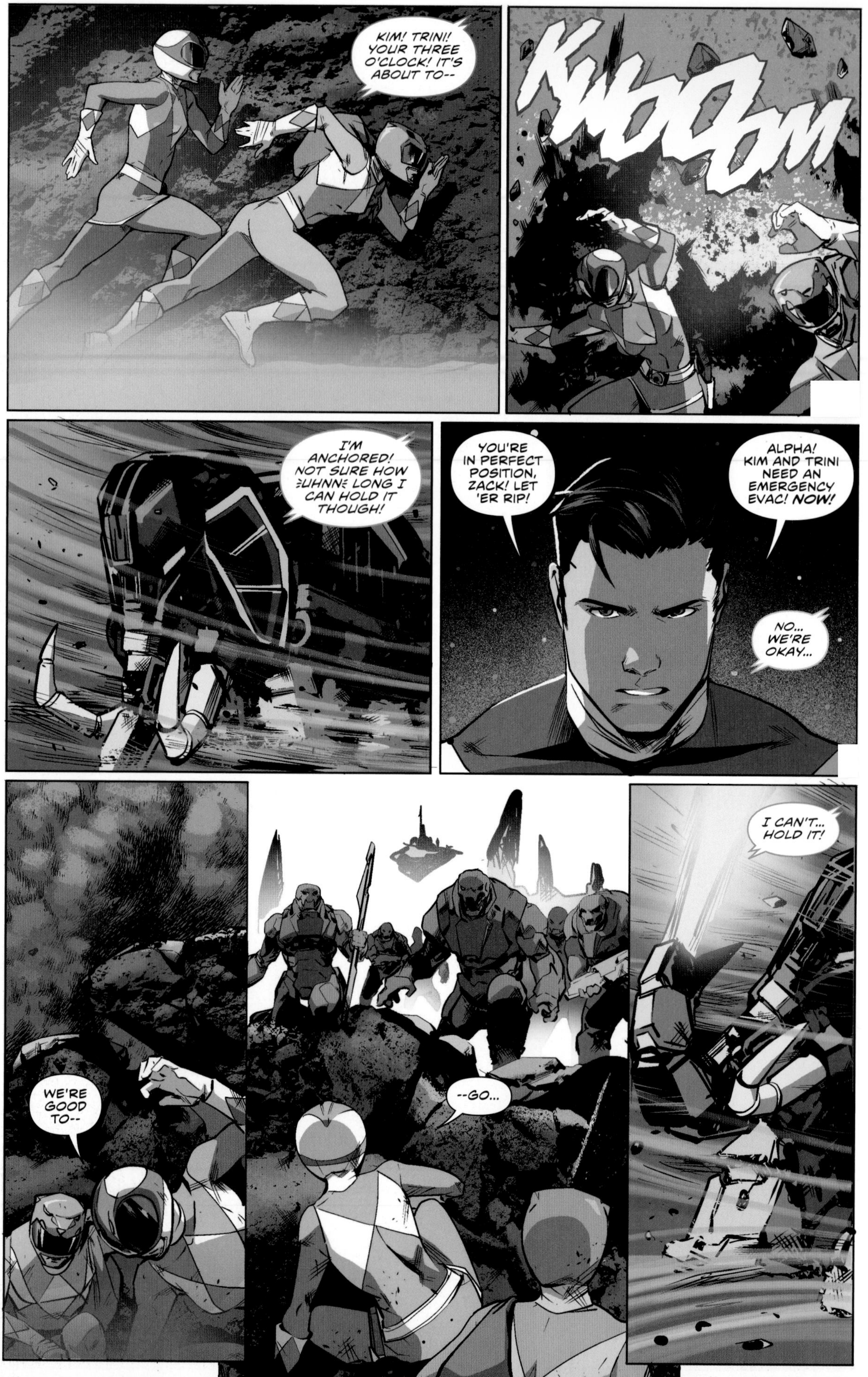
KIM! TRINI! YOUR THREE O'CLOCK! IT'S ABOUT TO--
KWOOOM
I'M ANCHORED! NOT SURE HOW ≥UHNN≤ LONG I CAN HOLD IT THOUGH!
YOU'RE IN PERFECT POSITION, ZACK! LET 'ER RIP!
ALPHA! KIM AND TRINI NEED AN EMERGENCY EVAC! **NOW!**
NO... WE'RE OKAY...
WE'RE GOOD TO--
--GO...
I CAN'T... HOLD IT!

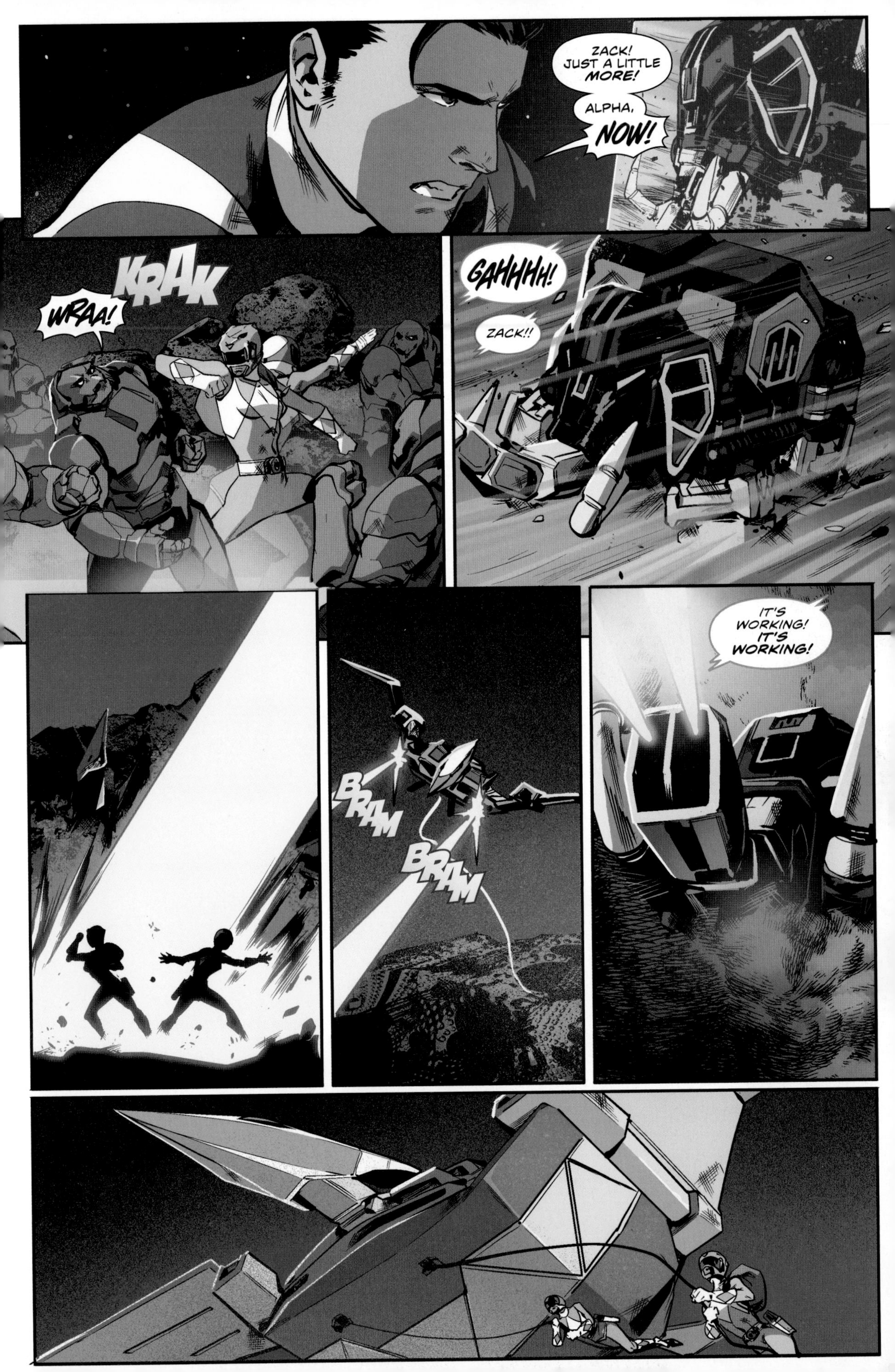
ZACK! JUST A LITTLE MORE!
ALPHA, NOW!
KRAK
WRAA!
GAHHHH!
ZACK!!
BRAM
BRAM
IT'S WORKING! IT'S WORKING!

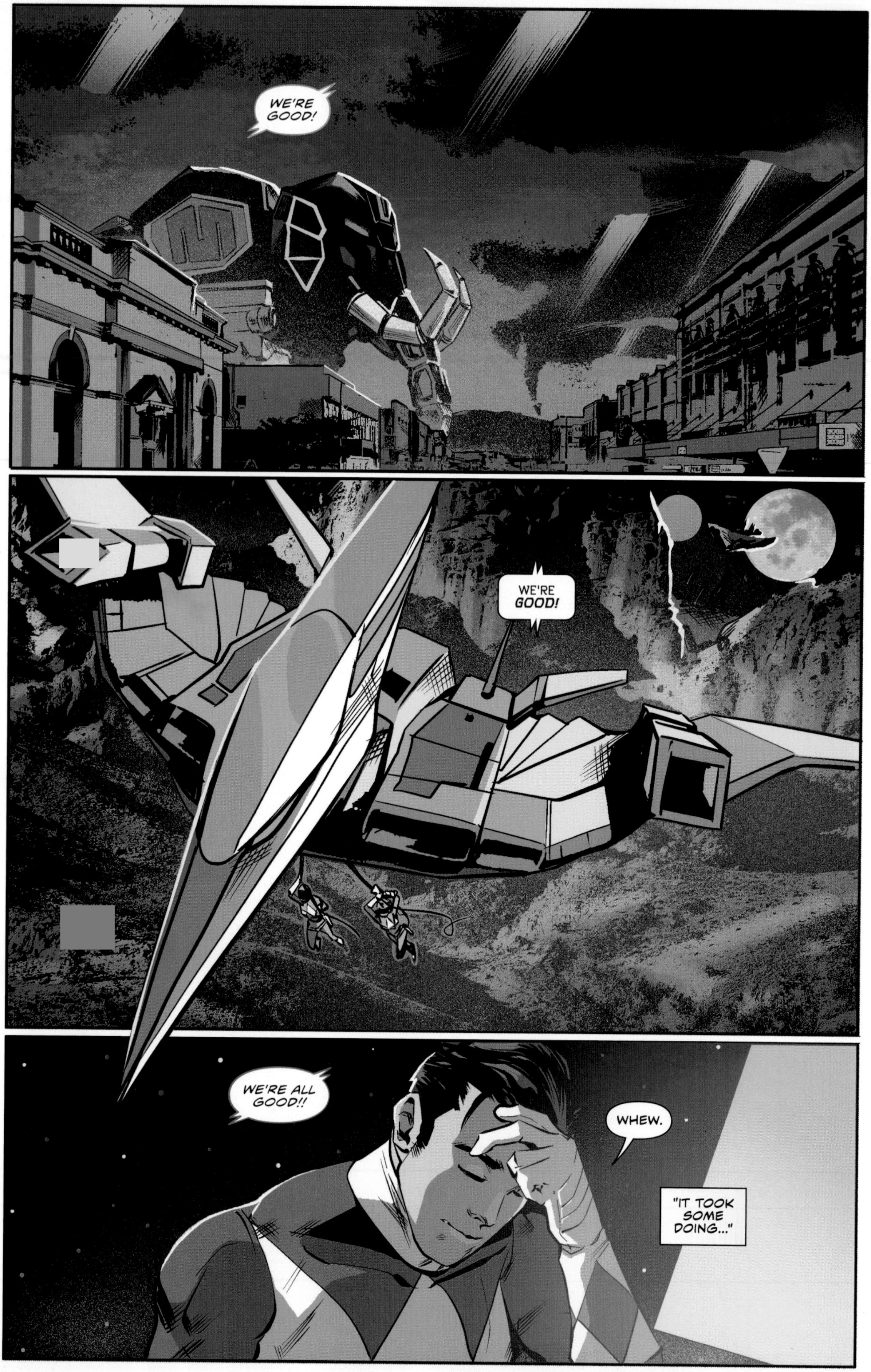
WE'RE GOOD!
WE'RE GOOD!
WE'RE ALL GOOD!!
WHEW.
"IT TOOK SOME DOING..."

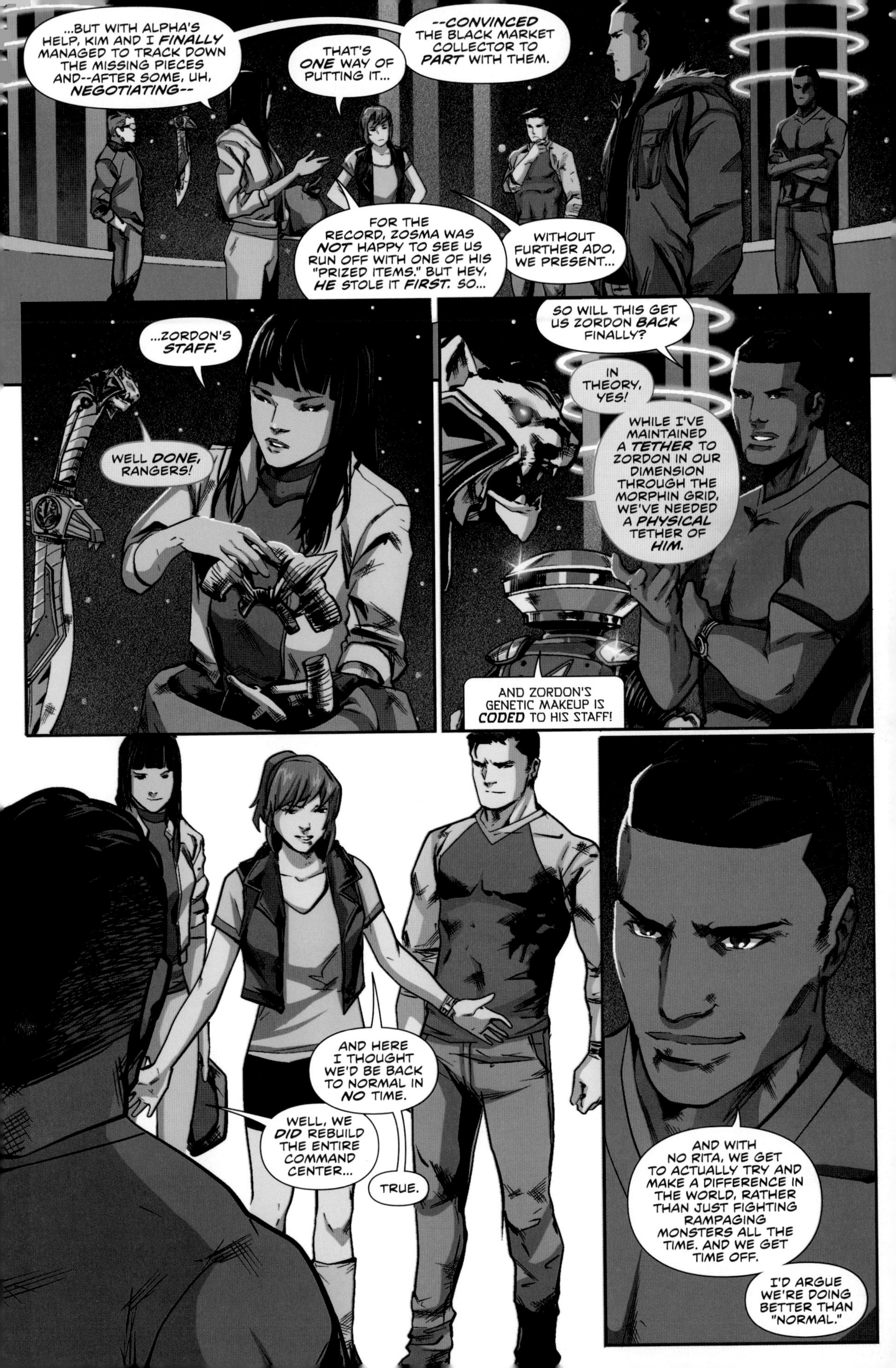

...BUT WITH ALPHA'S HELP, KIM AND I FINALLY MANAGED TO TRACK DOWN THE MISSING PIECES AND--AFTER SOME, UH, NEGOTIATING--
THAT'S ONE WAY OF PUTTING IT...
--CONVINCED THE BLACK MARKET COLLECTOR TO PART WITH THEM.
FOR THE RECORD, ZOSMA WAS NOT HAPPY TO SEE US RUN OFF WITH ONE OF HIS "PRIZED ITEMS." BUT HEY, HE STOLE IT FIRST. SO...
WITHOUT FURTHER ADO, WE PRESENT...
...ZORDON'S STAFF.
WELL DONE, RANGERS!
SO WILL THIS GET US ZORDON BACK FINALLY?
IN THEORY, YES!
WHILE I'VE MAINTAINED A TETHER TO ZORDON IN OUR DIMENSION THROUGH THE MORPHIN GRID, WE'VE NEEDED A PHYSICAL TETHER OF HIM.
AND ZORDON'S GENETIC MAKEUP IS CODED TO HIS STAFF!
AND HERE I THOUGHT WE'D BE BACK TO NORMAL IN NO TIME.
WELL, WE DID REBUILD THE ENTIRE COMMAND CENTER...
TRUE.
AND WITH NO RITA, WE GET TO ACTUALLY TRY AND MAKE A DIFFERENCE IN THE WORLD, RATHER THAN JUST FIGHTING RAMPAGING MONSTERS ALL THE TIME. AND WE GET TIME OFF.
I'D ARGUE WE'RE DOING BETTER THAN "NORMAL."

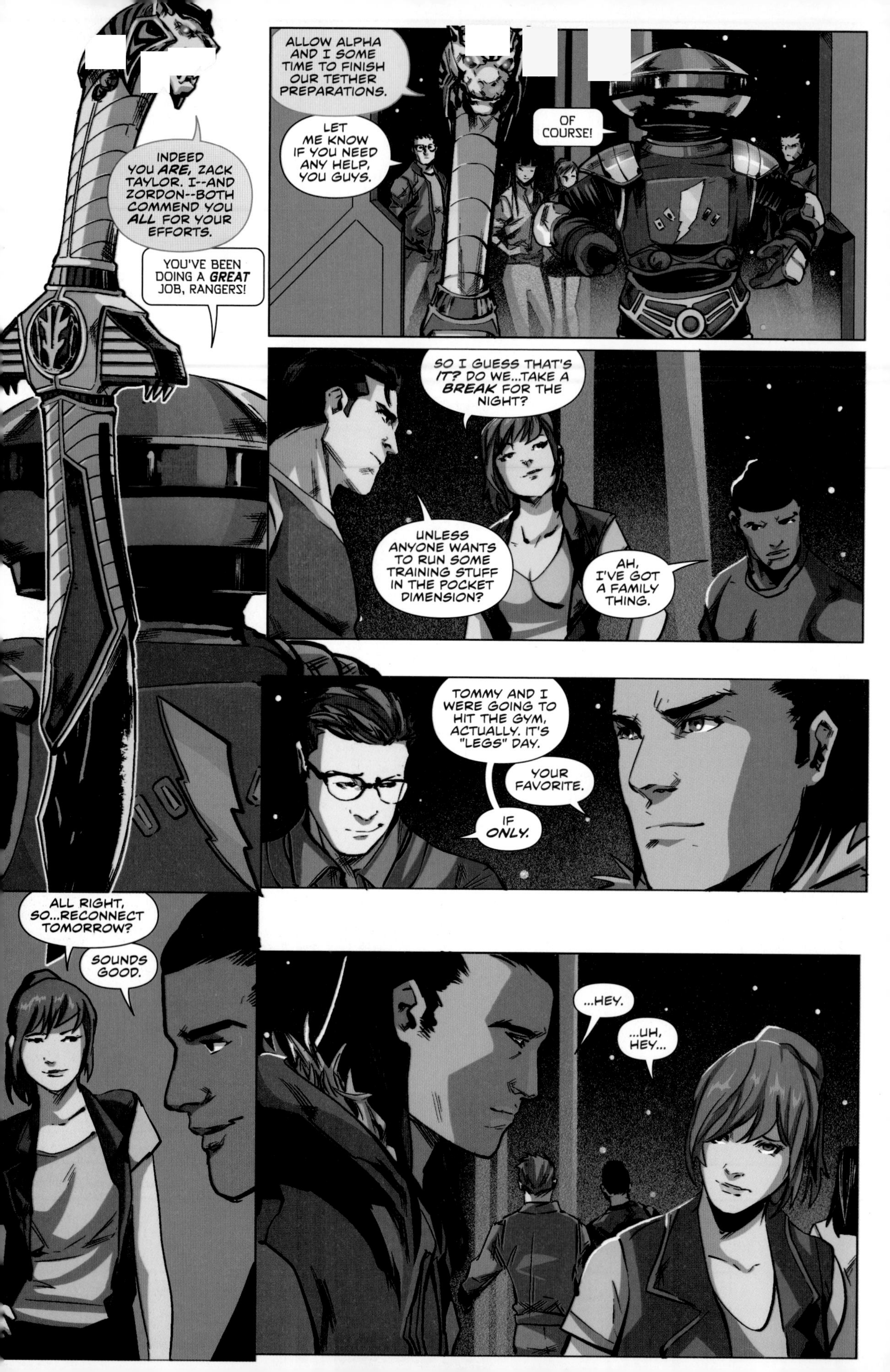
INDEED YOU ARE, ZACK TAYLOR. I--AND ZORDON--BOTH COMMEND YOU ALL FOR YOUR EFFORTS.
YOU'VE BEEN DOING A GREAT JOB, RANGERS!
ALLOW ALPHA AND I SOME TIME TO FINISH OUR TETHER PREPARATIONS.
LET ME KNOW IF YOU NEED ANY HELP, YOU GUYS.
OF COURSE!
SO I GUESS THAT'S IT? DO WE...TAKE A BREAK FOR THE NIGHT?
UNLESS ANYONE WANTS TO RUN SOME TRAINING STUFF IN THE POCKET DIMENSION?
AH, I'VE GOT A FAMILY THING.
TOMMY AND I WERE GOING TO HIT THE GYM, ACTUALLY. IT'S "LEGS" DAY.
YOUR FAVORITE.
IF ONLY.
ALL RIGHT, SO...RECONNECT TOMORROW?
SOUNDS GOOD.
...HEY.
...UH, HEY...

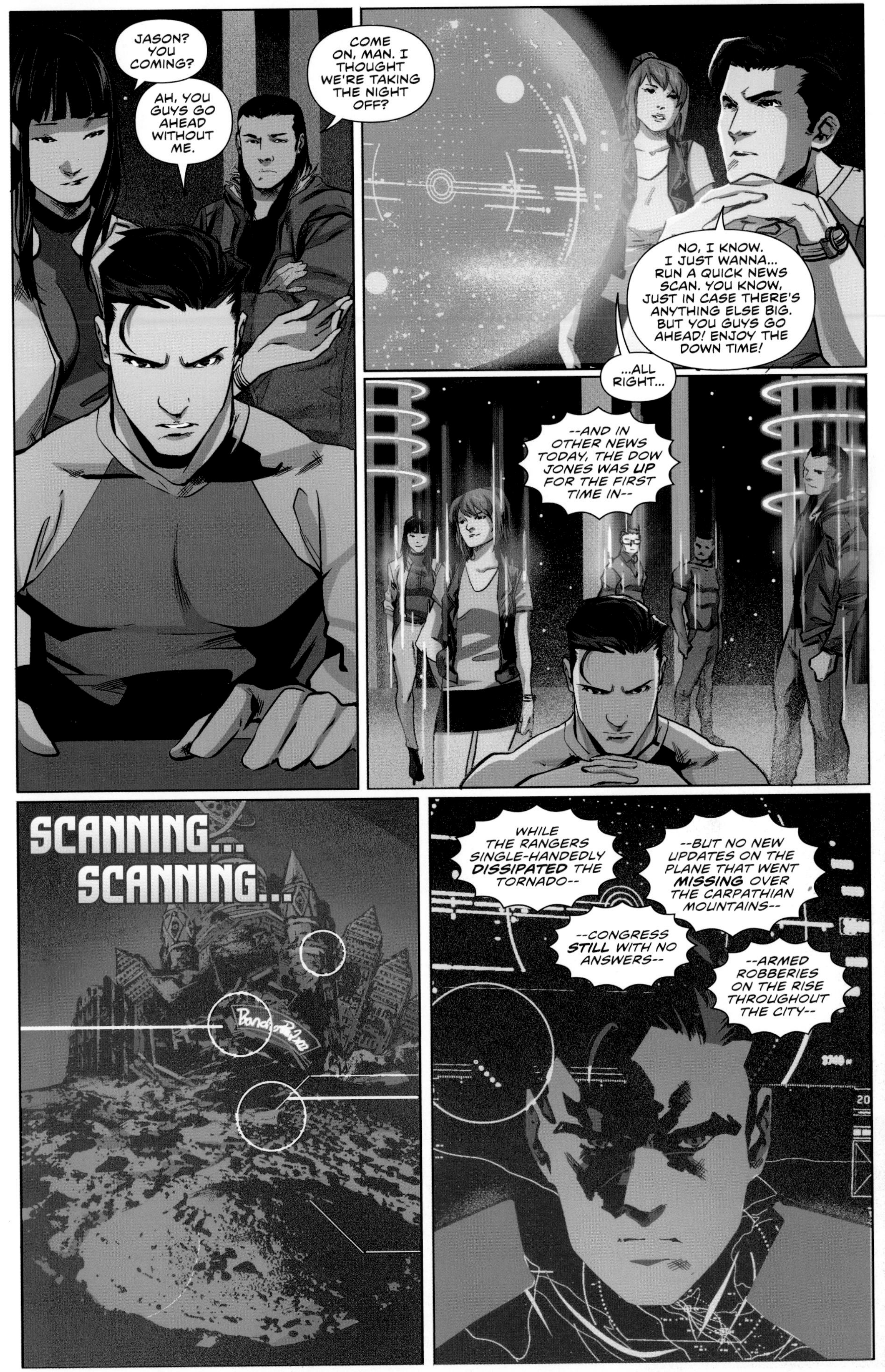
JASON? YOU COMING?
AH, YOU GUYS GO AHEAD WITHOUT ME.
COME ON, MAN. I THOUGHT WE'RE TAKING THE NIGHT OFF?
NO, I KNOW. I JUST WANNA... RUN A QUICK NEWS SCAN. YOU KNOW, JUST IN CASE THERE'S ANYTHING ELSE BIG. BUT YOU GUYS GO AHEAD! ENJOY THE DOWN TIME!
...ALL RIGHT...
--AND IN OTHER NEWS TODAY, THE DOW JONES WAS **UP** FOR THE FIRST TIME IN--
SCANNING... SCANNING...
WHILE THE RANGERS SINGLE-HANDEDLY **DISSIPATED** THE TORNADO--
--BUT NO NEW UPDATES ON THE PLANE THAT WENT **MISSING** OVER THE CARPATHIAN MOUNTAINS--
--CONGRESS **STILL** WITH NO ANSWERS--
--ARMED ROBBERIES ON THE RISE THROUGHOUT THE CITY--

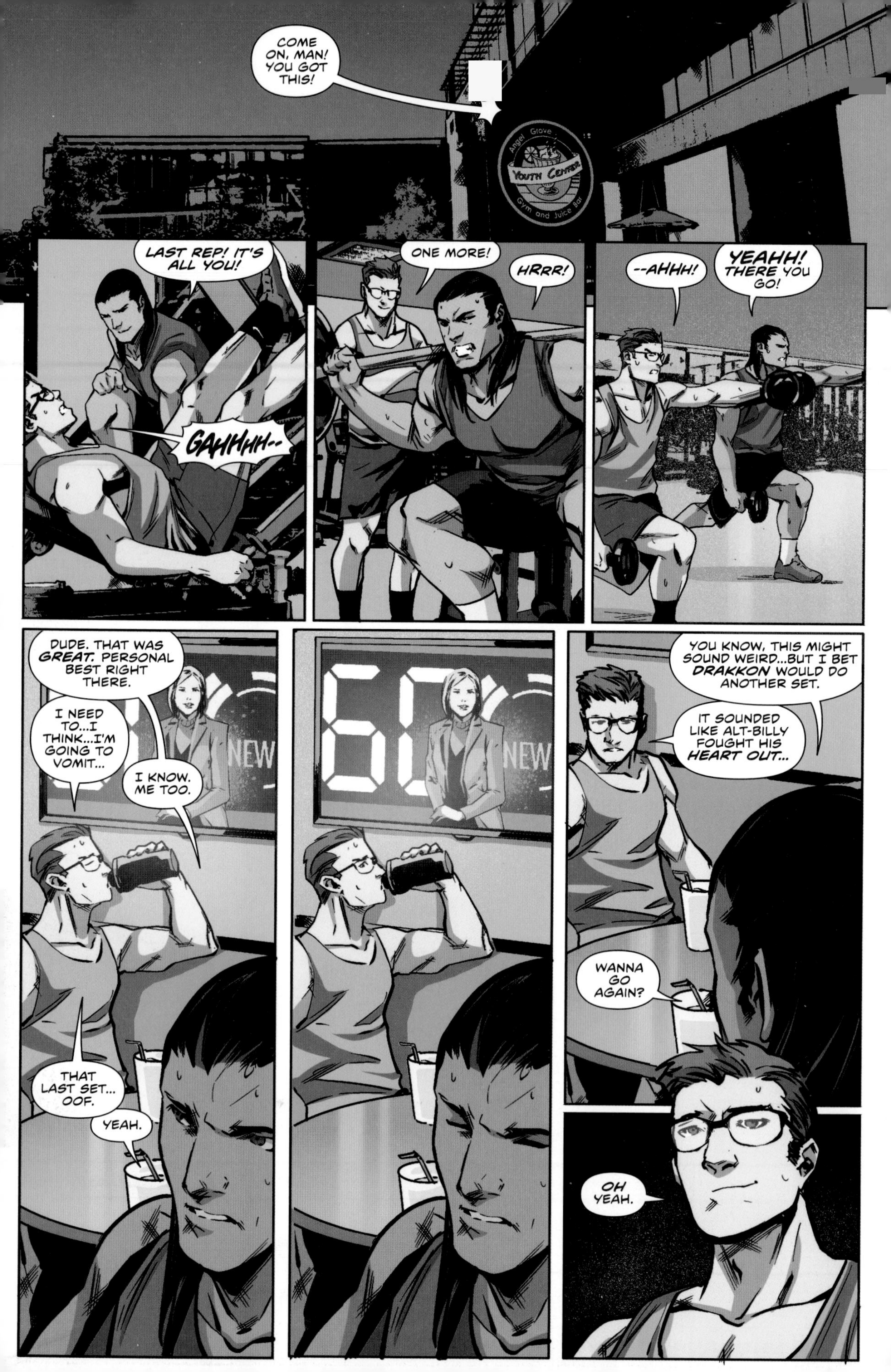
COME ON, MAN! YOU GOT THIS!
Angel Grove
YOUTH CENTER
Gym and Juice Bar
LAST REP! IT'S ALL YOU!
GAHHHH--
ONE MORE!
HRRR!
--AHHH!
YEAHH! THERE YOU GO!
DUDE. THAT WAS GREAT. PERSONAL BEST RIGHT THERE.
I NEED TO...I THINK...I'M GOING TO VOMIT...
I KNOW. ME TOO.
THAT LAST SET... OOF.
YEAH.
NEWS
YOU KNOW, THIS MIGHT SOUND WEIRD...BUT I BET DRAKKON WOULD DO ANOTHER SET.
IT SOUNDED LIKE ALT-BILLY FOUGHT HIS HEART OUT...
WANNA GO AGAIN?
OH YEAH.

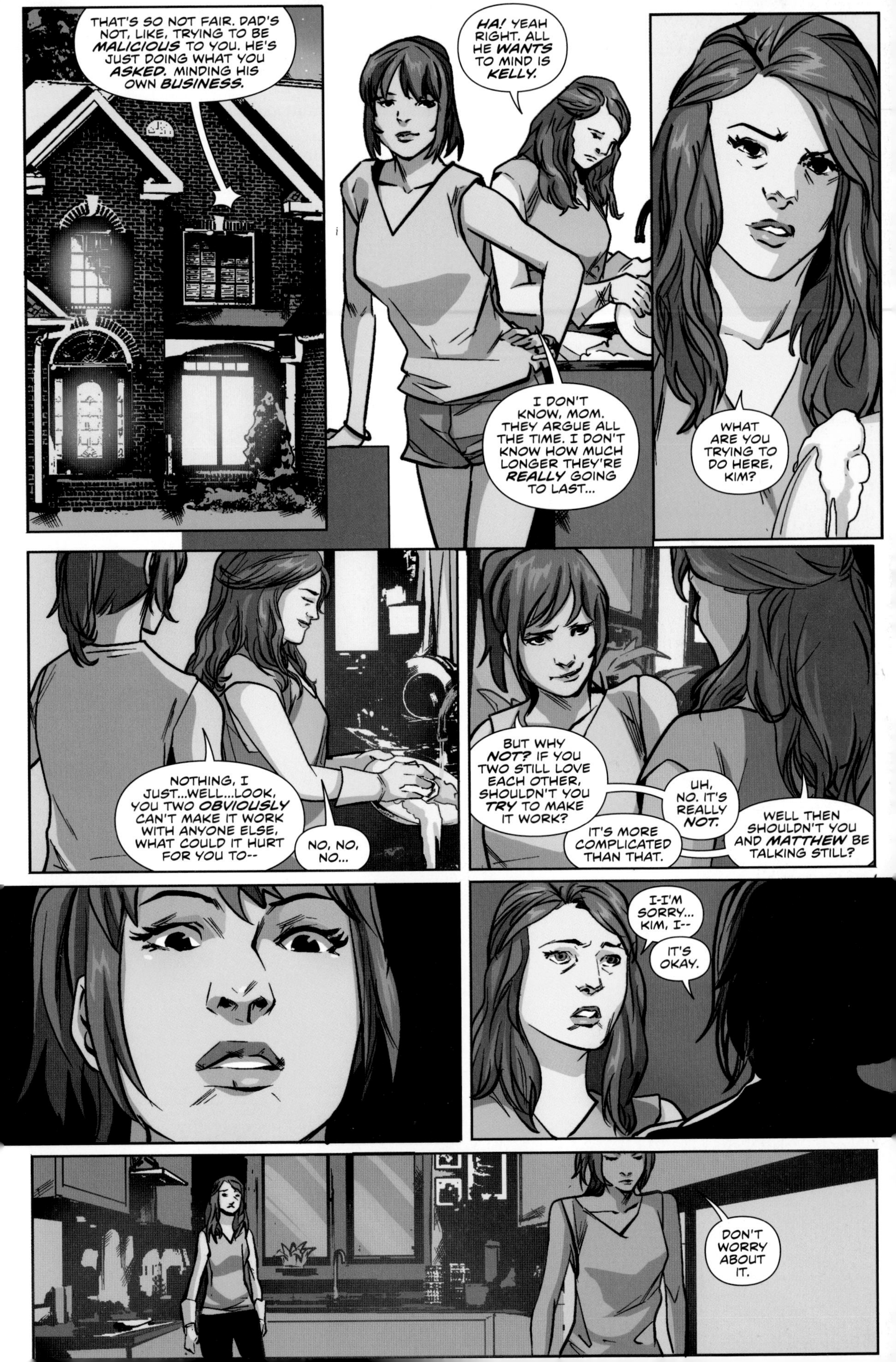
THAT'S SO NOT FAIR. DAD'S NOT, LIKE, TRYING TO BE MALICIOUS TO YOU. HE'S JUST DOING WHAT YOU ASKED. MINDING HIS OWN BUSINESS.
HA! YEAH RIGHT. ALL HE WANTS TO MIND IS KELLY.
I DON'T KNOW, MOM. THEY ARGUE ALL THE TIME. I DON'T KNOW HOW MUCH LONGER THEY'RE REALLY GOING TO LAST...
WHAT ARE YOU TRYING TO DO HERE, KIM?
NOTHING, I JUST...WELL...LOOK, YOU TWO OBVIOUSLY CAN'T MAKE IT WORK WITH ANYONE ELSE, WHAT COULD IT HURT FOR YOU TO--
NO, NO, NO...
BUT WHY NOT? IF YOU TWO STILL LOVE EACH OTHER, SHOULDN'T YOU TRY TO MAKE IT WORK?
IT'S MORE COMPLICATED THAN THAT.
UH, NO. IT'S REALLY NOT.
WELL THEN SHOULDN'T YOU AND MATTHEW BE TALKING STILL?
I-I'M SORRY... KIM, I--
IT'S OKAY.
DON'T WORRY ABOUT IT.

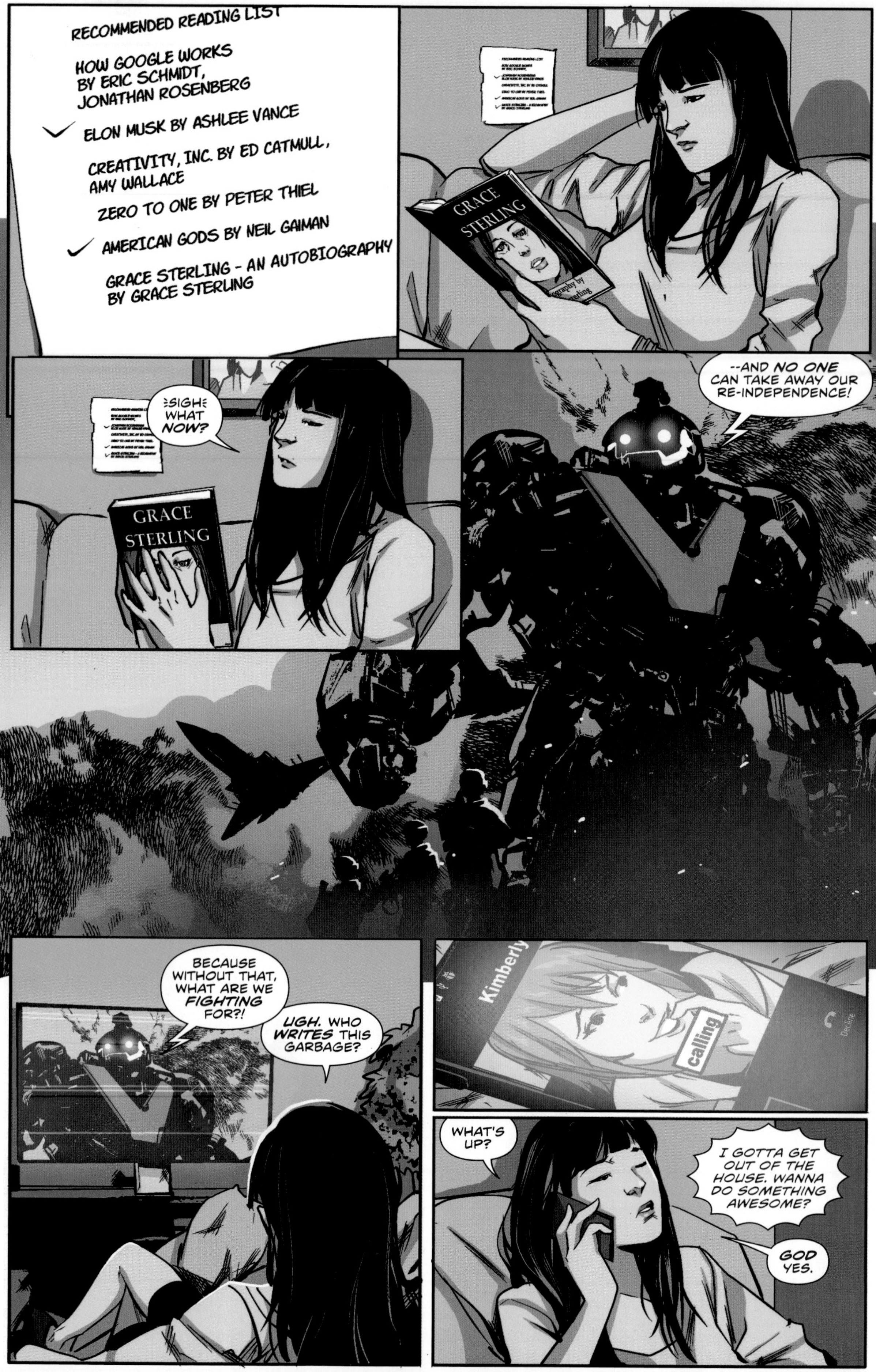
RECOMMENDED READING LIST
HOW GOOGLE WORKS BY ERIC SCHMIDT, JONATHAN ROSENBERG
ELON MUSK BY ASHLEE VANCE
CREATIVITY, INC. BY ED CATMULL, AMY WALLACE
ZERO TO ONE BY PETER THIEL
AMERICAN GODS BY NEIL GAIMAN
GRACE STERLING - AN AUTOBIOGRAPHY BY GRACE STERLING
GRACE STERLING
SIGH WHAT NOW?
GRACE STERLING
--AND NO ONE CAN TAKE AWAY OUR RE-INDEPENDENCE!
BECAUSE WITHOUT THAT, WHAT ARE WE FIGHTING FOR?!
UGH. WHO WRITES THIS GARBAGE?
Kimberly
calling
Decline
WHAT'S UP?
I GOTTA GET OUT OF THE HOUSE. WANNA DO SOMETHING AWESOME?
GOD YES.

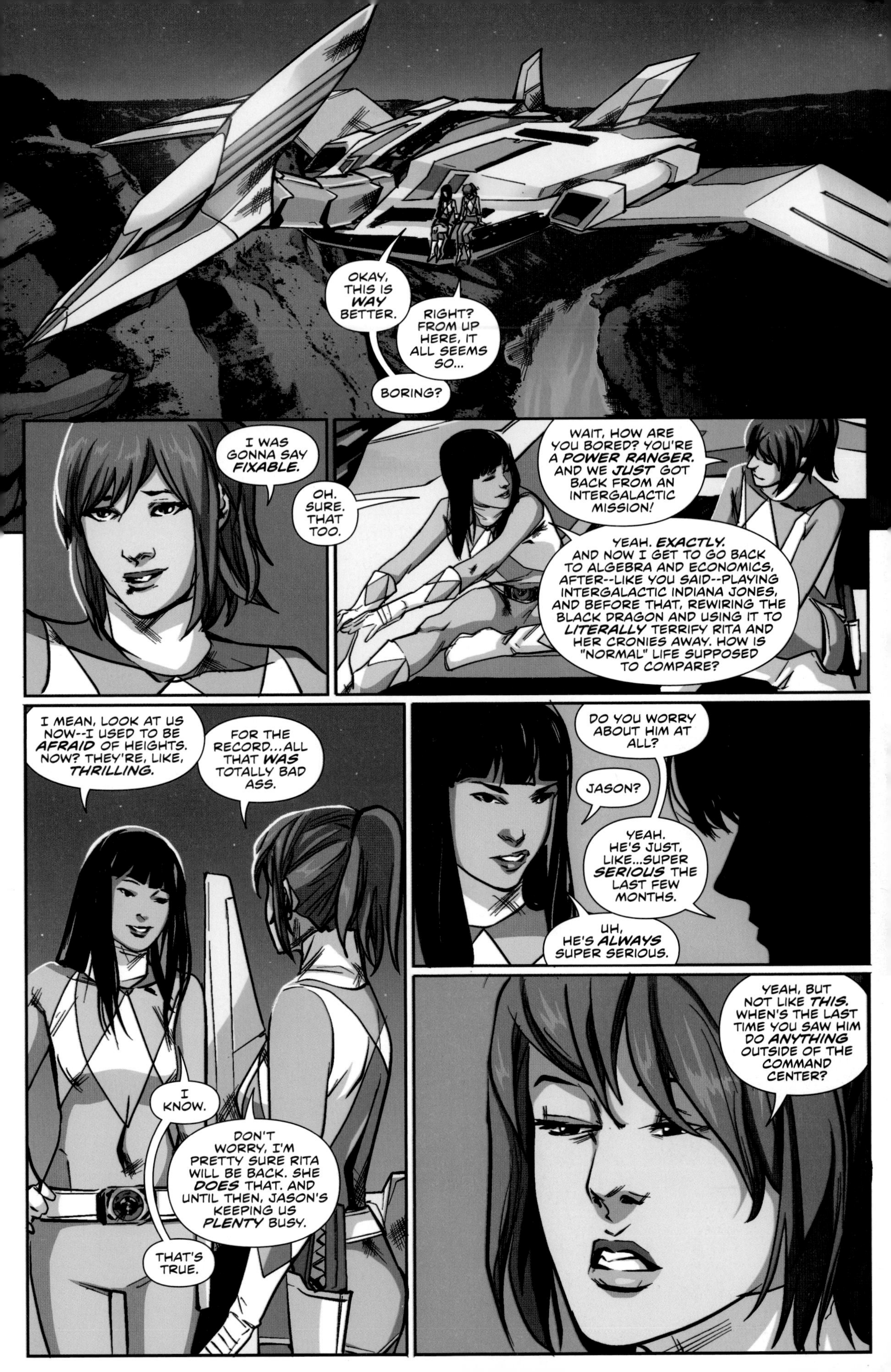
OKAY, THIS IS WAY BETTER.
RIGHT? FROM UP HERE, IT ALL SEEMS SO...
BORING?
I WAS GONNA SAY FIXABLE.
OH. SURE. THAT TOO.
WAIT, HOW ARE YOU BORED? YOU'RE A POWER RANGER. AND WE JUST GOT BACK FROM AN INTERGALACTIC MISSION!
YEAH. EXACTLY. AND NOW I GET TO GO BACK TO ALGEBRA AND ECONOMICS, AFTER--LIKE YOU SAID--PLAYING INTERGALACTIC INDIANA JONES, AND BEFORE THAT, REWIRING THE BLACK DRAGON AND USING IT TO LITERALLY TERRIFY RITA AND HER CRONIES AWAY. HOW IS "NORMAL" LIFE SUPPOSED TO COMPARE?
I MEAN, LOOK AT US NOW--I USED TO BE AFRAID OF HEIGHTS. NOW? THEY'RE, LIKE, THRILLING.
FOR THE RECORD...ALL THAT WAS TOTALLY BAD ASS.
I KNOW.
DON'T WORRY, I'M PRETTY SURE RITA WILL BE BACK. SHE DOES THAT. AND UNTIL THEN, JASON'S KEEPING US PLENTY BUSY.
THAT'S TRUE.
DO YOU WORRY ABOUT HIM AT ALL?
JASON?
YEAH. HE'S JUST, LIKE...SUPER SERIOUS THE LAST FEW MONTHS.
UH, HE'S ALWAYS SUPER SERIOUS.
YEAH, BUT NOT LIKE THIS. WHEN'S THE LAST TIME YOU SAW HIM DO ANYTHING OUTSIDE OF THE COMMAND CENTER?

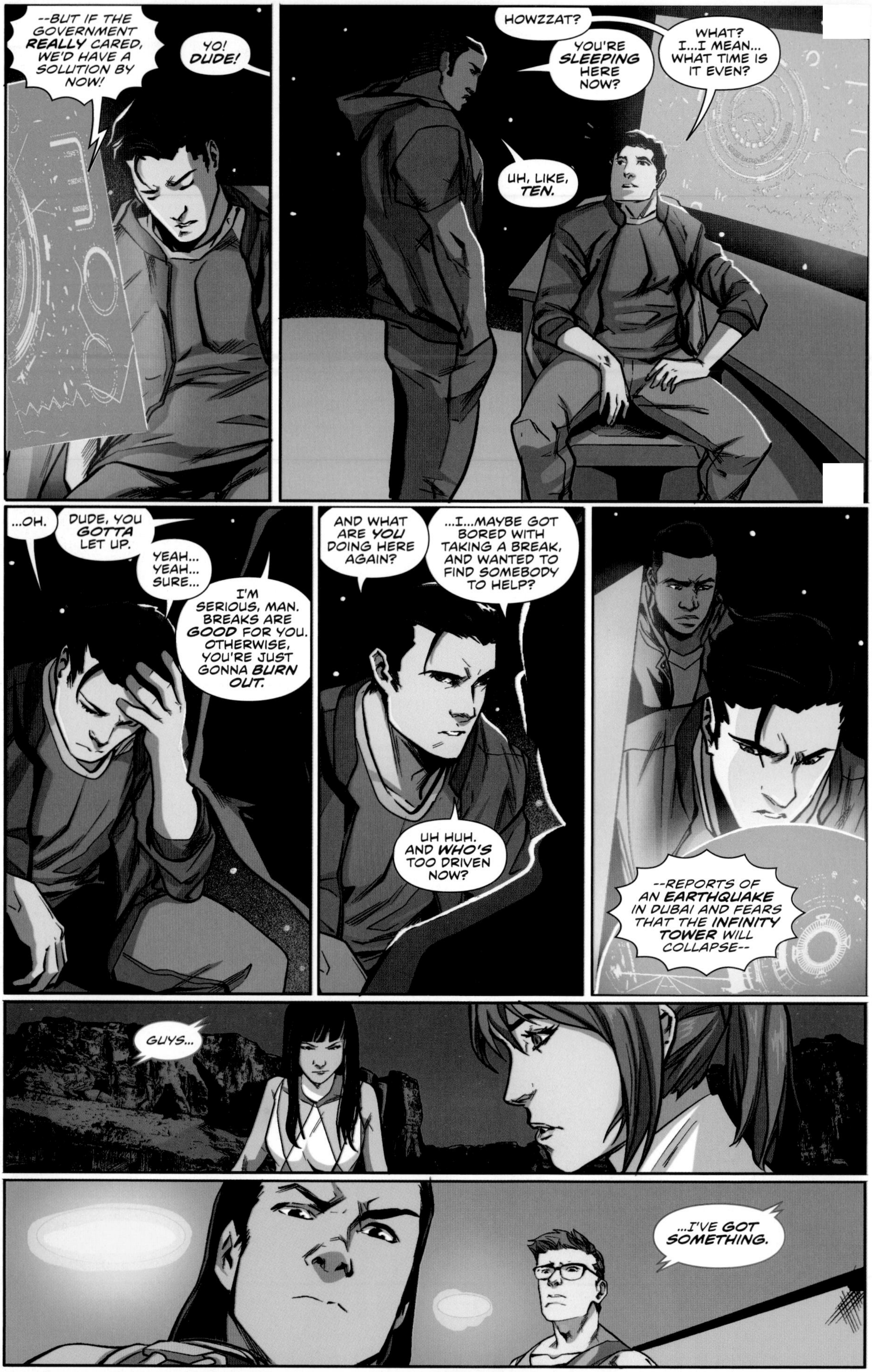
--BUT IF THE GOVERNMENT REALLY CARED, WE'D HAVE A SOLUTION BY NOW!
YO! DUDE!
HOWZZAT?
YOU'RE SLEEPING HERE NOW?
WHAT? I...I MEAN... WHAT TIME IS IT EVEN?
UH, LIKE, TEN.
...OH.
DUDE, YOU GOTTA LET UP.
YEAH... YEAH... SURE...
I'M SERIOUS, MAN. BREAKS ARE GOOD FOR YOU. OTHERWISE, YOU'RE JUST GONNA BURN OUT.
AND WHAT ARE YOU DOING HERE AGAIN?
...I...MAYBE GOT BORED WITH TAKING A BREAK, AND WANTED TO FIND SOMEBODY TO HELP?
UH HUH. AND WHO'S TOO DRIVEN NOW?
--REPORTS OF AN EARTHQUAKE IN DUBAI AND FEARS THAT THE INFINITY TOWER WILL COLLAPSE--
GUYS...
...I'VE GOT SOMETHING.

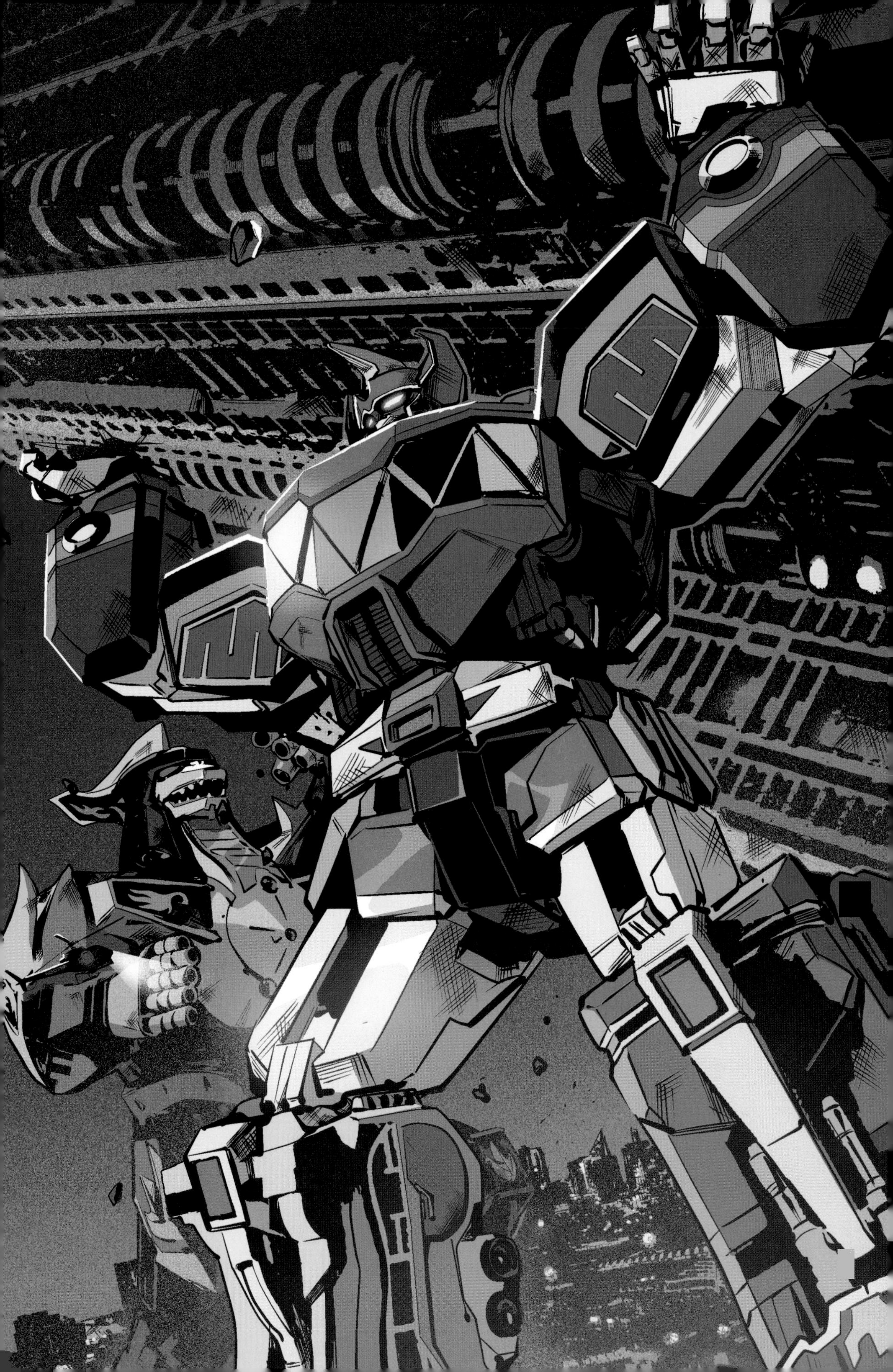

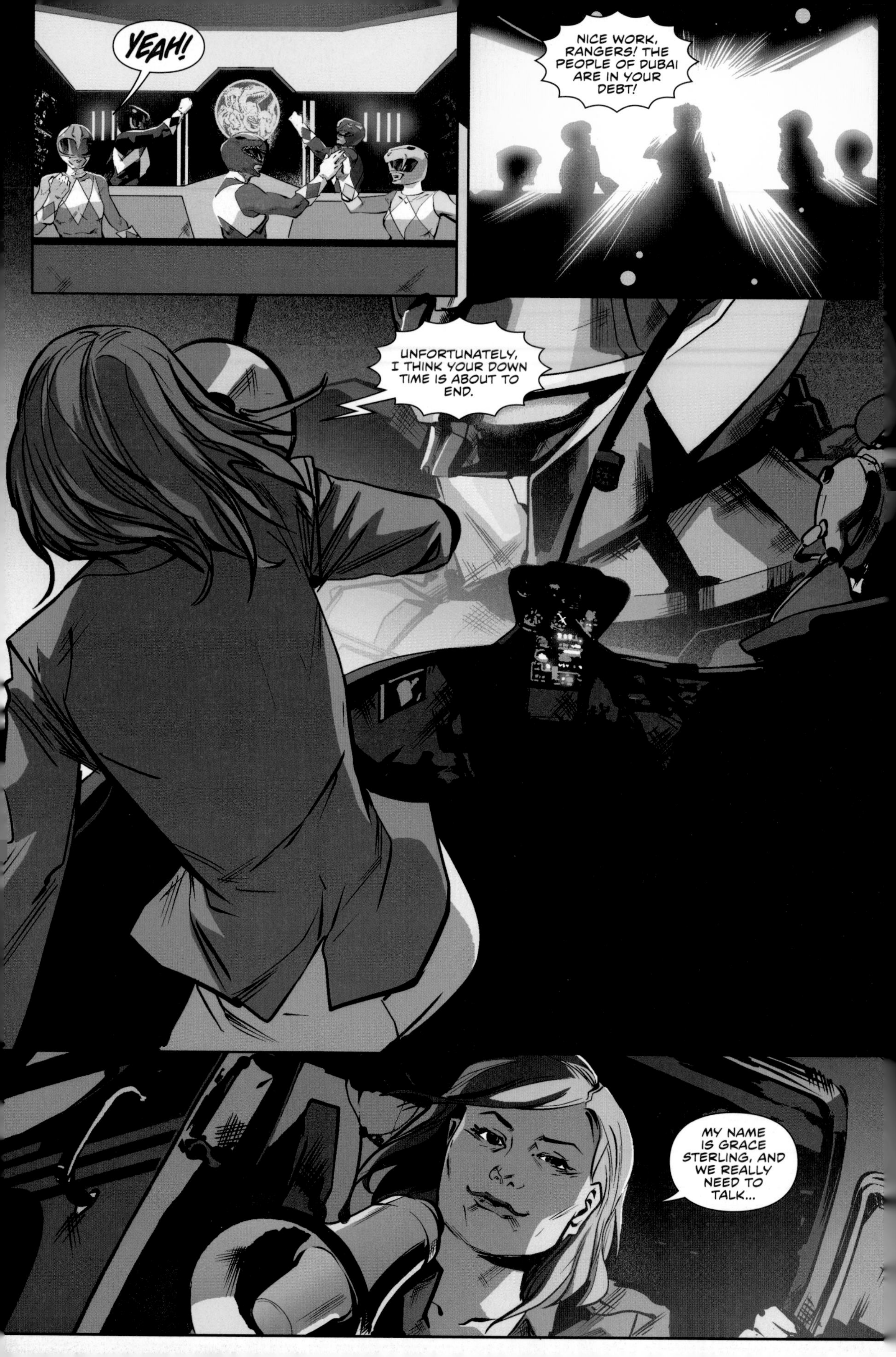
YEAH!
NICE WORK, RANGERS! THE PEOPLE OF DUBAI ARE IN YOUR DEBT!
UNFORTUNATELY, I THINK YOUR DOWN TIME IS ABOUT TO END.
MY NAME IS GRACE STERLING, AND WE REALLY NEED TO TALK...

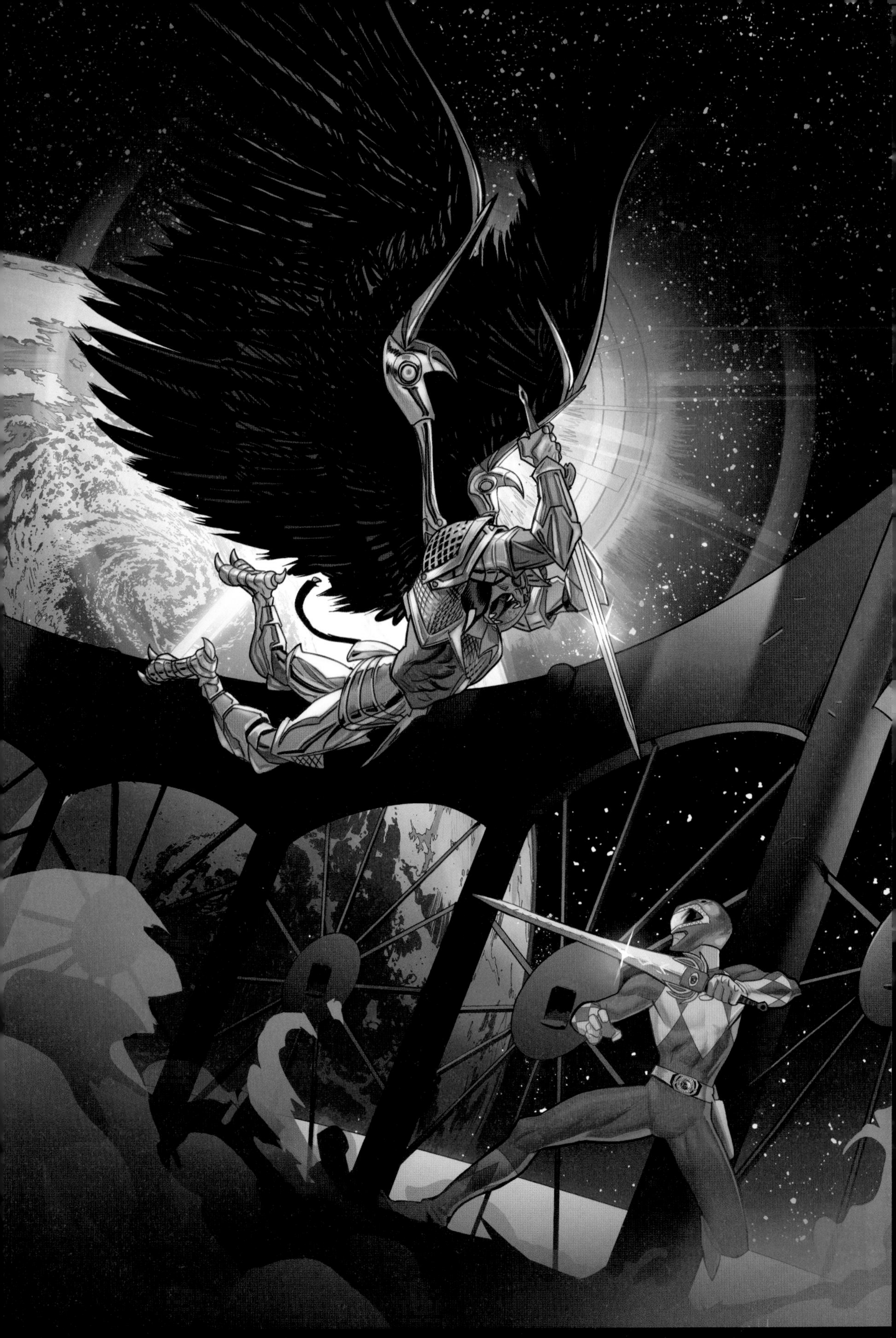

DAN MORA | ISSUE SEVENTEEN VERSUS VARIANT COVER

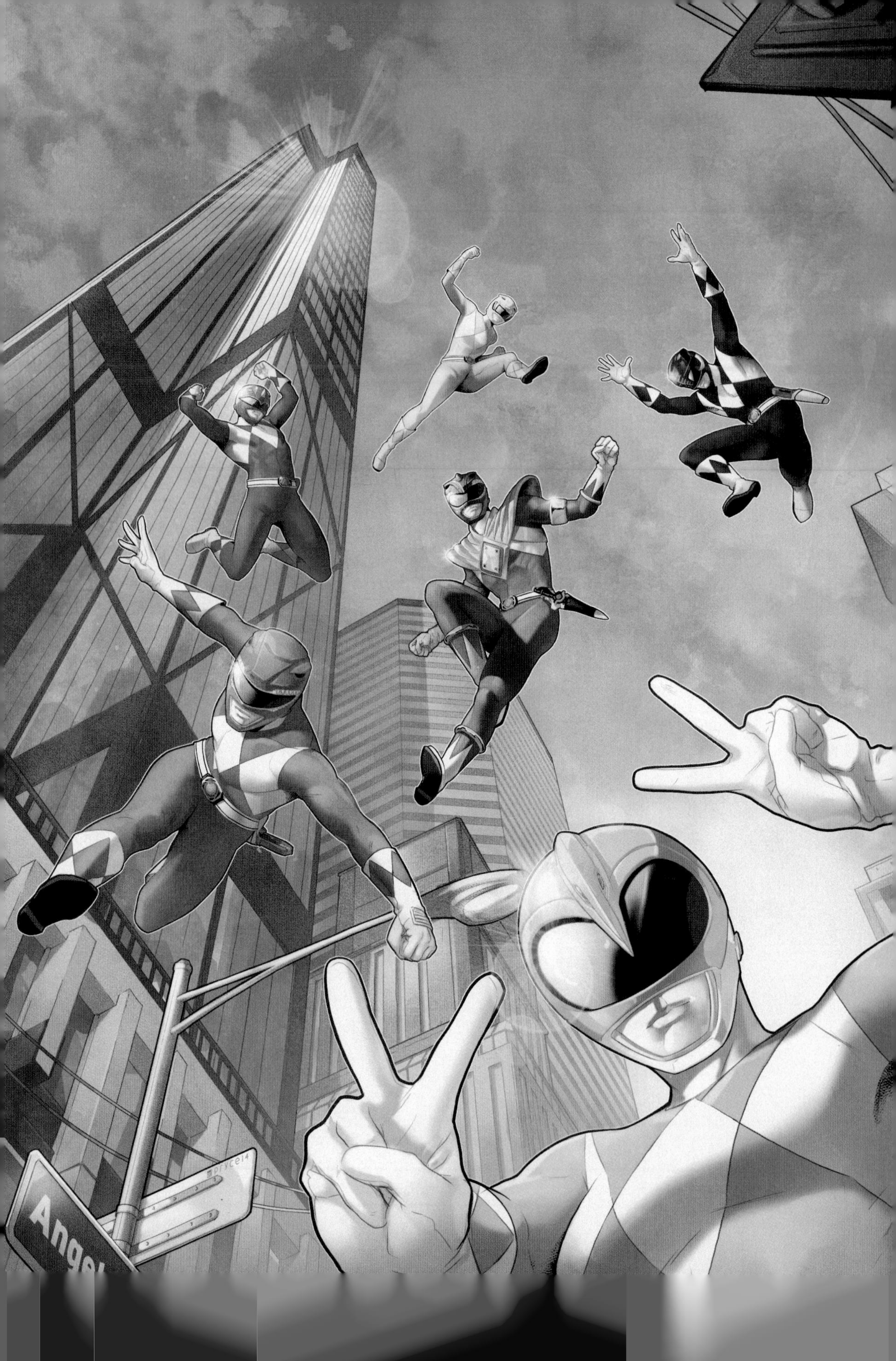

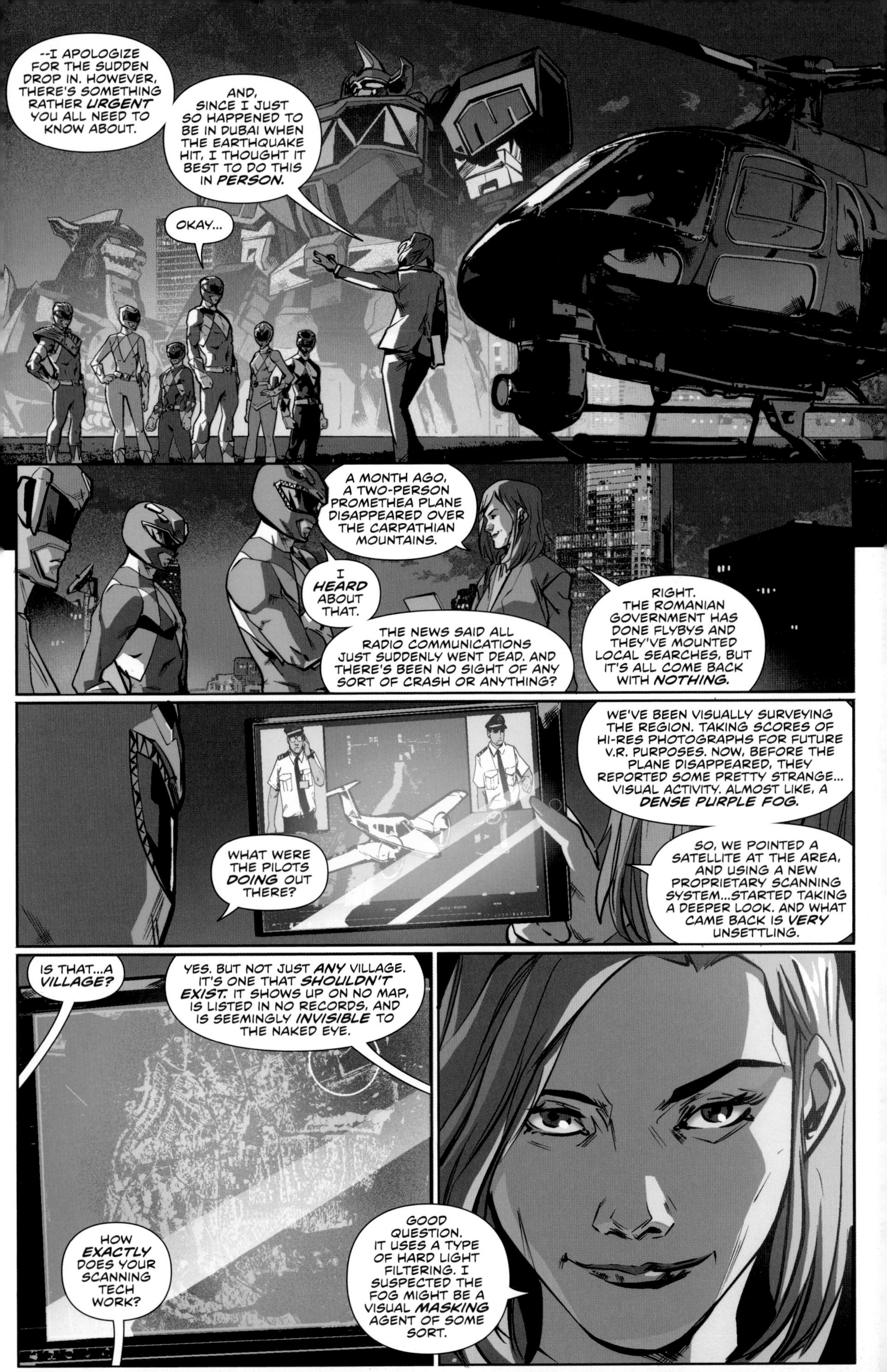
--I APOLOGIZE FOR THE SUDDEN DROP IN. HOWEVER, THERE'S SOMETHING RATHER URGENT YOU ALL NEED TO KNOW ABOUT.
AND, SINCE I JUST SO HAPPENED TO BE IN DUBAI WHEN THE EARTHQUAKE HIT, I THOUGHT IT BEST TO DO THIS IN PERSON.
OKAY...
A MONTH AGO, A TWO-PERSON PROMETHEA PLANE DISAPPEARED OVER THE CARPATHIAN MOUNTAINS.
I HEARD ABOUT THAT.
THE NEWS SAID ALL RADIO COMMUNICATIONS JUST SUDDENLY WENT DEAD. AND THERE'S BEEN NO SIGHT OF ANY SORT OF CRASH OR ANYTHING?
RIGHT. THE ROMANIAN GOVERNMENT HAS DONE FLYBYS AND THEY'VE MOUNTED LOCAL SEARCHES, BUT IT'S ALL COME BACK WITH NOTHING.
WE'VE BEEN VISUALLY SURVEYING THE REGION. TAKING SCORES OF HI-RES PHOTOGRAPHS FOR FUTURE V.R. PURPOSES. NOW, BEFORE THE PLANE DISAPPEARED, THEY REPORTED SOME PRETTY STRANGE... VISUAL ACTIVITY. ALMOST LIKE, A DENSE PURPLE FOG.
WHAT WERE THE PILOTS DOING OUT THERE?
SO, WE POINTED A SATELLITE AT THE AREA, AND USING A NEW PROPRIETARY SCANNING SYSTEM...STARTED TAKING A DEEPER LOOK. AND WHAT CAME BACK IS VERY UNSETTLING.
IS THAT...A VILLAGE?
YES. BUT NOT JUST ANY VILLAGE. IT'S ONE THAT SHOULDN'T EXIST. IT SHOWS UP ON NO MAP, IS LISTED IN NO RECORDS, AND IS SEEMINGLY INVISIBLE TO THE NAKED EYE.
HOW EXACTLY DOES YOUR SCANNING TECH WORK?
GOOD QUESTION. IT USES A TYPE OF HARD LIGHT FILTERING. I SUSPECTED THE FOG MIGHT BE A VISUAL MASKING AGENT OF SOME SORT.

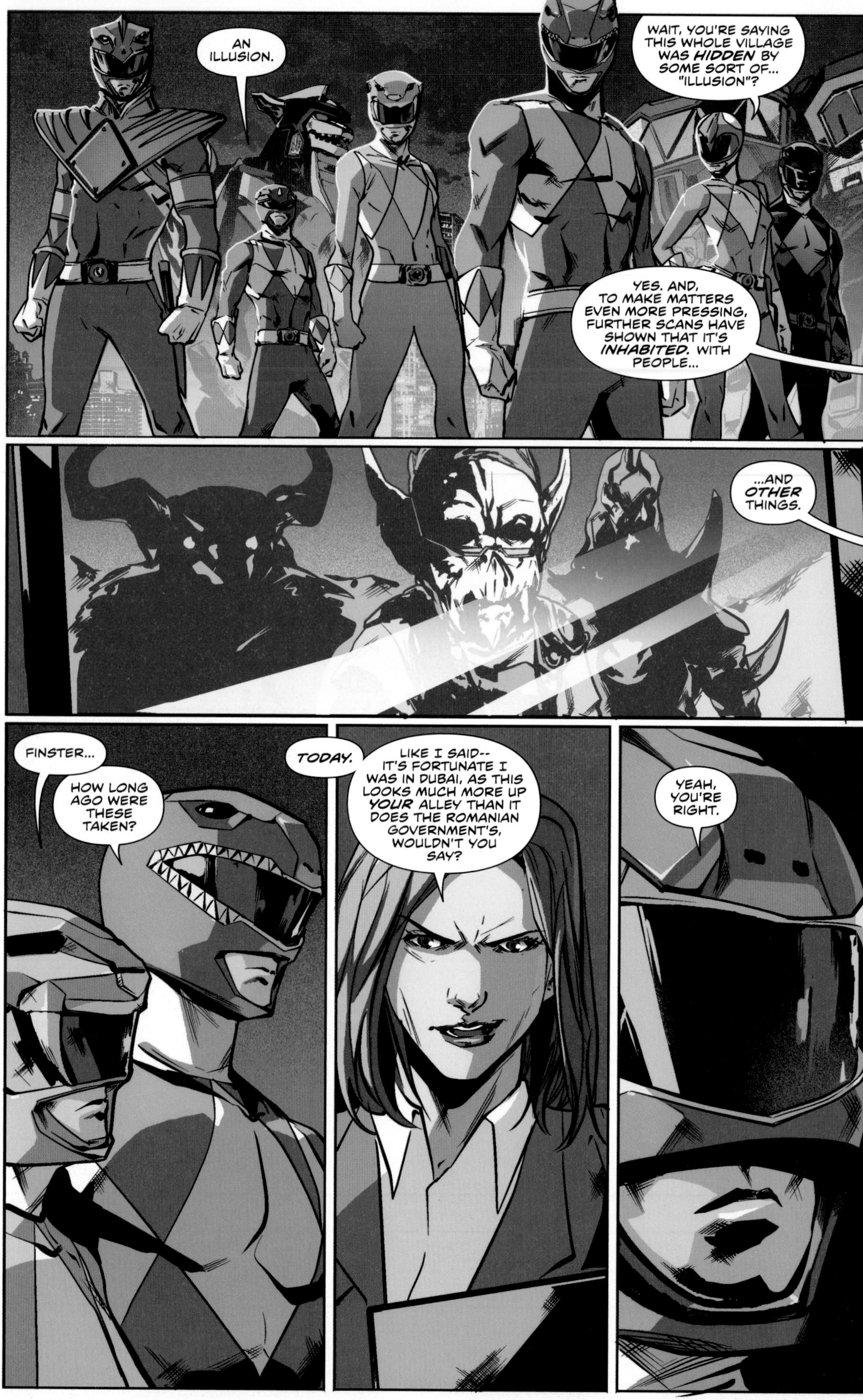
AN ILLUSION.
WAIT, YOU'RE SAYING THIS WHOLE VILLAGE WAS *HIDDEN* BY SOME SORT OF... "ILLUSION"?
YES. AND, TO MAKE MATTERS EVEN MORE PRESSING, FURTHER SCANS HAVE SHOWN THAT IT'S *INHABITED.* WITH PEOPLE...
...AND *OTHER* THINGS.
FINSTER...
HOW LONG AGO WERE THESE TAKEN?
TODAY.
LIKE I SAID-- IT'S FORTUNATE I WAS IN DUBAI, AS THIS LOOKS MUCH MORE UP *YOUR* ALLEY THAN IT DOES THE ROMANIAN GOVERNMENT'S, WOULDN'T YOU SAY?
YEAH, YOU'RE RIGHT.

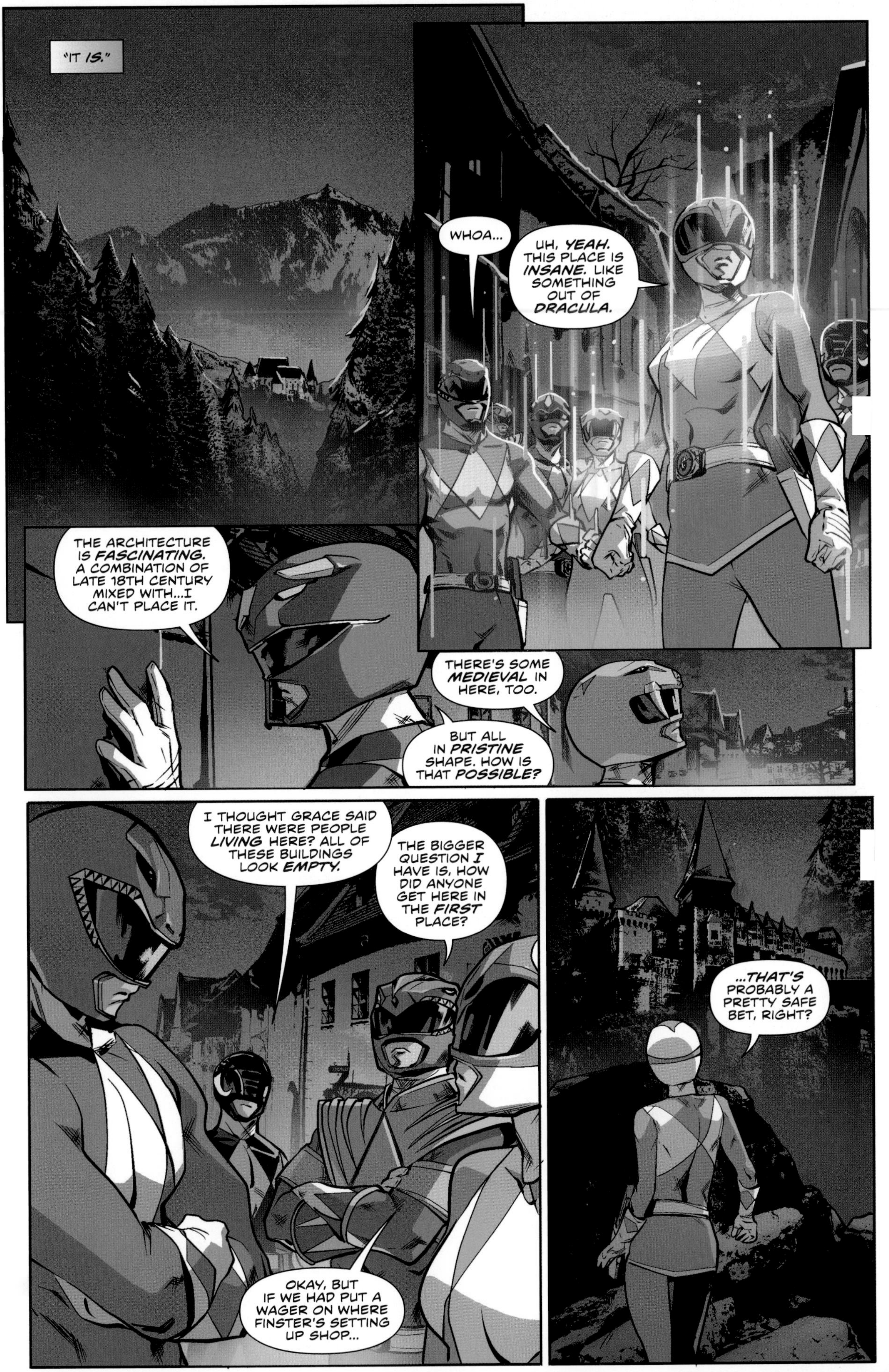
"IT IS."
WHOA...
UH, YEAH. THIS PLACE IS INSANE. LIKE SOMETHING OUT OF DRACULA.
THE ARCHITECTURE IS FASCINATING. A COMBINATION OF LATE 18TH CENTURY MIXED WITH...I CAN'T PLACE IT.
THERE'S SOME MEDIEVAL IN HERE, TOO.
BUT ALL IN PRISTINE SHAPE. HOW IS THAT POSSIBLE?
I THOUGHT GRACE SAID THERE WERE PEOPLE LIVING HERE? ALL OF THESE BUILDINGS LOOK EMPTY.
THE BIGGER QUESTION I HAVE IS, HOW DID ANYONE GET HERE IN THE FIRST PLACE?
OKAY, BUT IF WE HAD PUT A WAGER ON WHERE FINSTER'S SETTING UP SHOP...
...THAT'S PROBABLY A PRETTY SAFE BET, RIGHT?

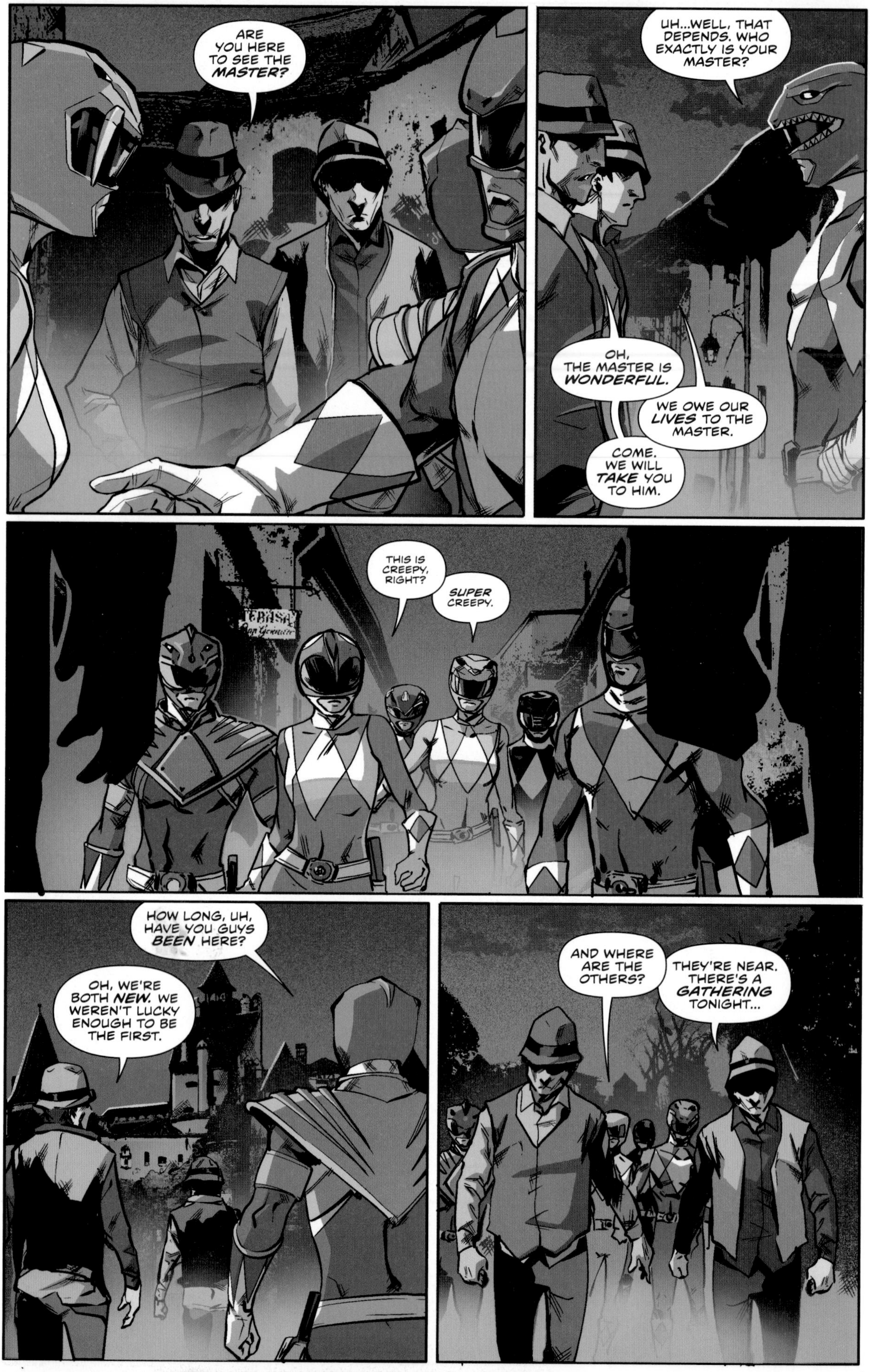
ARE YOU HERE TO SEE THE MASTER?
UH...WELL, THAT DEPENDS. WHO EXACTLY IS YOUR MASTER?
OH, THE MASTER IS WONDERFUL.
WE OWE OUR LIVES TO THE MASTER.
COME. WE WILL TAKE YOU TO HIM.
THIS IS CREEPY, RIGHT?
SUPER CREEPY.
HOW LONG, UH, HAVE YOU GUYS BEEN HERE?
OH, WE'RE BOTH NEW. WE WEREN'T LUCKY ENOUGH TO BE THE FIRST.
AND WHERE ARE THE OTHERS?
THEY'RE NEAR. THERE'S A GATHERING TONIGHT...

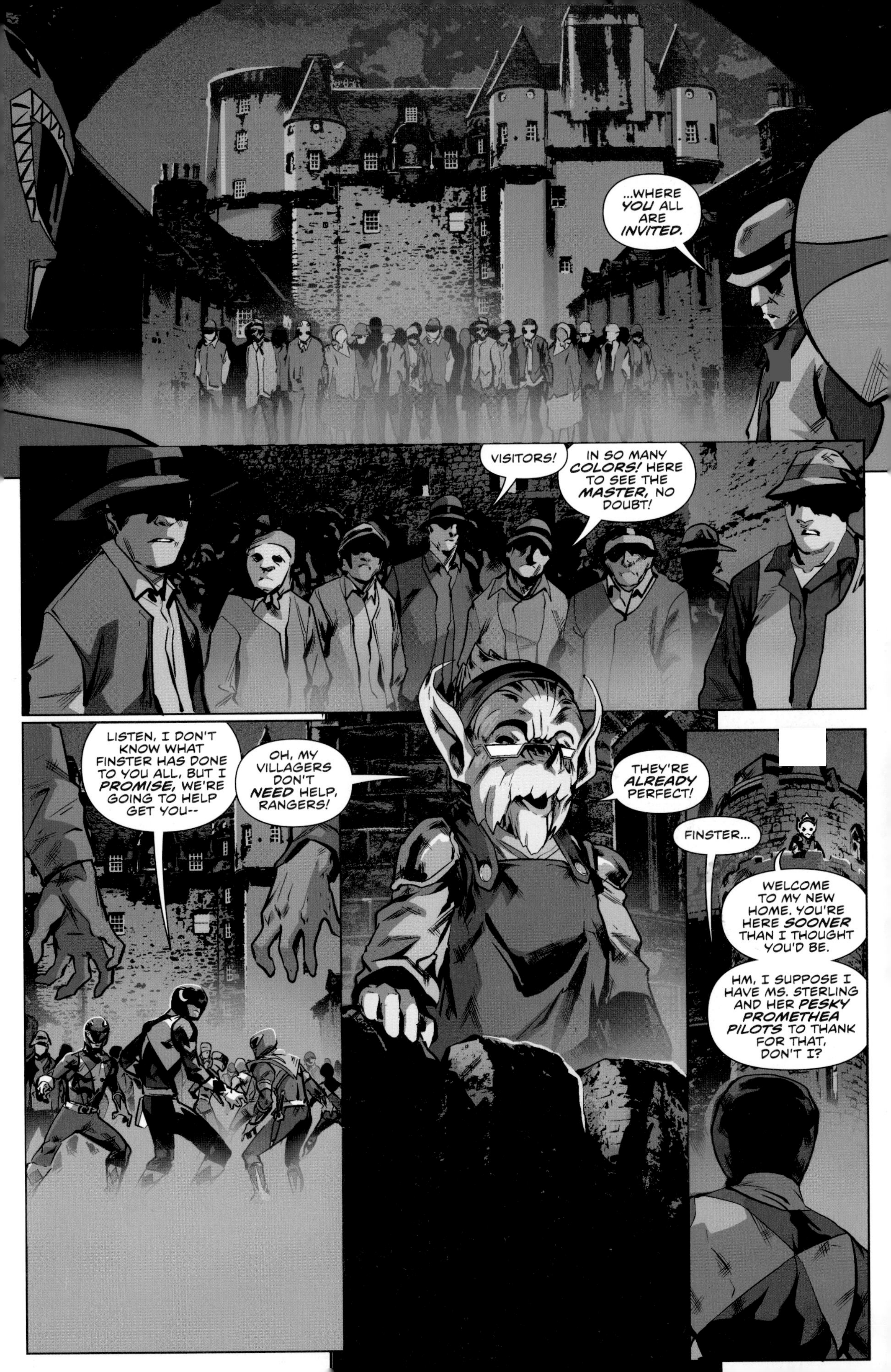
...WHERE YOU ALL ARE INVITED.
VISITORS!
IN SO MANY COLORS! HERE TO SEE THE MASTER, NO DOUBT!
LISTEN, I DON'T KNOW WHAT FINSTER HAS DONE TO YOU ALL, BUT I PROMISE, WE'RE GOING TO HELP GET YOU--
OH, MY VILLAGERS DON'T NEED HELP, RANGERS!
THEY'RE ALREADY PERFECT!
FINSTER...
WELCOME TO MY NEW HOME. YOU'RE HERE SOONER THAN I THOUGHT YOU'D BE.
HM, I SUPPOSE I HAVE MS. STERLING AND HER PESKY PROMETHEA PILOTS TO THANK FOR THAT, DON'T I?

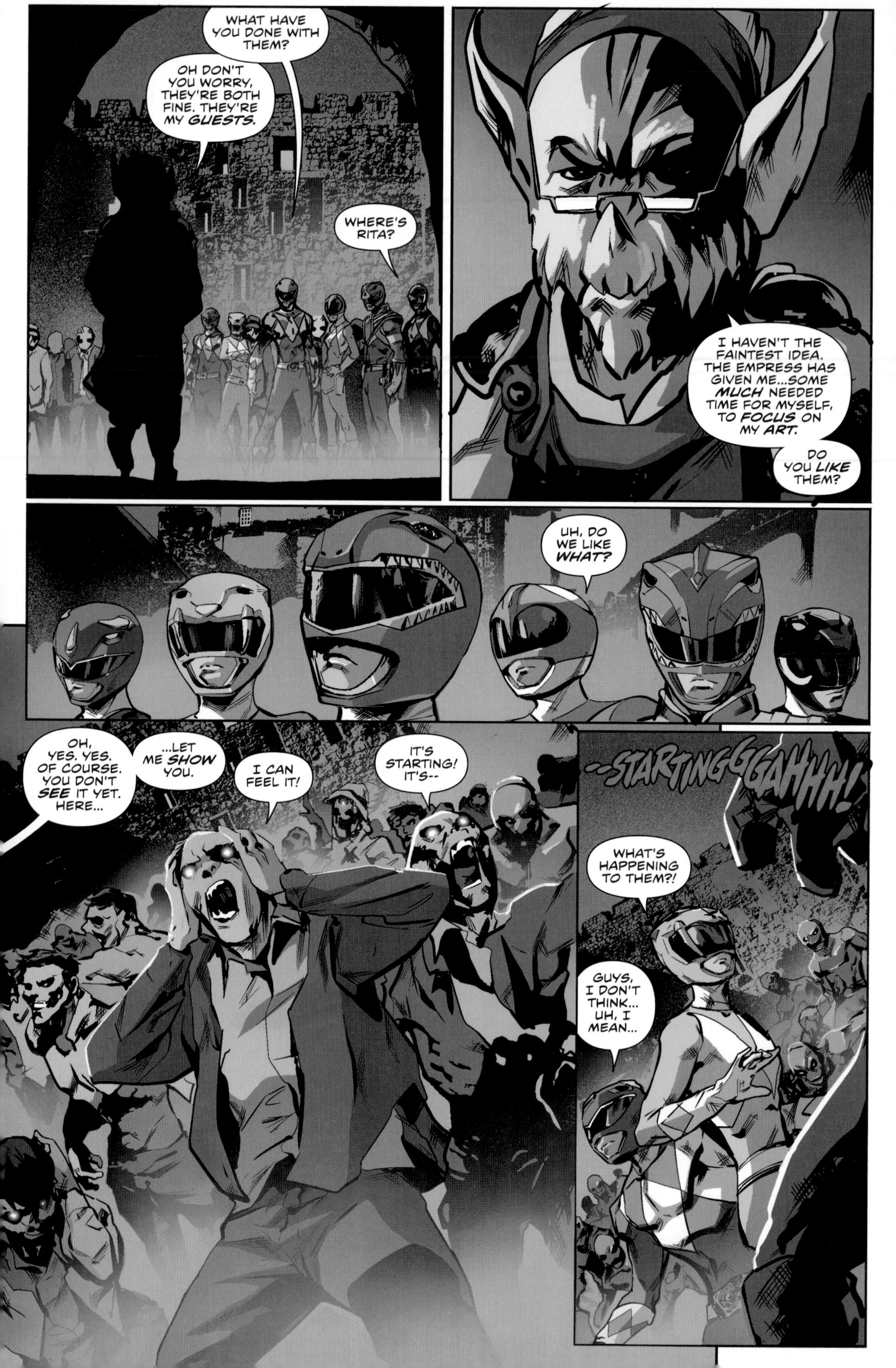
WHAT HAVE YOU DONE WITH THEM?
OH DON'T YOU WORRY, THEY'RE BOTH FINE. THEY'RE MY GUESTS.
WHERE'S RITA?
I HAVEN'T THE FAINTEST IDEA. THE EMPRESS HAS GIVEN ME...SOME MUCH NEEDED TIME FOR MYSELF, TO FOCUS ON MY ART.
DO YOU LIKE THEM?
UH, DO WE LIKE WHAT?
OH, YES. YES. OF COURSE. YOU DON'T SEE IT YET. HERE...
...LET ME SHOW YOU.
I CAN FEEL IT!
IT'S STARTING! IT'S--
--STARTINGGGAHHH!
WHAT'S HAPPENING TO THEM?!
GUYS, I DON'T THINK... UH, I MEAN...

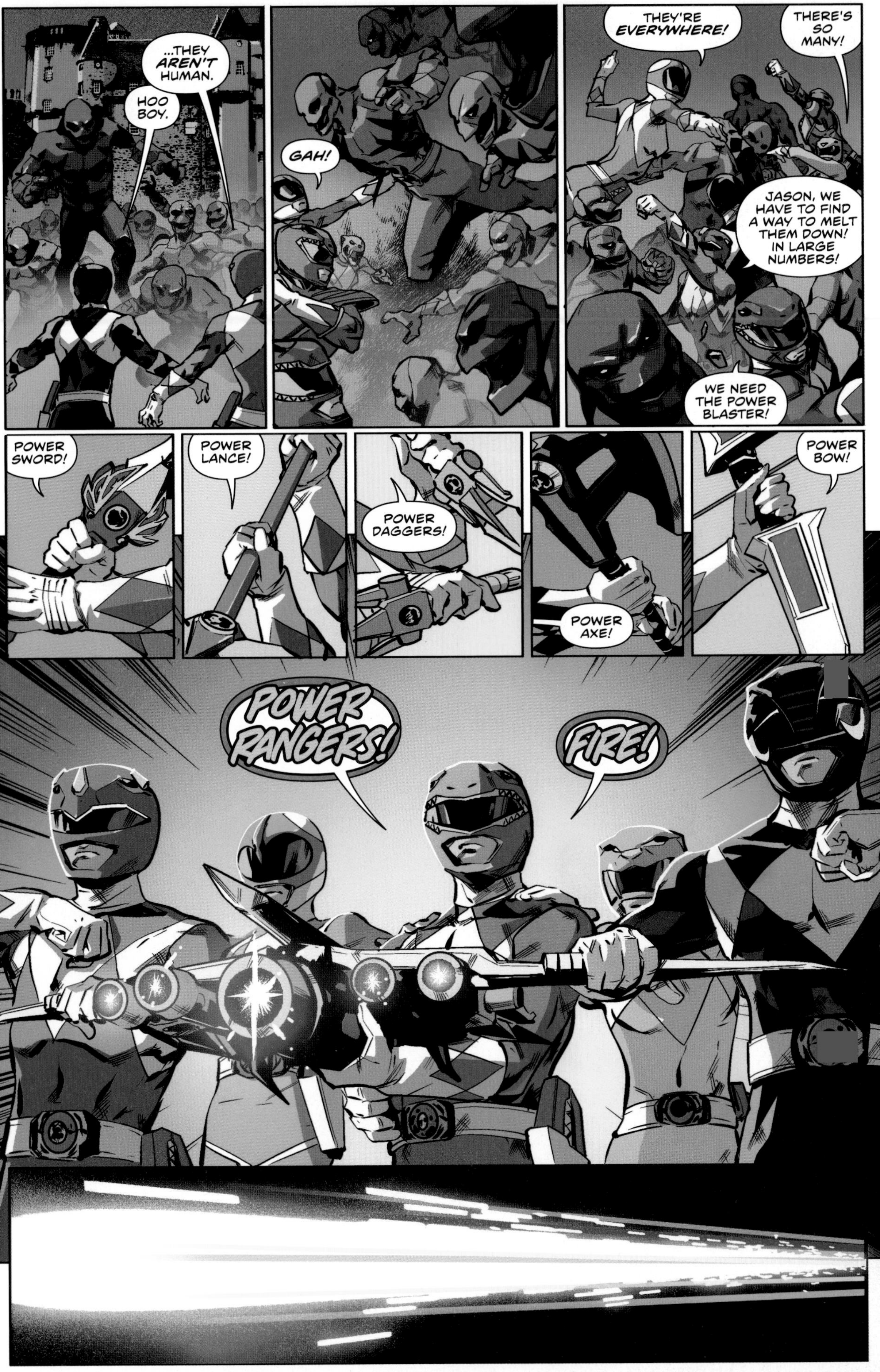
...THEY AREN'T HUMAN.
HOO BOY.
GAH!
THEY'RE EVERYWHERE!
THERE'S SO MANY!
JASON, WE HAVE TO FIND A WAY TO MELT THEM DOWN! IN LARGE NUMBERS!
WE NEED THE POWER BLASTER!
POWER SWORD!
POWER LANCE!
POWER DAGGERS!
POWER AXE!
POWER BOW!
POWER RANGERS!
FIRE!

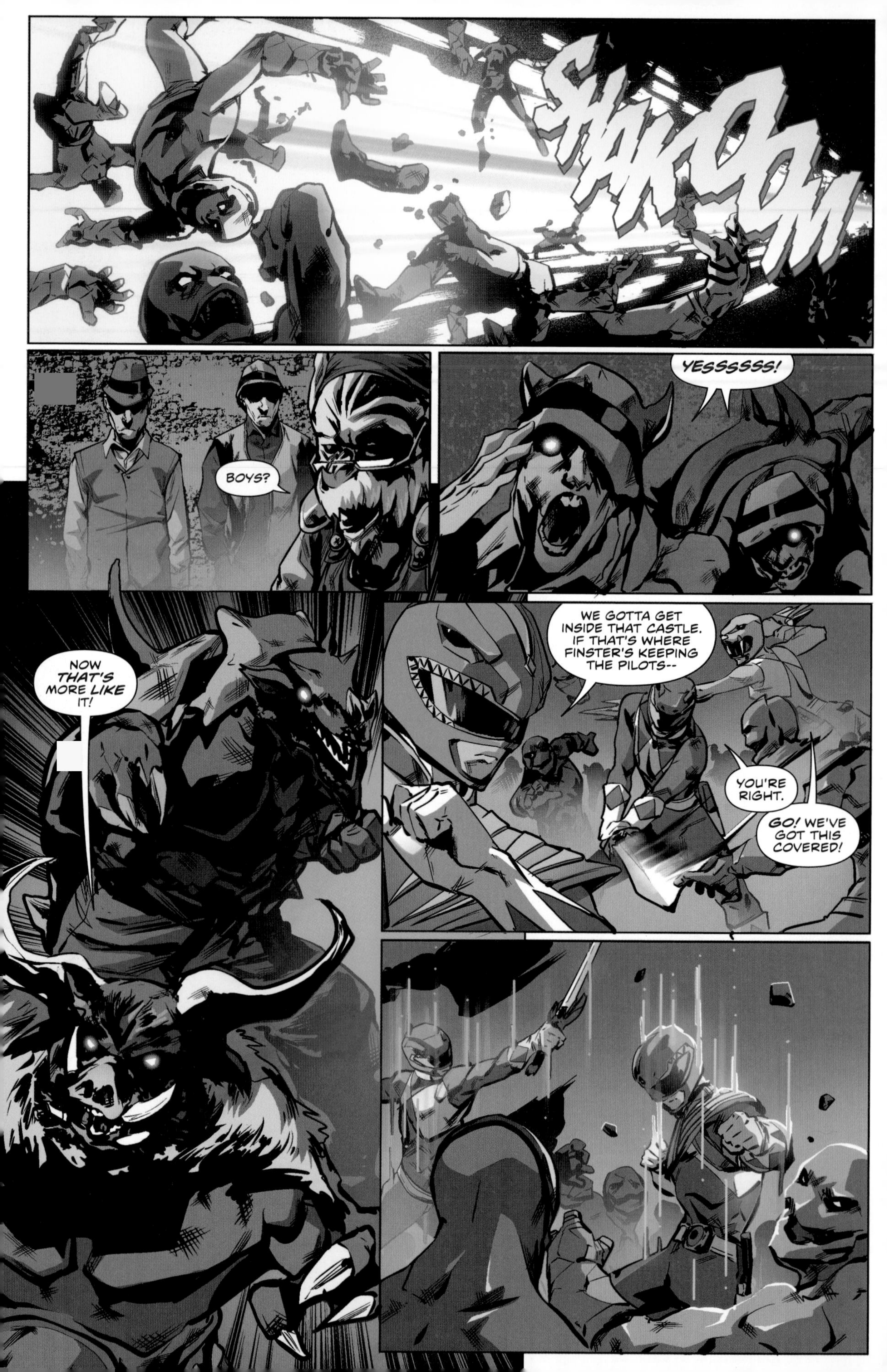
SHAKOOM
BOYS?
YESSSSSS!
NOW THAT'S MORE LIKE IT!
WE GOTTA GET INSIDE THAT CASTLE. IF THAT'S WHERE FINSTER'S KEEPING THE PILOTS--
YOU'RE RIGHT.
GO! WE'VE GOT THIS COVERED!

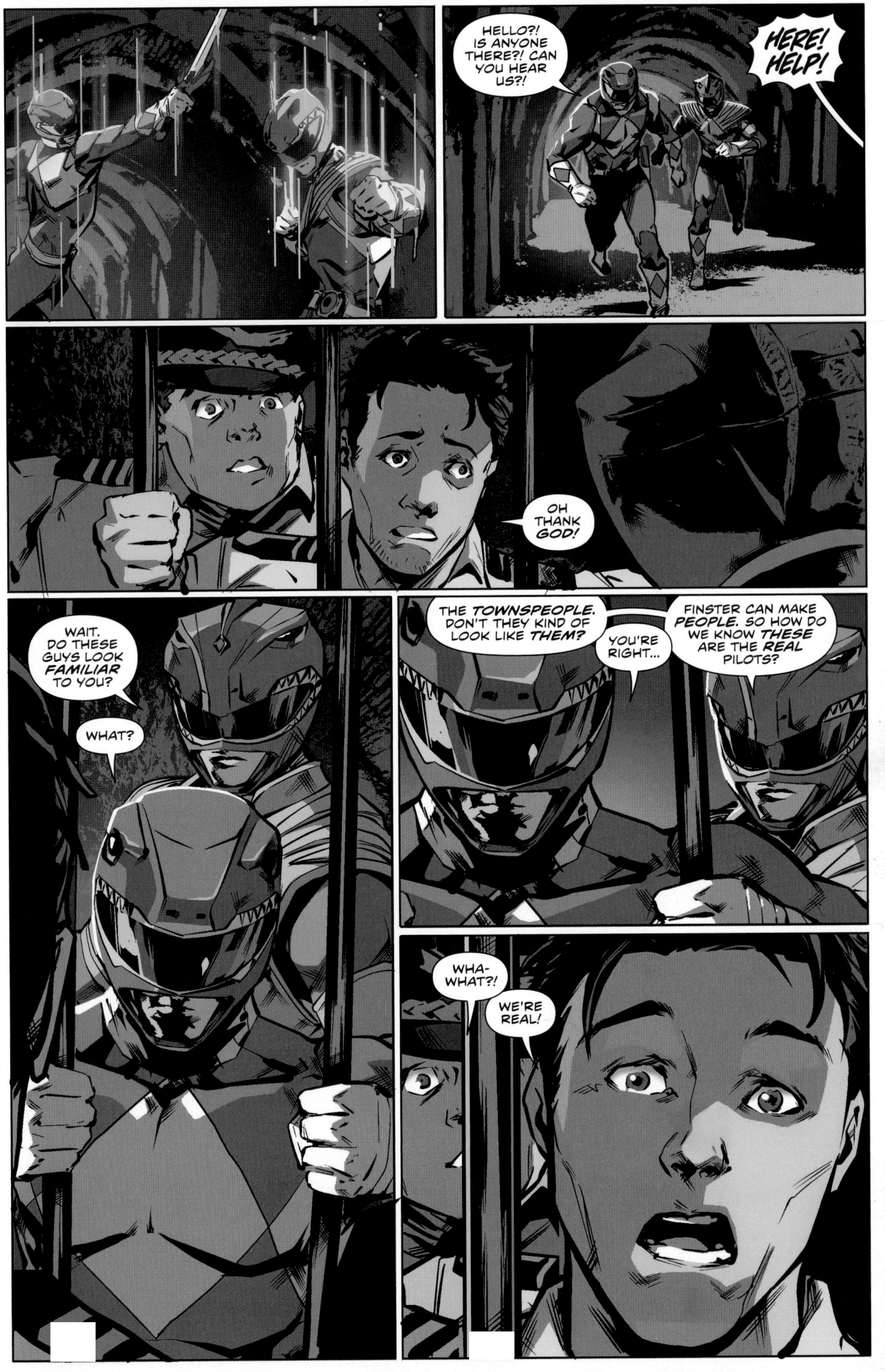
HELLO?! IS ANYONE THERE?! CAN YOU HEAR US?!
HERE! HELP!
OH THANK GOD!
WAIT. DO THESE GUYS LOOK FAMILIAR TO YOU?
WHAT?
THE TOWNSPEOPLE. DON'T THEY KIND OF LOOK LIKE THEM?
YOU'RE RIGHT...
FINSTER CAN MAKE PEOPLE. SO HOW DO WE KNOW THESE ARE THE REAL PILOTS?
WHA-WHAT?!
WE'RE REAL!

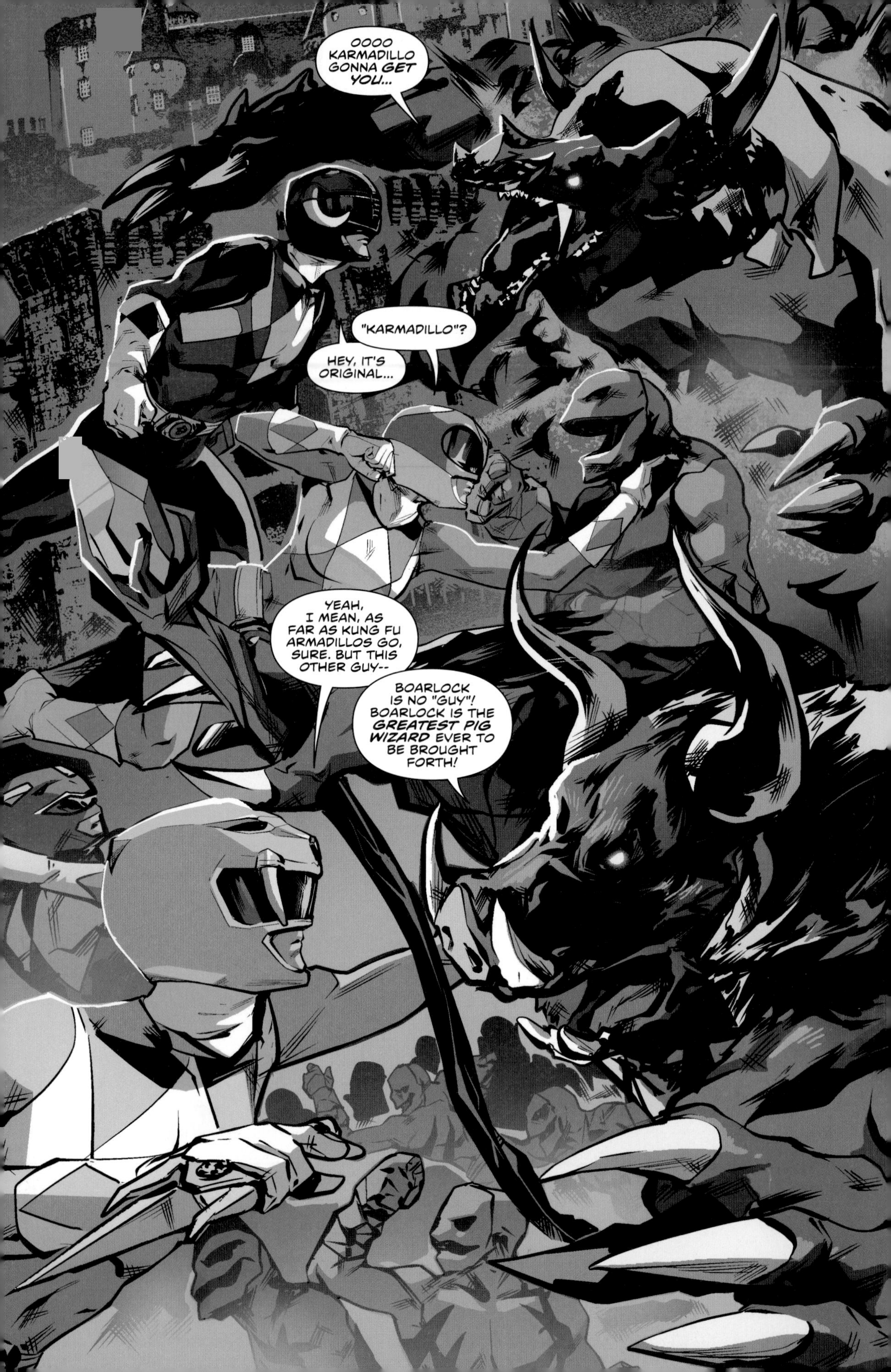
OOOO KARMADILLO GONNA GET YOU...
"KARMADILLO"?
HEY, IT'S ORIGINAL...
YEAH, I MEAN, AS FAR AS KUNG FU ARMADILLOS GO, SURE. BUT THIS OTHER GUY--
BOARLOCK IS NO "GUY"! BOARLOCK IS THE GREATEST PIG WIZARD EVER TO BE BROUGHT FORTH!

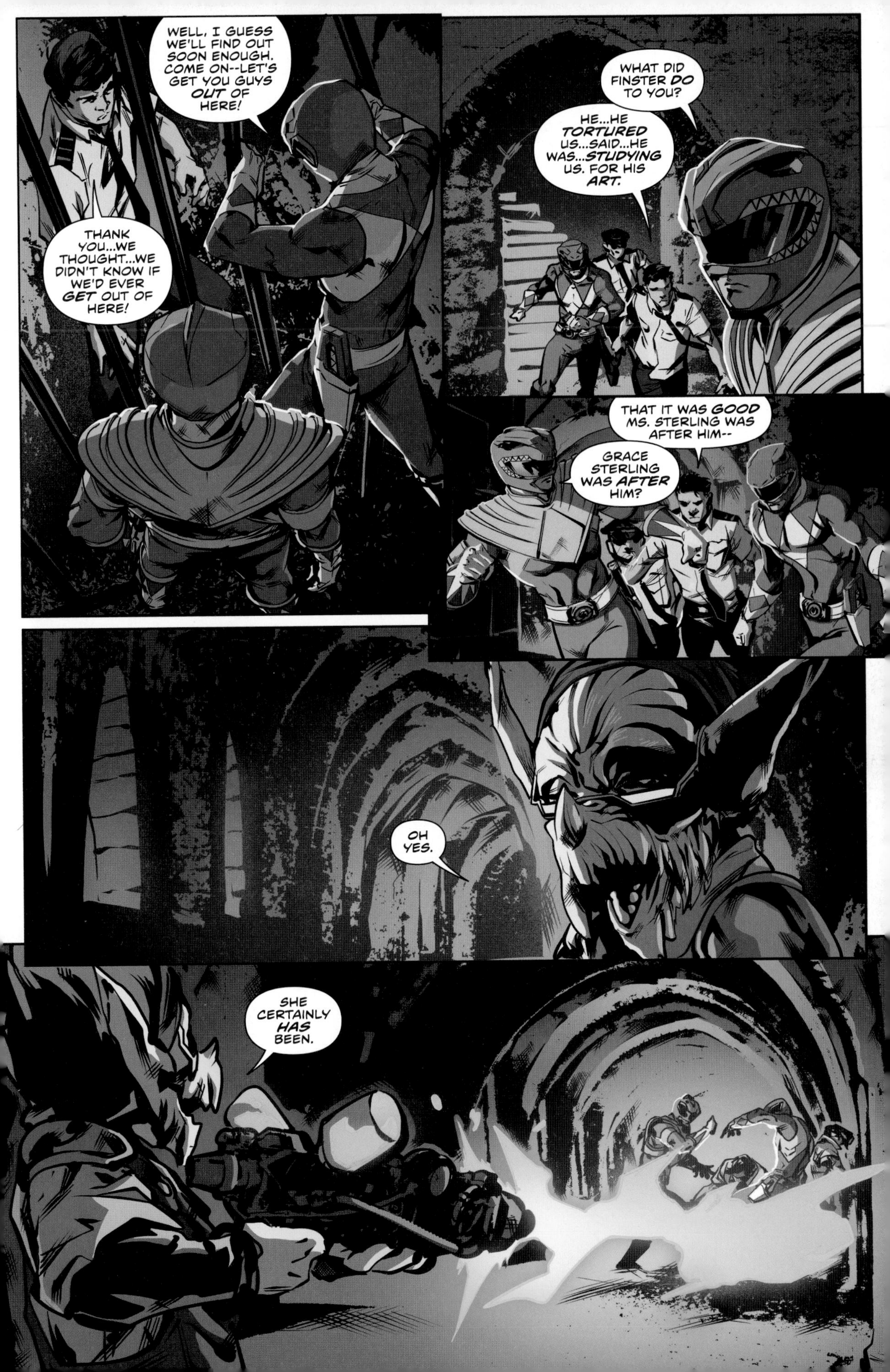
WELL, I GUESS WE'LL FIND OUT SOON ENOUGH. COME ON--LET'S GET YOU GUYS OUT OF HERE!
THANK YOU...WE THOUGHT...WE DIDN'T KNOW IF WE'D EVER GET OUT OF HERE!
WHAT DID FINSTER DO TO YOU?
HE...HE TORTURED US...SAID...HE WAS...STUDYING US. FOR HIS ART.
THAT IT WAS GOOD MS. STERLING WAS AFTER HIM--
GRACE STERLING WAS AFTER HIM?
OH YES.
SHE CERTAINLY HAS BEEN.

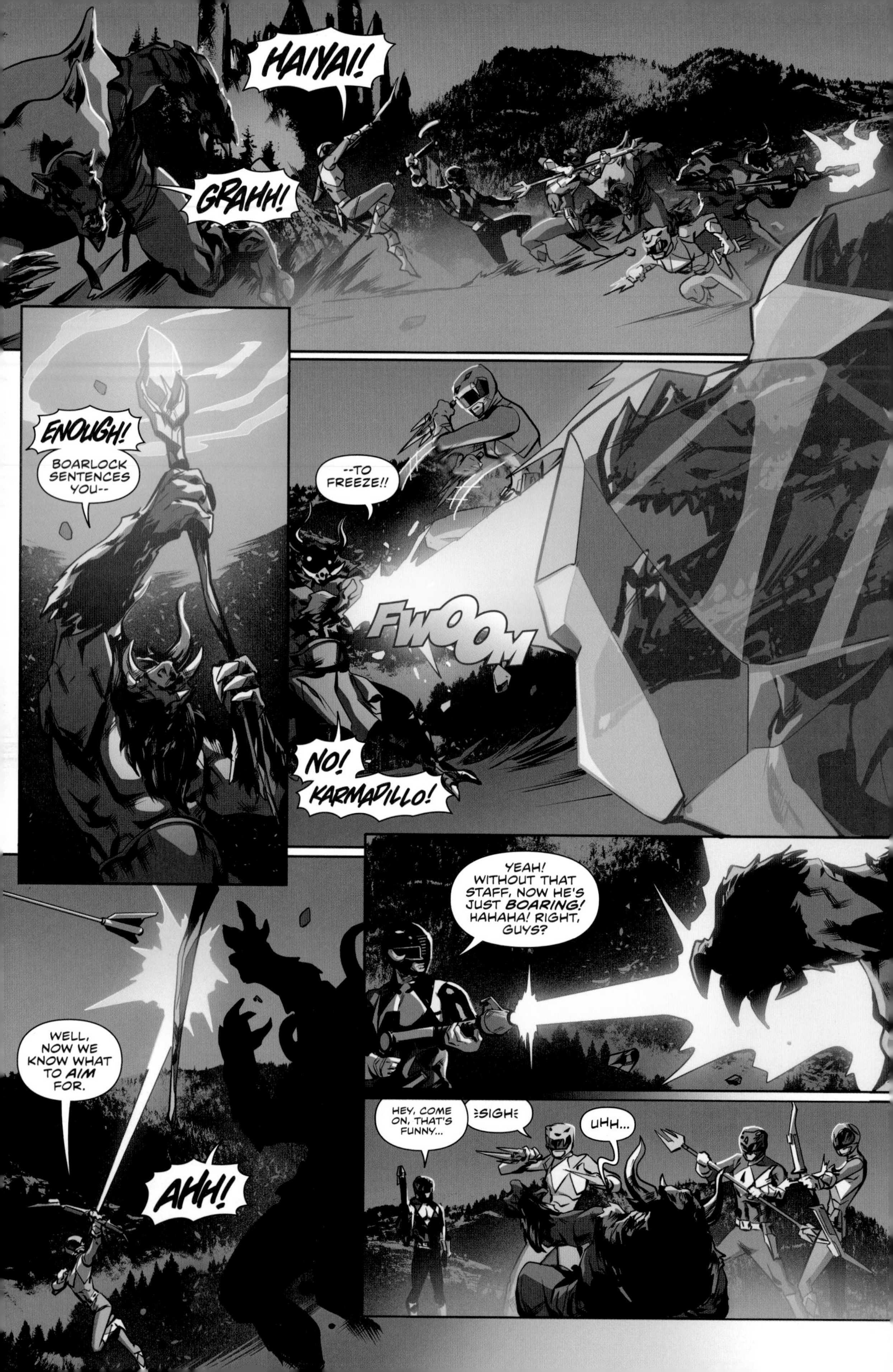
HAIYAI!
GRAHH!
ENOUGH!
BOARLOCK SENTENCES YOU--
--TO FREEZE!!
FWOOM
NO! KARMADILLO!
WELL, NOW WE KNOW WHAT TO AIM FOR.
AHH!
YEAH! WITHOUT THAT STAFF, NOW HE'S JUST BOARING! HAHAHA! RIGHT, GUYS?
HEY, COME ON, THAT'S FUNNY...
SIGH
UHH...

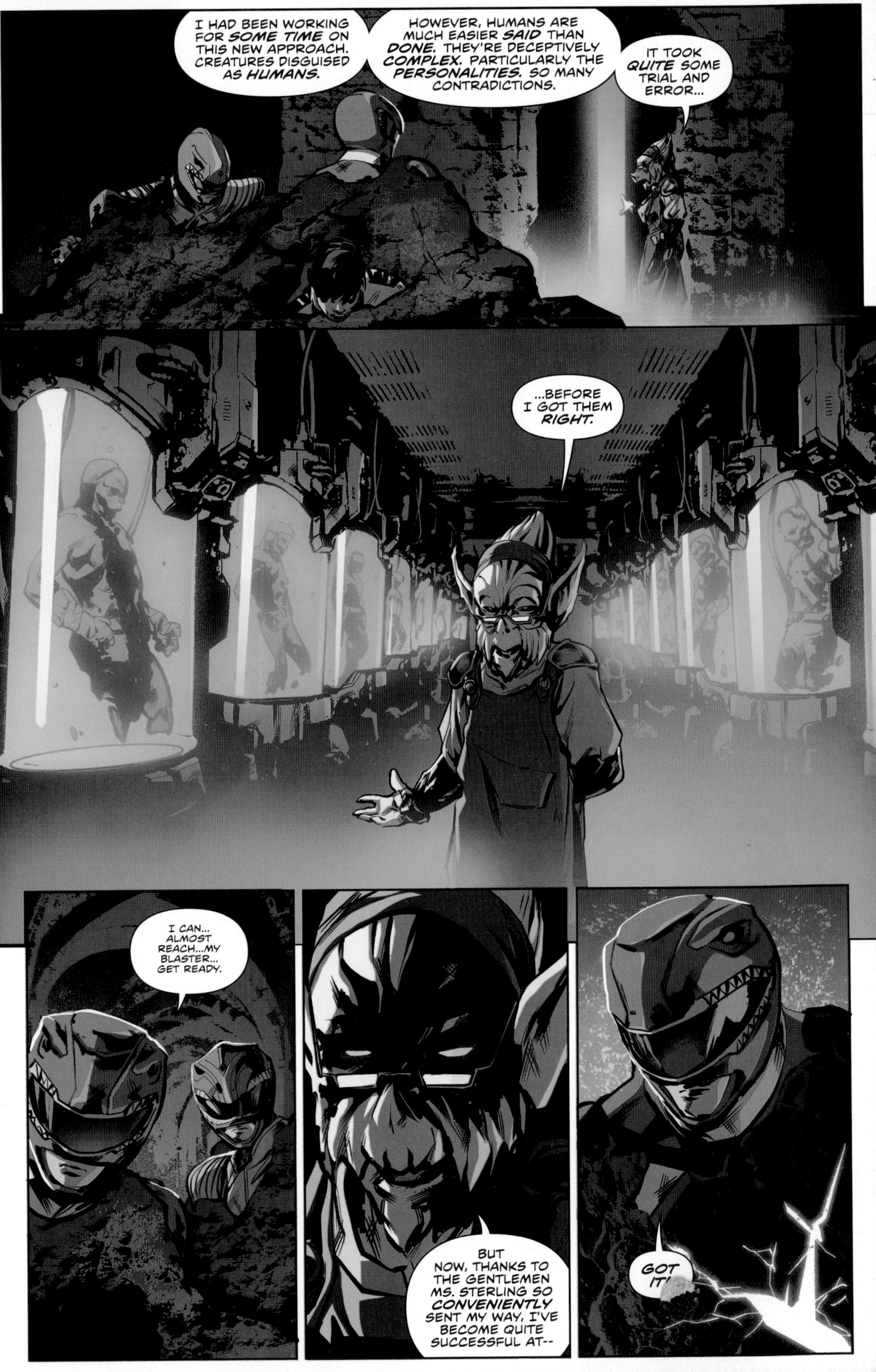

I HAD BEEN WORKING FOR SOME TIME ON THIS NEW APPROACH. CREATURES DISGUISED AS HUMANS.
HOWEVER, HUMANS ARE MUCH EASIER SAID THAN DONE. THEY'RE DECEPTIVELY COMPLEX. PARTICULARLY THE PERSONALITIES. SO MANY CONTRADICTIONS.
IT TOOK QUITE SOME TRIAL AND ERROR...
...BEFORE I GOT THEM RIGHT.
I CAN... ALMOST REACH...MY BLASTER... GET READY.
BUT NOW, THANKS TO THE GENTLEMEN MS. STERLING SO CONVENIENTLY SENT MY WAY, I'VE BECOME QUITE SUCCESSFUL AT--
GOT IT!

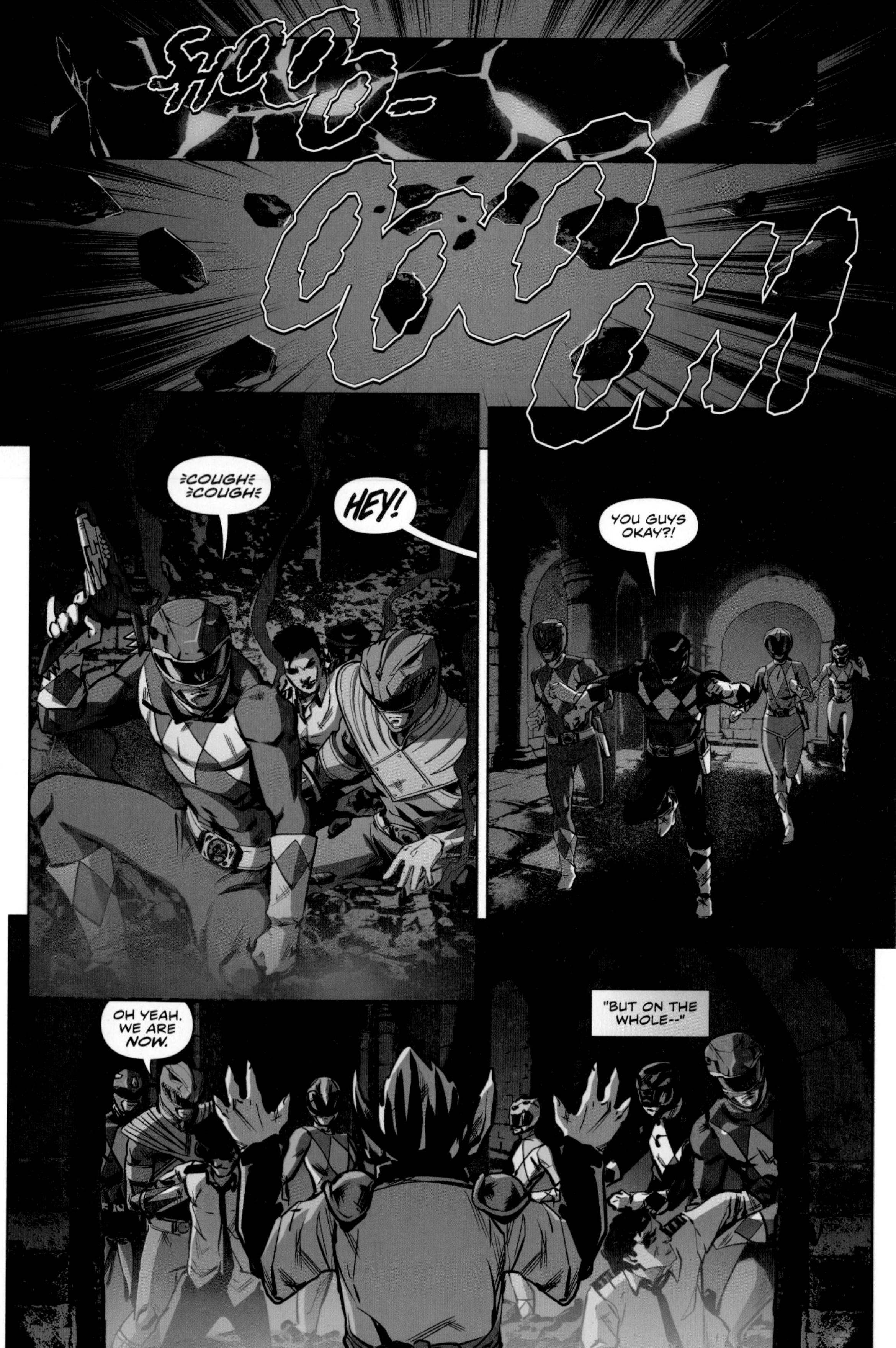
SHOOO-
OOOM
COUGH COUGH
HEY!
YOU GUYS OKAY?!
OH YEAH. WE ARE NOW.
"BUT ON THE WHOLE--"

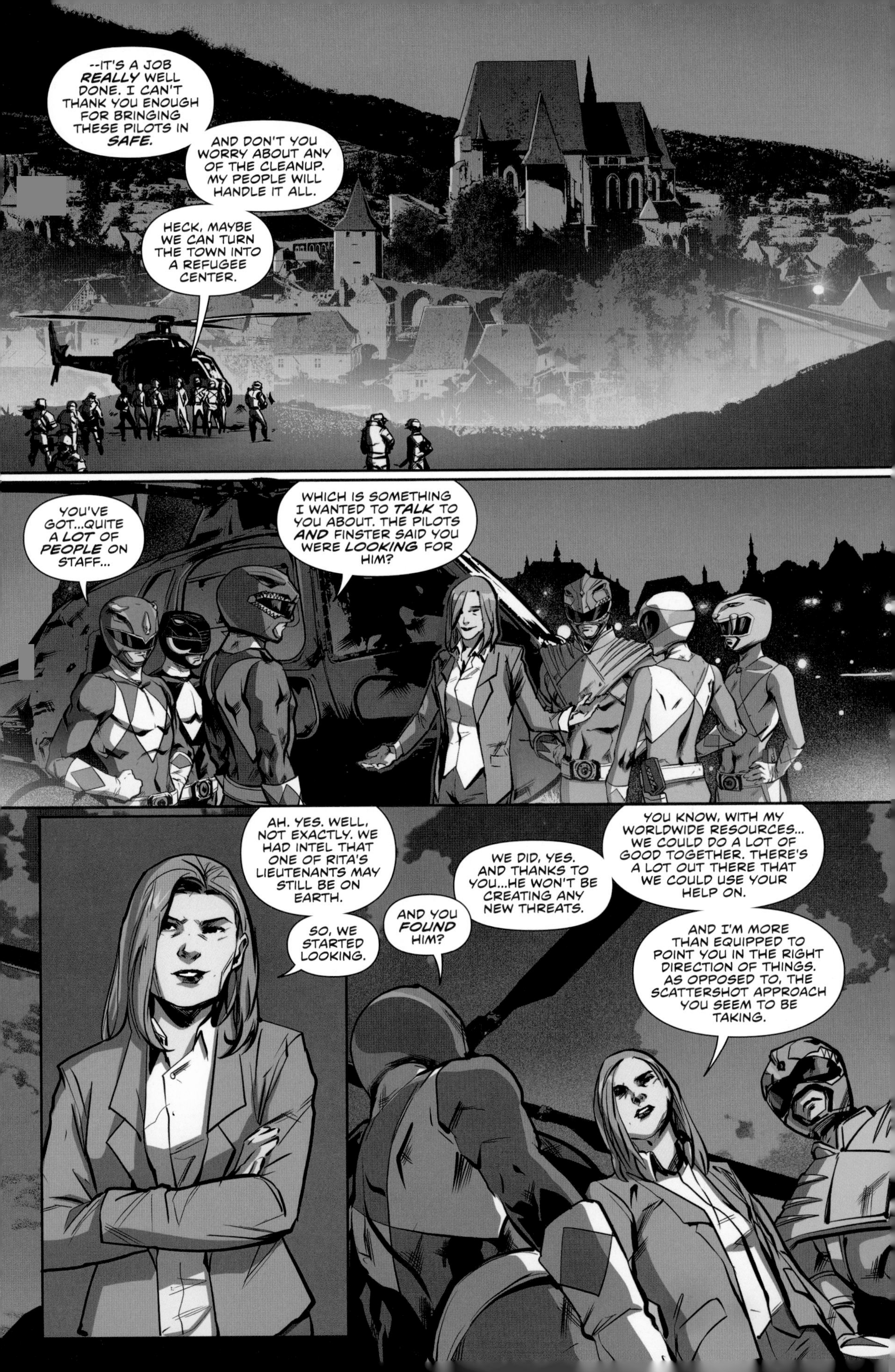
--IT'S A JOB REALLY WELL DONE. I CAN'T THANK YOU ENOUGH FOR BRINGING THESE PILOTS IN SAFE.
AND DON'T YOU WORRY ABOUT ANY OF THE CLEANUP. MY PEOPLE WILL HANDLE IT ALL.
HECK, MAYBE WE CAN TURN THE TOWN INTO A REFUGEE CENTER.
YOU'VE GOT...QUITE A LOT OF PEOPLE ON STAFF...
WHICH IS SOMETHING I WANTED TO TALK TO YOU ABOUT. THE PILOTS AND FINSTER SAID YOU WERE LOOKING FOR HIM?
AH. YES. WELL, NOT EXACTLY. WE HAD INTEL THAT ONE OF RITA'S LIEUTENANTS MAY STILL BE ON EARTH.
SO, WE STARTED LOOKING.
AND YOU FOUND HIM?
WE DID, YES. AND THANKS TO YOU...HE WON'T BE CREATING ANY NEW THREATS.
YOU KNOW, WITH MY WORLDWIDE RESOURCES... WE COULD DO A LOT OF GOOD TOGETHER. THERE'S A LOT OUT THERE THAT WE COULD USE YOUR HELP ON.
AND I'M MORE THAN EQUIPPED TO POINT YOU IN THE RIGHT DIRECTION OF THINGS. AS OPPOSED TO, THE SCATTERSHOT APPROACH YOU SEEM TO BE TAKING.

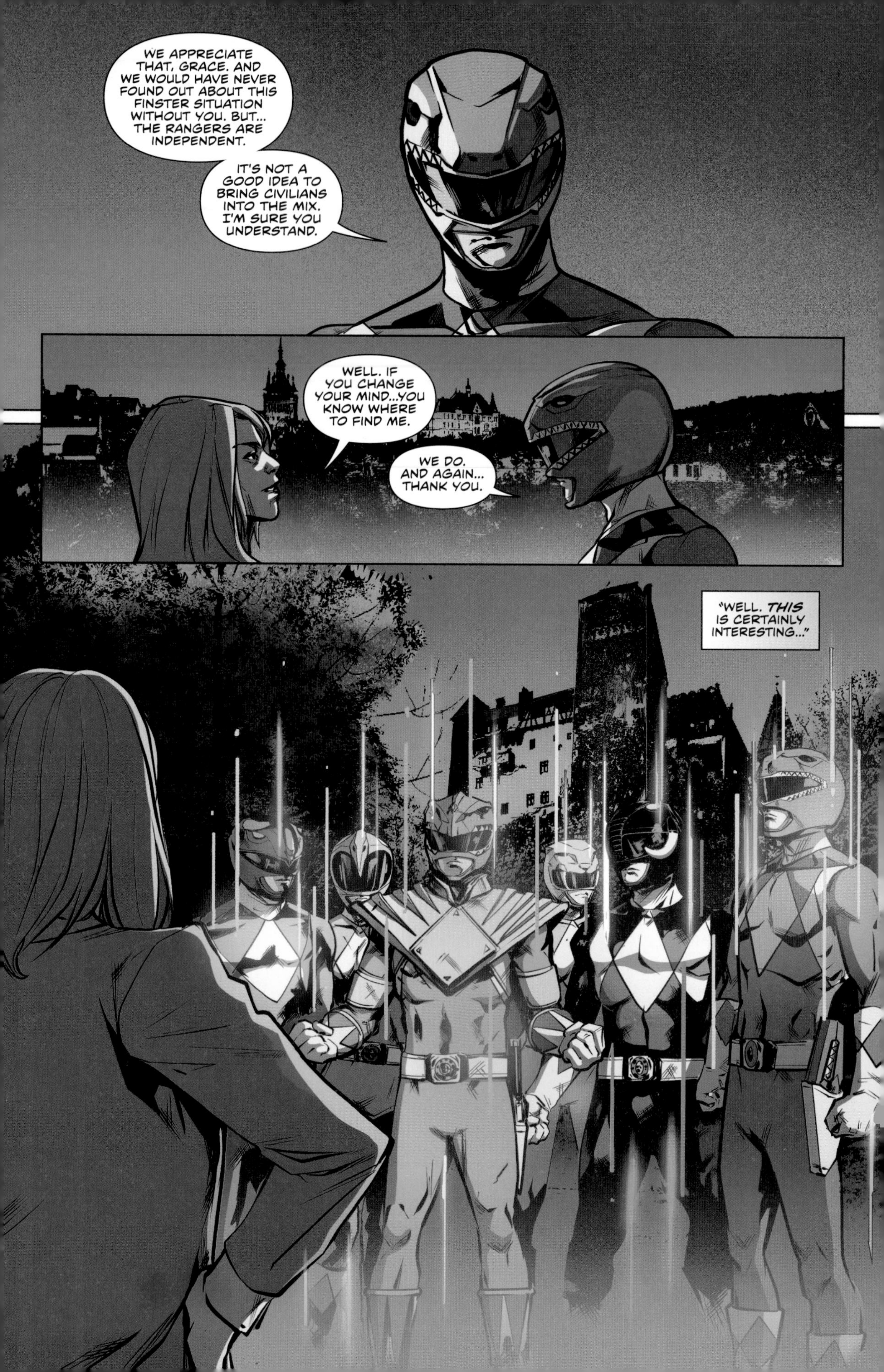
WE APPRECIATE THAT, GRACE. AND WE WOULD HAVE NEVER FOUND OUT ABOUT THIS FINSTER SITUATION WITHOUT YOU. BUT... THE RANGERS ARE INDEPENDENT.
IT'S NOT A GOOD IDEA TO BRING CIVILIANS INTO THE MIX. I'M SURE YOU UNDERSTAND.
WELL. IF YOU CHANGE YOUR MIND...YOU KNOW WHERE TO FIND ME.
WE DO. AND AGAIN... THANK YOU.
"WELL. *THIS* IS CERTAINLY INTERESTING..."

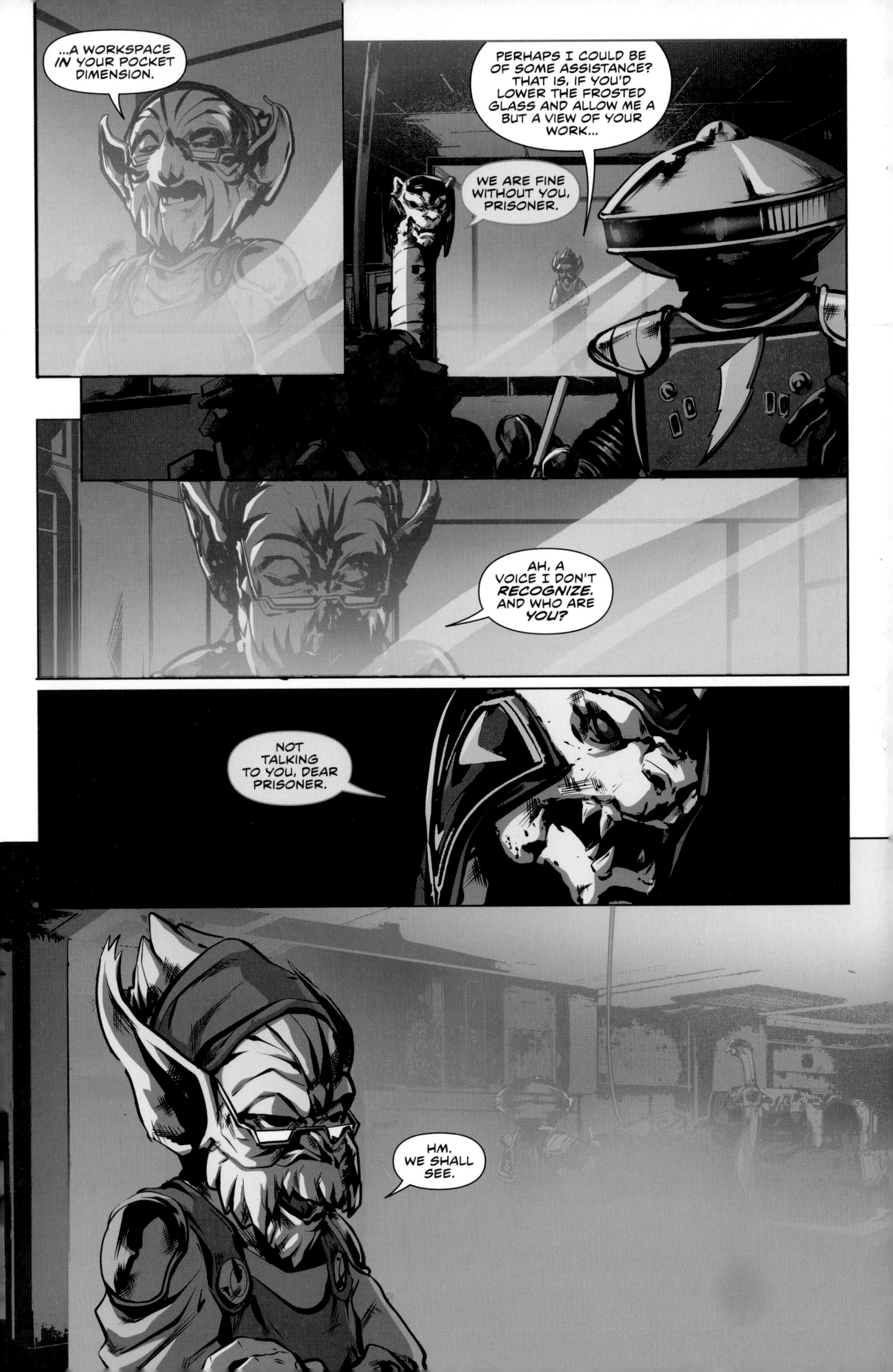
...A WORKSPACE *IN* YOUR POCKET DIMENSION.
PERHAPS I COULD BE OF SOME ASSISTANCE? THAT IS, IF YOU'D LOWER THE FROSTED GLASS AND ALLOW ME A BUT A VIEW OF YOUR WORK...
WE ARE FINE WITHOUT YOU, PRISONER.
AH, A VOICE I DON'T *RECOGNIZE.* AND WHO ARE *YOU?*
NOT TALKING TO YOU, DEAR PRISONER.
HM. WE SHALL SEE.

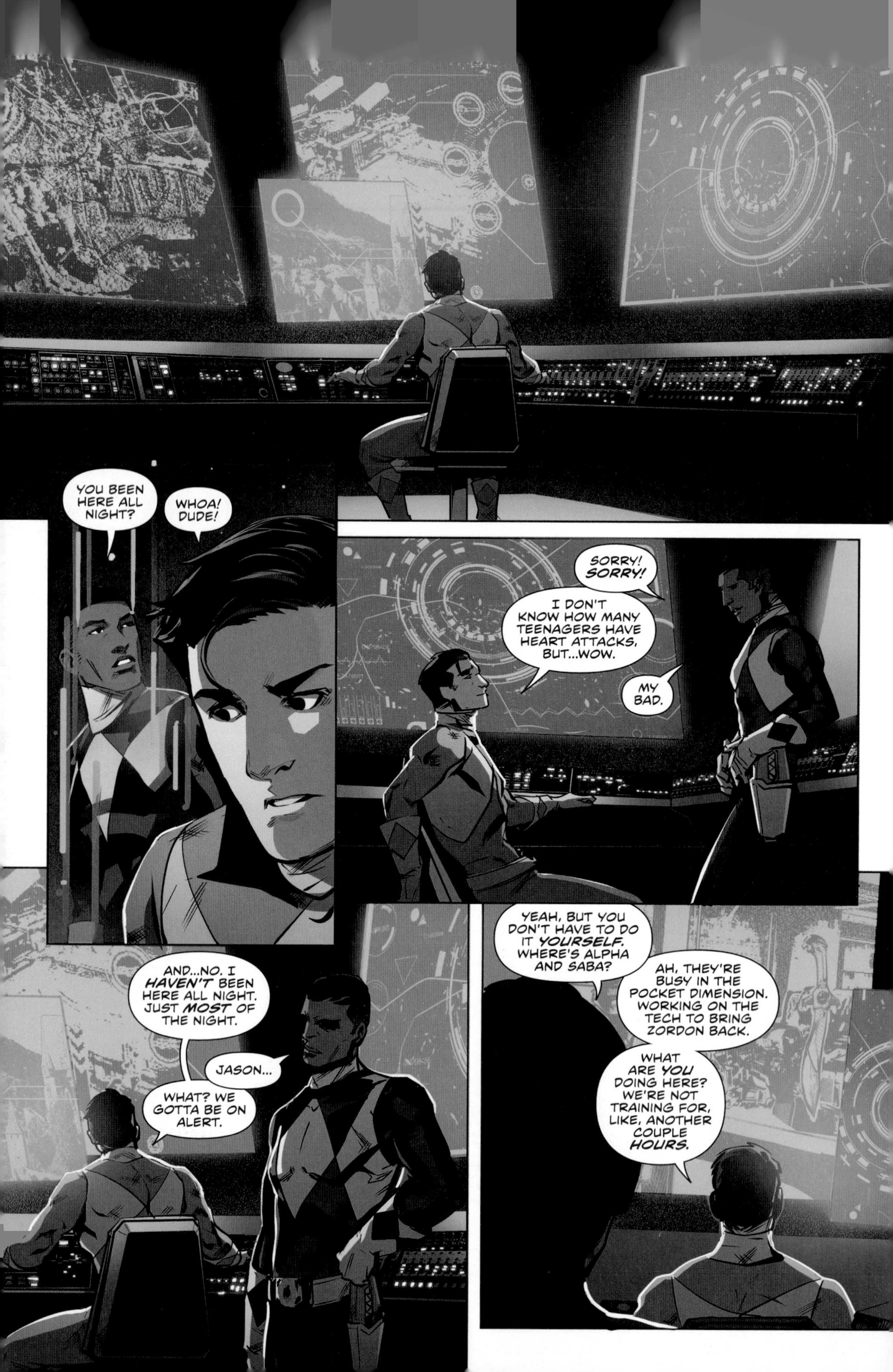
YOU BEEN HERE ALL NIGHT?
WHOA! DUDE!
SORRY! SORRY!
I DON'T KNOW HOW MANY TEENAGERS HAVE HEART ATTACKS, BUT...WOW.
MY BAD.
AND...NO. I HAVEN'T BEEN HERE ALL NIGHT. JUST MOST OF THE NIGHT.
JASON...
WHAT? WE GOTTA BE ON ALERT.
YEAH, BUT YOU DON'T HAVE TO DO IT YOURSELF. WHERE'S ALPHA AND SABA?
AH, THEY'RE BUSY IN THE POCKET DIMENSION. WORKING ON THE TECH TO BRING ZORDON BACK.
WHAT ARE YOU DOING HERE? WE'RE NOT TRAINING FOR, LIKE, ANOTHER COUPLE HOURS.

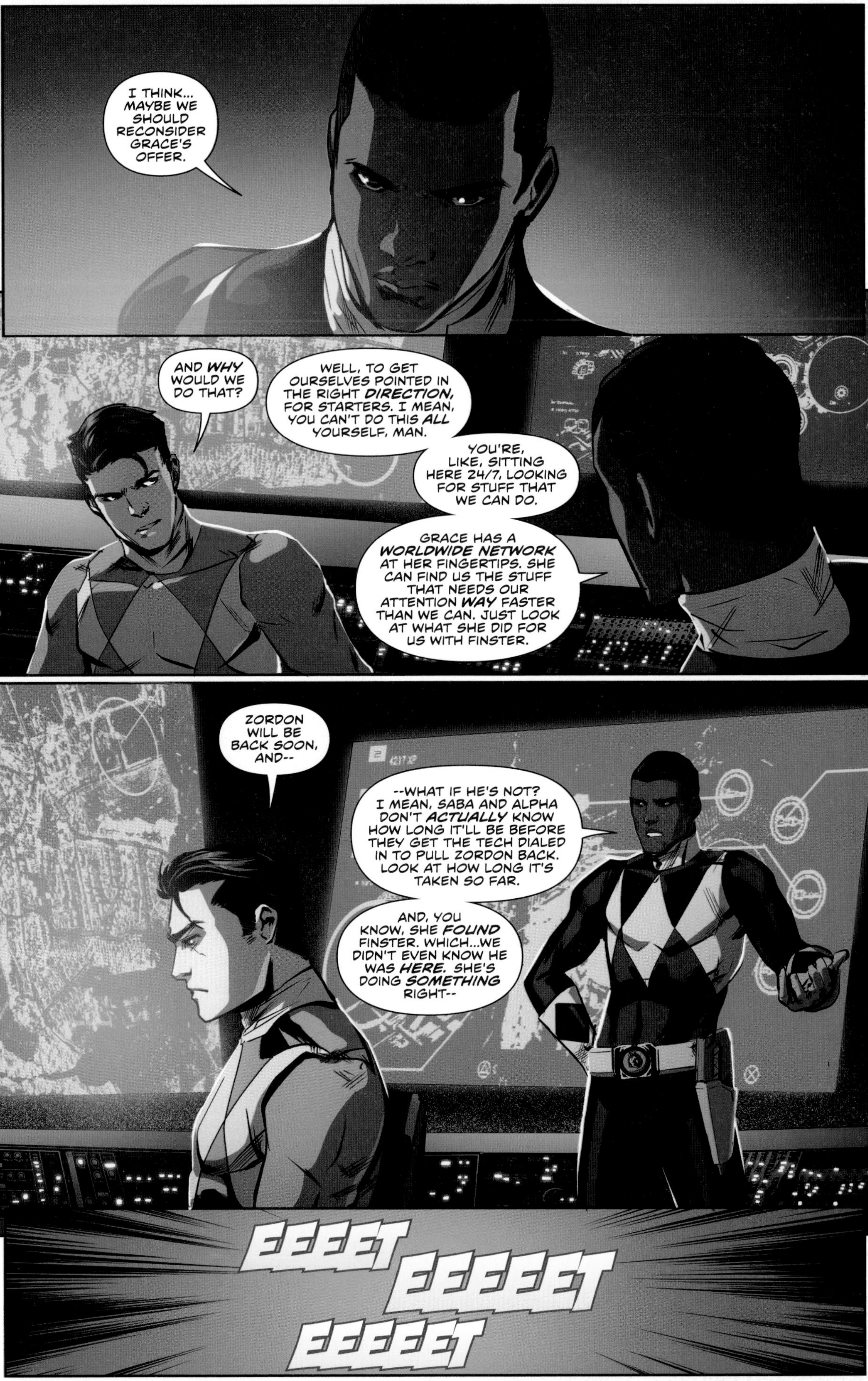
I THINK... MAYBE WE SHOULD RECONSIDER GRACE'S OFFER.
AND WHY WOULD WE DO THAT?
WELL, TO GET OURSELVES POINTED IN THE RIGHT DIRECTION, FOR STARTERS. I MEAN, YOU CAN'T DO THIS ALL YOURSELF, MAN.
YOU'RE, LIKE, SITTING HERE 24/7, LOOKING FOR STUFF THAT WE CAN DO.
GRACE HAS A WORLDWIDE NETWORK AT HER FINGERTIPS. SHE CAN FIND US THE STUFF THAT NEEDS OUR ATTENTION WAY FASTER THAN WE CAN. JUST LOOK AT WHAT SHE DID FOR US WITH FINSTER.
ZORDON WILL BE BACK SOON, AND--
--WHAT IF HE'S NOT? I MEAN, SABA AND ALPHA DON'T ACTUALLY KNOW HOW LONG IT'LL BE BEFORE THEY GET THE TECH DIALED IN TO PULL ZORDON BACK. LOOK AT HOW LONG IT'S TAKEN SO FAR.
AND, YOU KNOW, SHE FOUND FINSTER. WHICH...WE DIDN'T EVEN KNOW HE WAS HERE. SHE'S DOING SOMETHING RIGHT--
EEEET
EEEEET
EEEEET

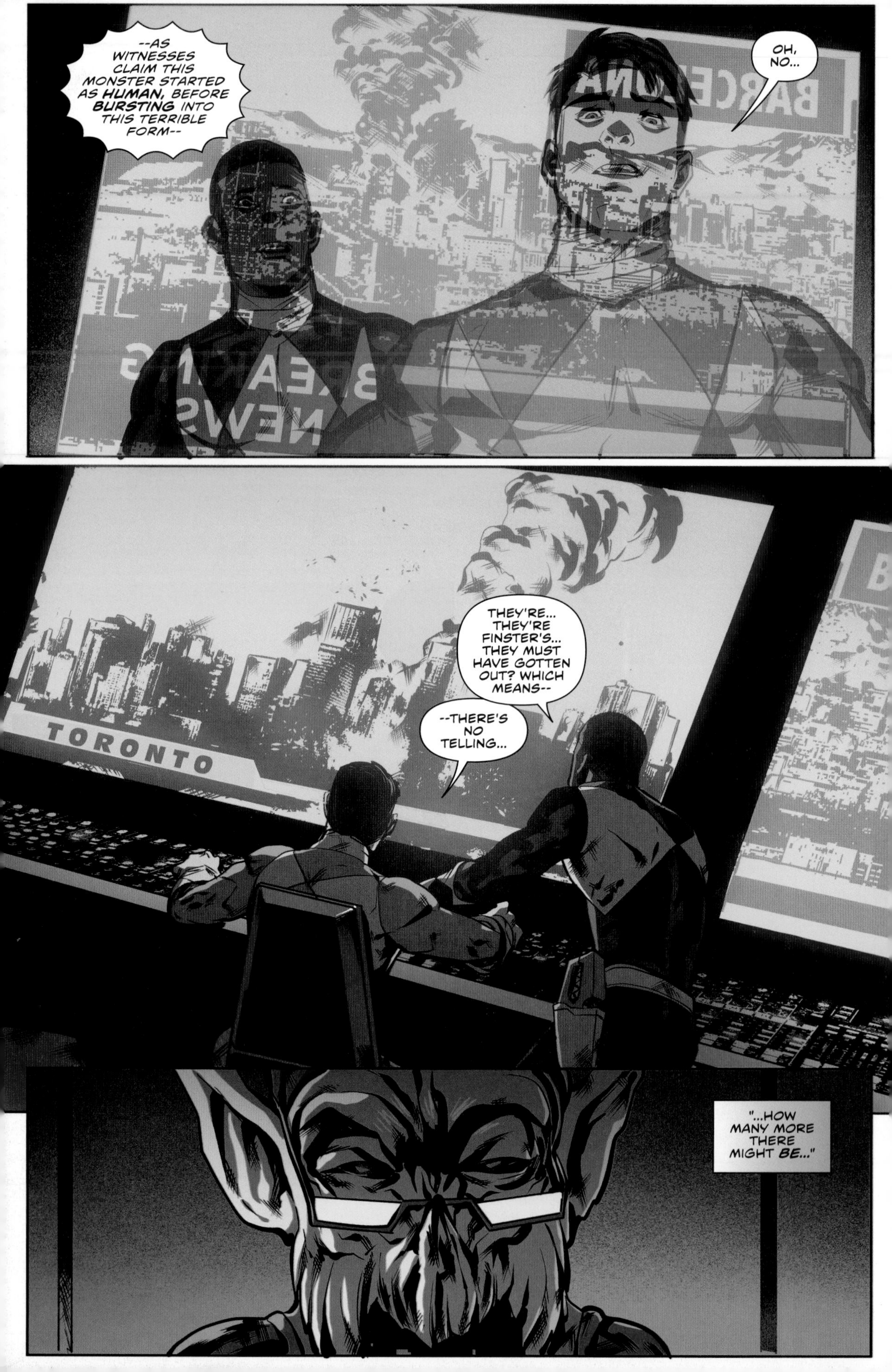
--AS WITNESSES CLAIM THIS MONSTER STARTED AS HUMAN, BEFORE BURSTING INTO THIS TERRIBLE FORM--
OH, NO...
BARCELONA
BREAKING NEWS
TORONTO
THEY'RE... THEY'RE FINSTER'S... THEY MUST HAVE GOTTEN OUT? WHICH MEANS--
--THERE'S NO TELLING...
"...HOW MANY MORE THERE MIGHT BE..."

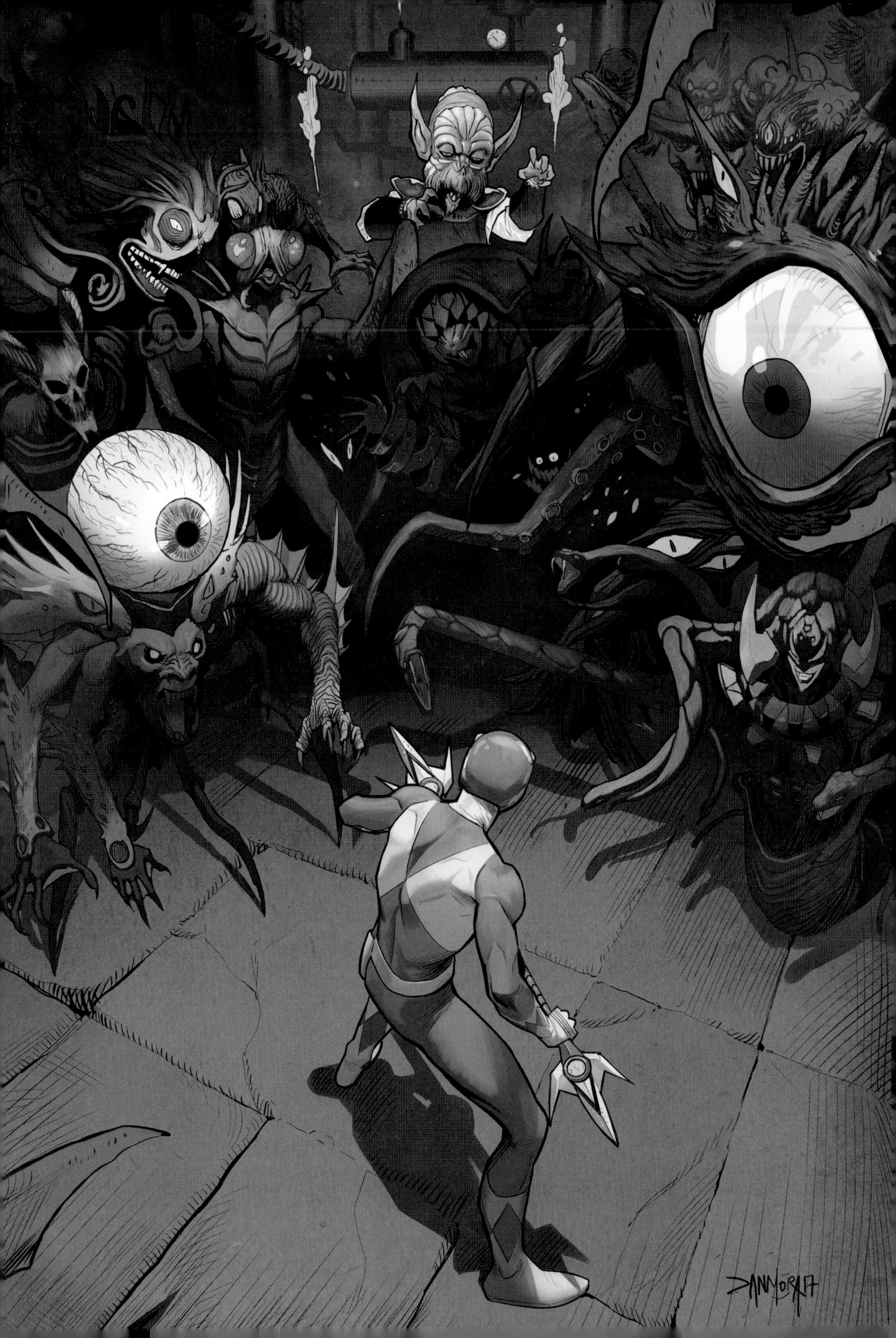
DANMORA17

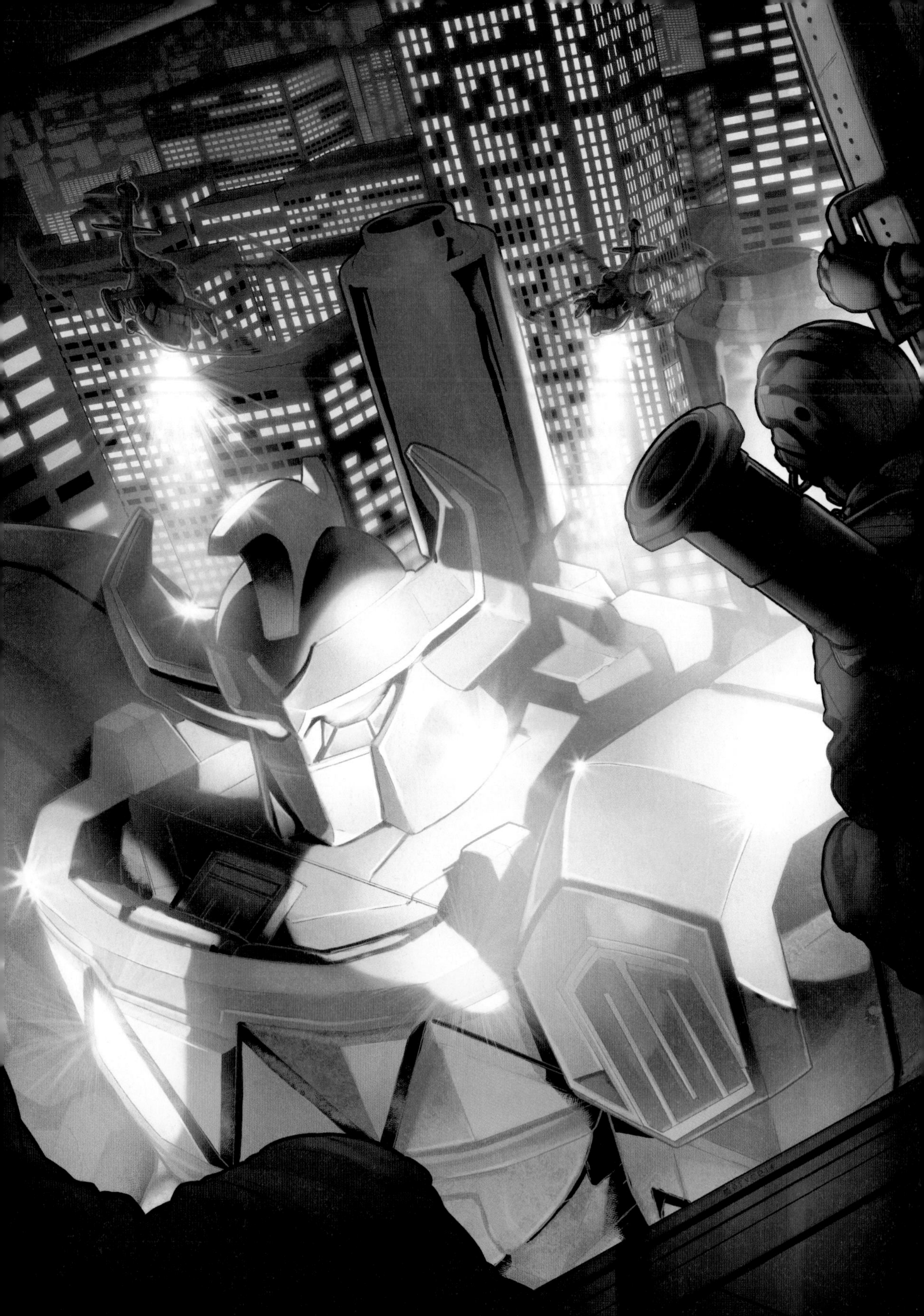

CHAPTER **NINETEEN**

JAMAL CAMPBELL | ISSUE NINETEEN COVER

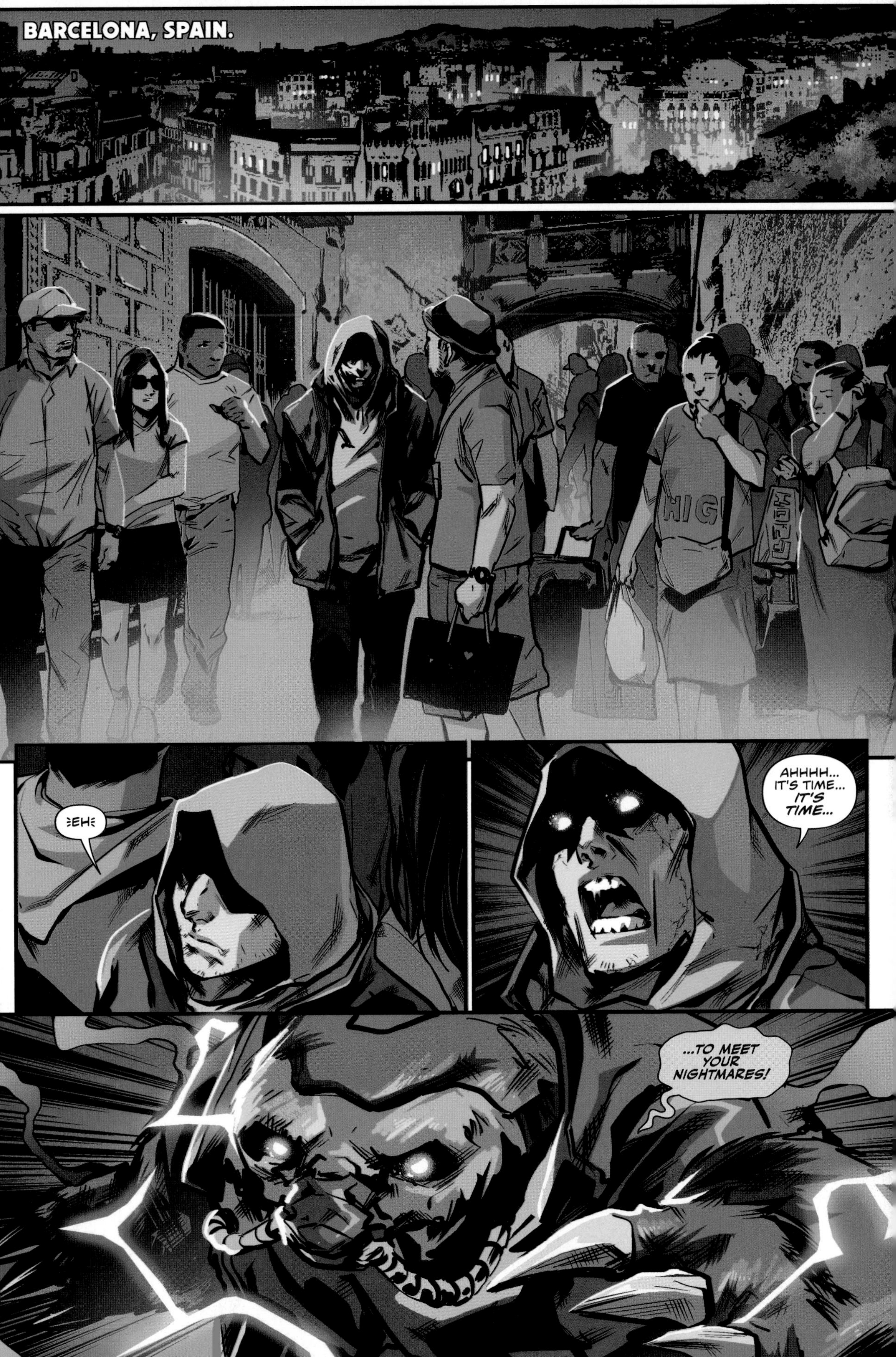
BARCELONA, SPAIN.
EH
AHHHH... IT'S TIME... IT'S TIME...
...TO MEET YOUR NIGHTMARES!

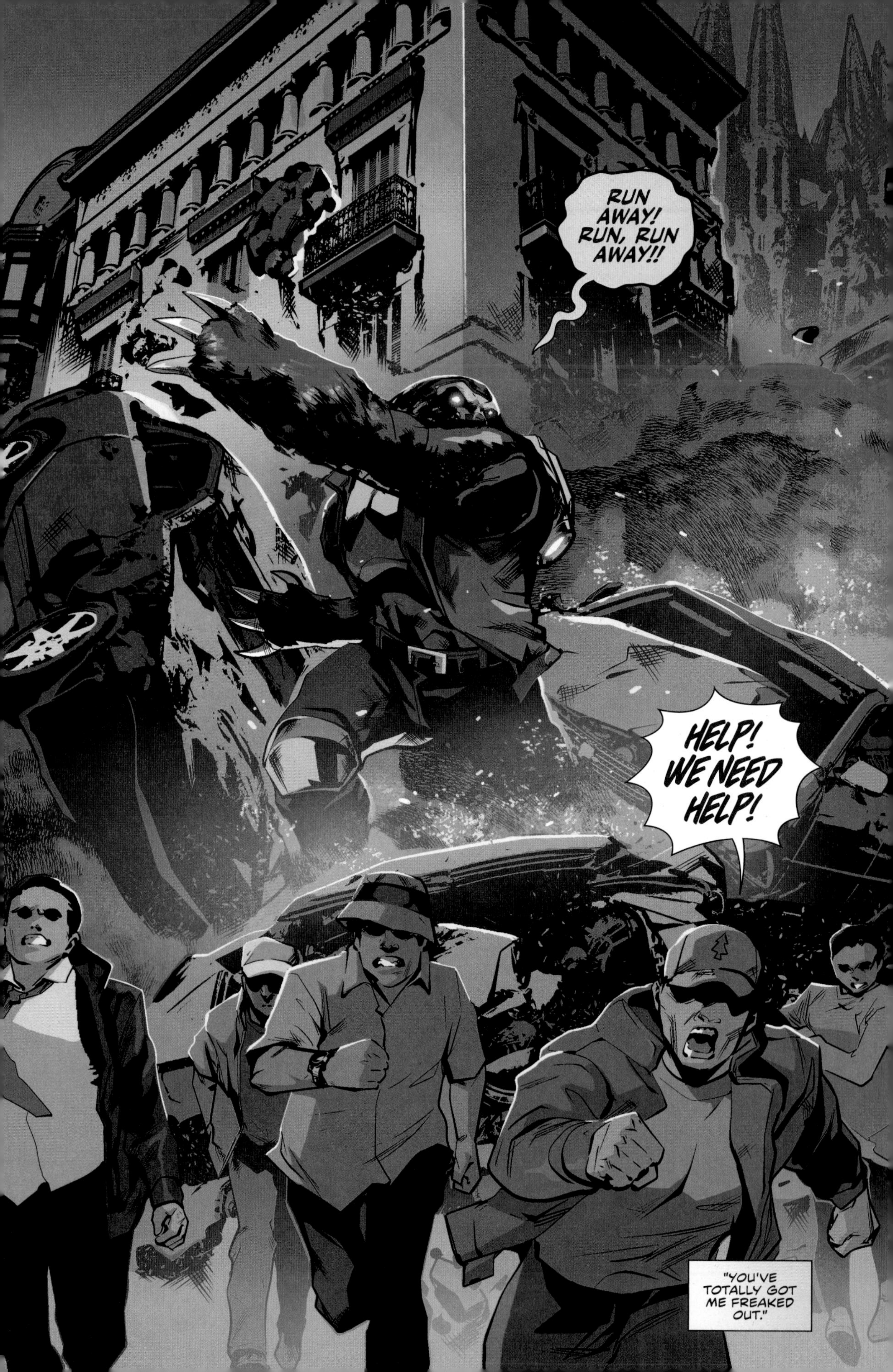
RUN AWAY! RUN, RUN AWAY!!
HELP! WE NEED HELP!
"YOU'VE TOTALLY GOT ME FREAKED OUT."

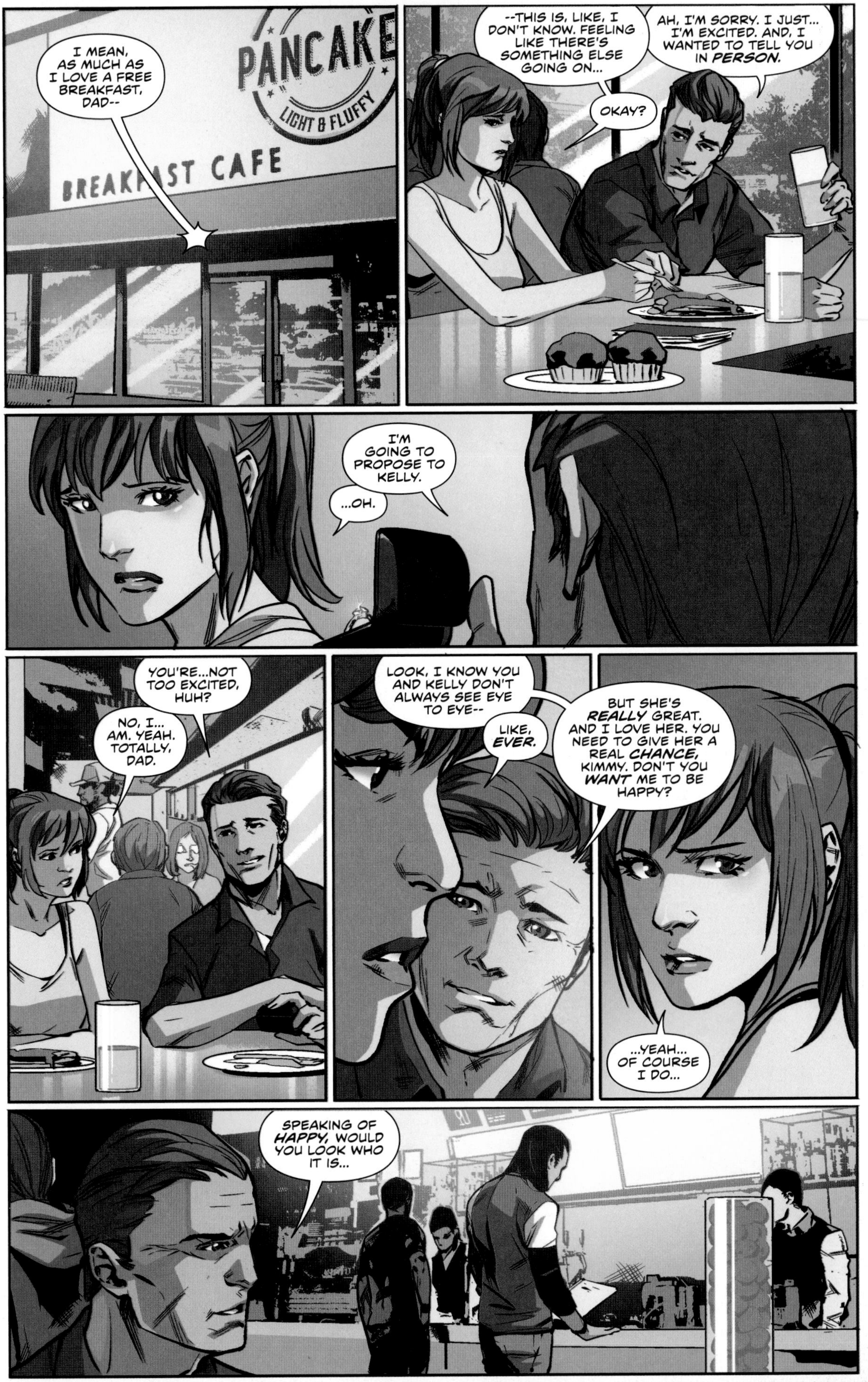
PANCAKE
LIGHT & FLUFFY
BREAKFAST CAFE
I MEAN, AS MUCH AS I LOVE A FREE BREAKFAST, DAD--
--THIS IS, LIKE, I DON'T KNOW. FEELING LIKE THERE'S SOMETHING ELSE GOING ON...
OKAY?
AH, I'M SORRY. I JUST... I'M EXCITED. AND, I WANTED TO TELL YOU IN PERSON.
I'M GOING TO PROPOSE TO KELLY.
...OH.
YOU'RE...NOT TOO EXCITED, HUH?
NO, I... AM. YEAH. TOTALLY, DAD.
LOOK, I KNOW YOU AND KELLY DON'T ALWAYS SEE EYE TO EYE--
LIKE, EVER.
BUT SHE'S REALLY GREAT. AND I LOVE HER. YOU NEED TO GIVE HER A REAL CHANCE, KIMMY. DON'T YOU WANT ME TO BE HAPPY?
...YEAH... OF COURSE I DO...
SPEAKING OF HAPPY, WOULD YOU LOOK WHO IT IS...

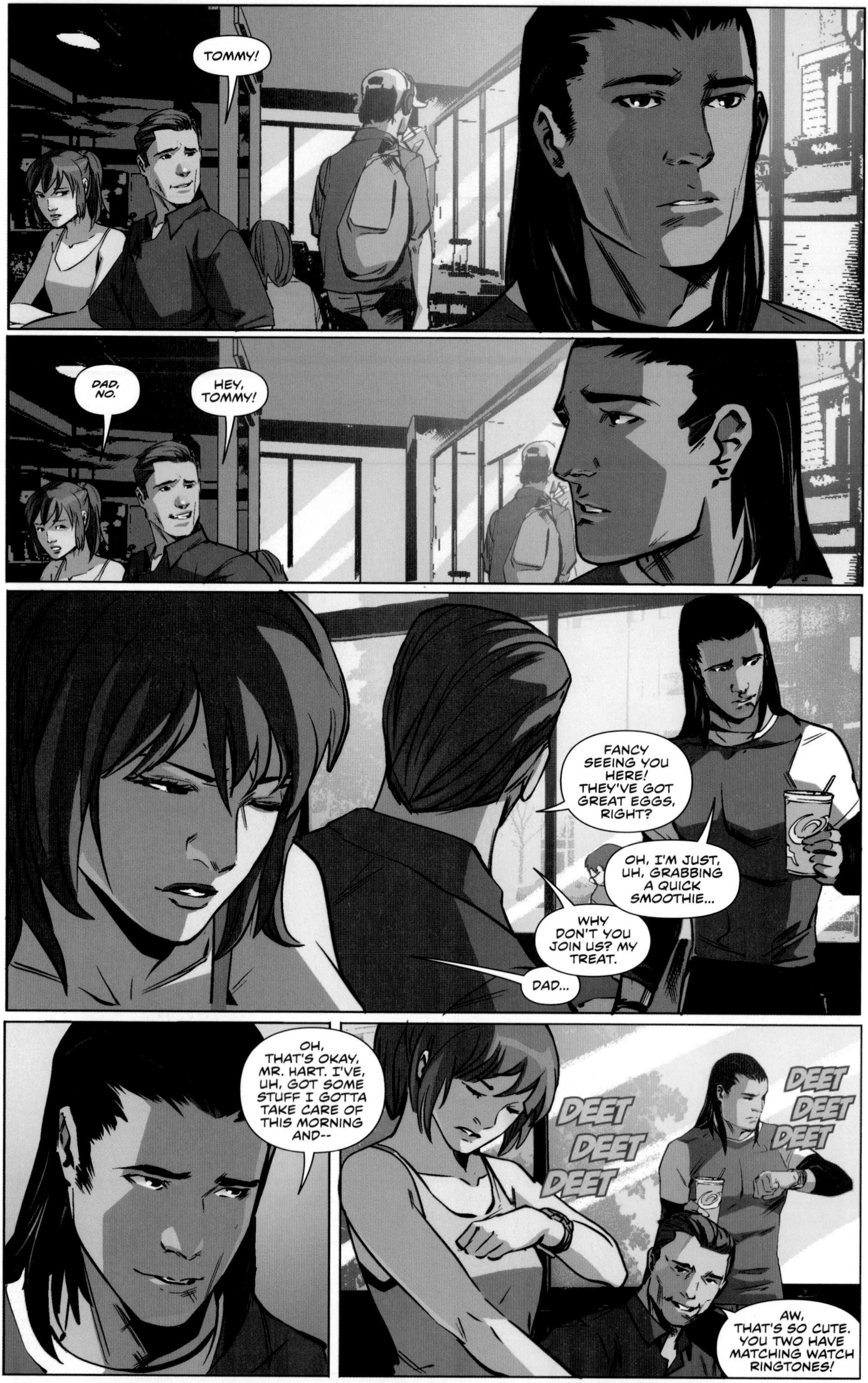

TOMMY!
DAD, NO.
HEY, TOMMY!
FANCY SEEING YOU HERE! THEY'VE GOT GREAT EGGS, RIGHT?
OH, I'M JUST, UH, GRABBING A QUICK SMOOTHIE...
WHY DON'T YOU JOIN US? MY TREAT.
DAD...
OH, THAT'S OKAY, MR. HART. I'VE, UH, GOT SOME STUFF I GOTTA TAKE CARE OF THIS MORNING AND--
DEET DEET DEET
DEET DEET DEET
AW, THAT'S SO CUTE. YOU TWO HAVE MATCHING WATCH RINGTONES!

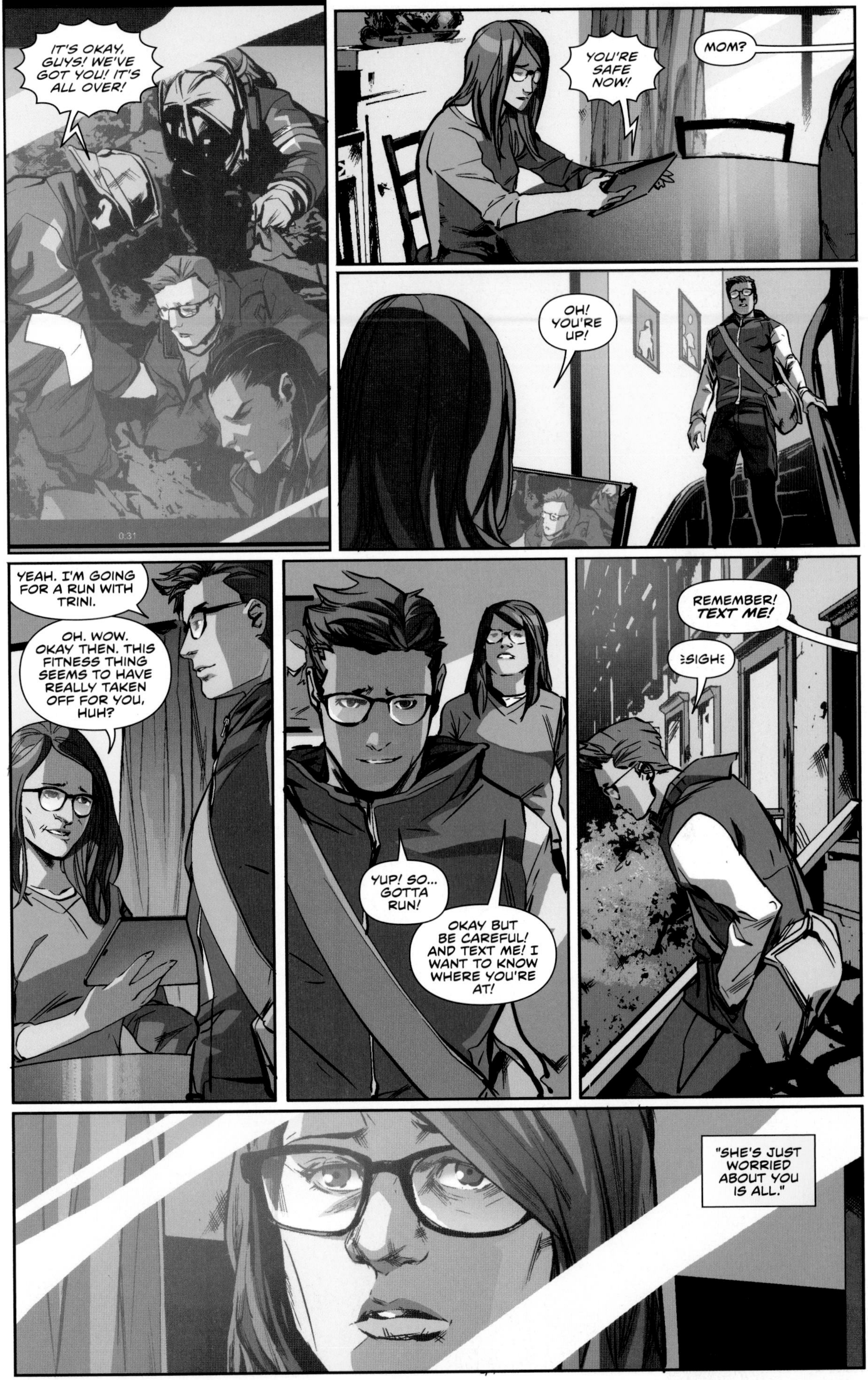
IT'S OKAY, GUYS! WE'VE GOT YOU! IT'S ALL OVER!
0:31
YOU'RE SAFE NOW!
MOM?
OH! YOU'RE UP!
YEAH. I'M GOING FOR A RUN WITH TRINI.
OH. WOW. OKAY THEN. THIS FITNESS THING SEEMS TO HAVE REALLY TAKEN OFF FOR YOU, HUH?
YUP! SO... GOTTA RUN!
OKAY BUT BE CAREFUL! AND TEXT ME! I WANT TO KNOW WHERE YOU'RE AT!
REMEMBER! TEXT ME!
SIGH
"SHE'S JUST WORRIED ABOUT YOU IS ALL."

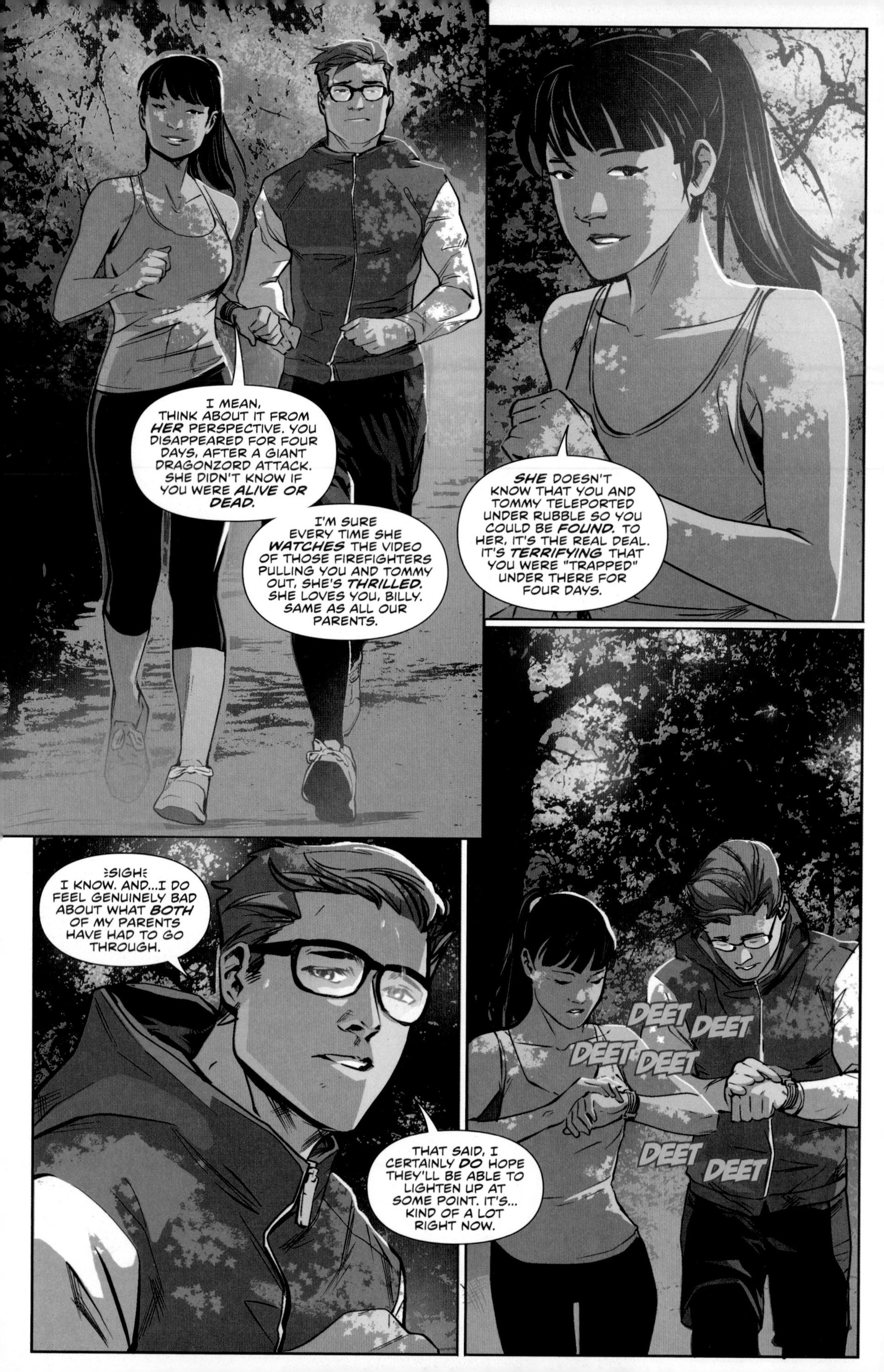
I MEAN, THINK ABOUT IT FROM HER PERSPECTIVE. YOU DISAPPEARED FOR FOUR DAYS, AFTER A GIANT DRAGONZORD ATTACK. SHE DIDN'T KNOW IF YOU WERE ALIVE OR DEAD.
I'M SURE EVERY TIME SHE WATCHES THE VIDEO OF THOSE FIREFIGHTERS PULLING YOU AND TOMMY OUT, SHE'S THRILLED. SHE LOVES YOU, BILLY. SAME AS ALL OUR PARENTS.
SHE DOESN'T KNOW THAT YOU AND TOMMY TELEPORTED UNDER RUBBLE SO YOU COULD BE FOUND. TO HER, IT'S THE REAL DEAL. IT'S TERRIFYING THAT YOU WERE "TRAPPED" UNDER THERE FOR FOUR DAYS.
ƐSIGHƐ I KNOW. AND...I DO FEEL GENUINELY BAD ABOUT WHAT BOTH OF MY PARENTS HAVE HAD TO GO THROUGH.
THAT SAID, I CERTAINLY DO HOPE THEY'LL BE ABLE TO LIGHTEN UP AT SOME POINT. IT'S... KIND OF A LOT RIGHT NOW.
DEET DEET
DEET DEET
DEET DEET

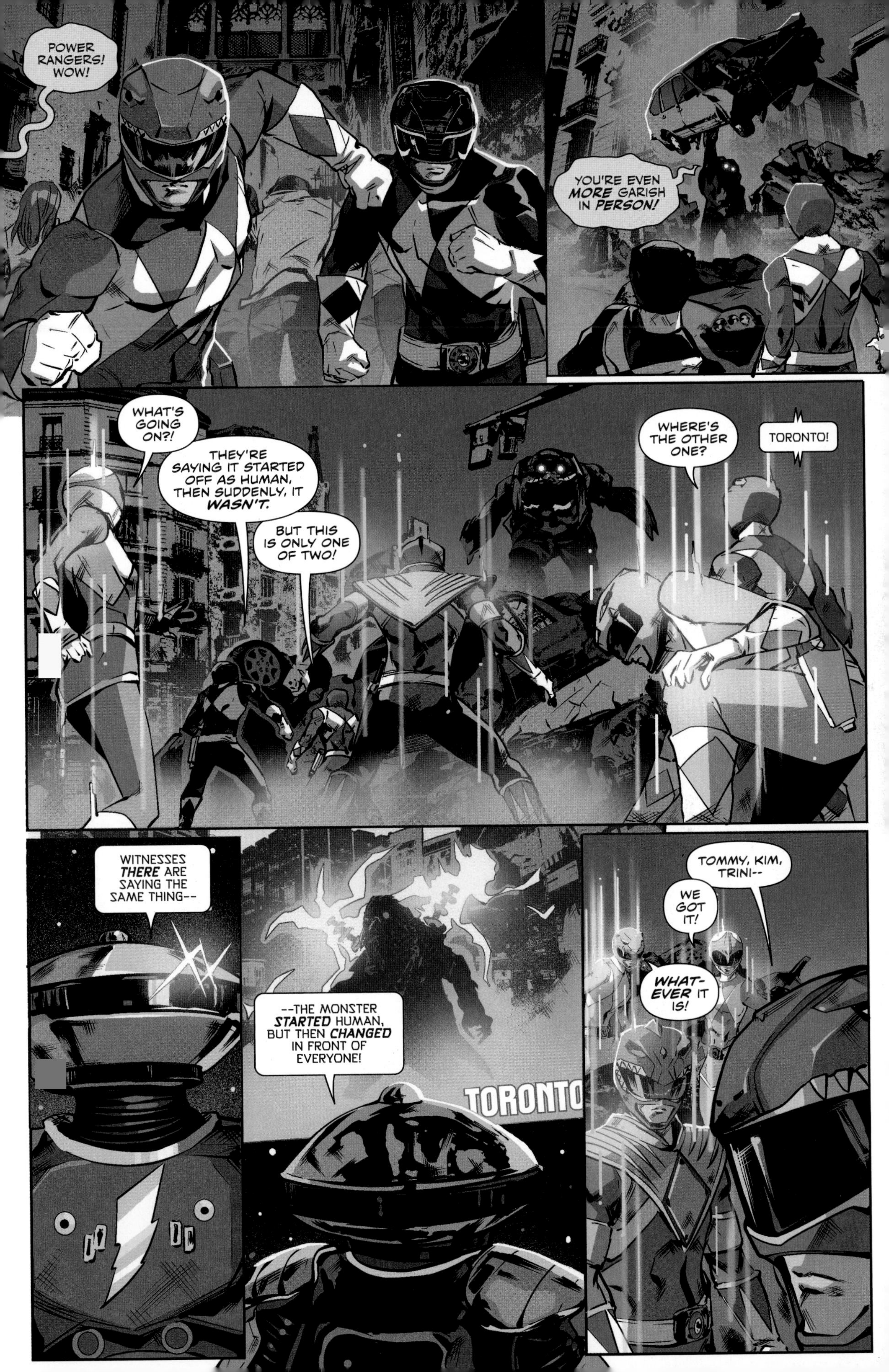
POWER RANGERS! WOW!
YOU'RE EVEN MORE GARISH IN PERSON!
WHAT'S GOING ON?!
THEY'RE SAYING IT STARTED OFF AS HUMAN, THEN SUDDENLY, IT WASN'T.
BUT THIS IS ONLY ONE OF TWO!
WHERE'S THE OTHER ONE?
TORONTO!
WITNESSES THERE ARE SAYING THE SAME THING--
--THE MONSTER STARTED HUMAN, BUT THEN CHANGED IN FRONT OF EVERYONE!
TORONTO
TOMMY, KIM, TRINI--
WE GOT IT!
WHATEVER IT IS!

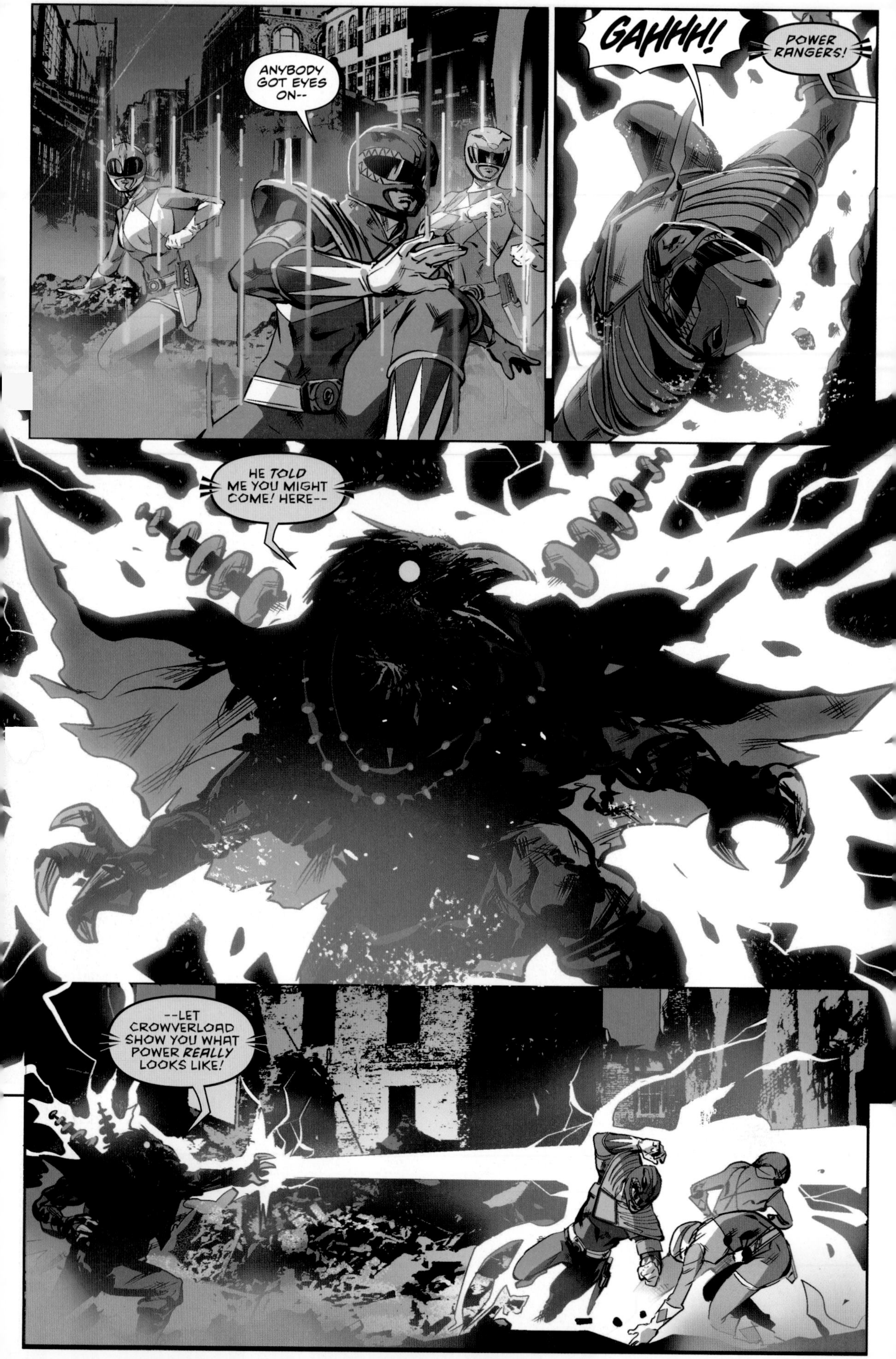
ANYBODY GOT EYES ON--
GAHHH!
POWER RANGERS!
HE TOLD ME YOU MIGHT COME! HERE--
--LET CROWVERLOAD SHOW YOU WHAT POWER REALLY LOOKS LIKE!

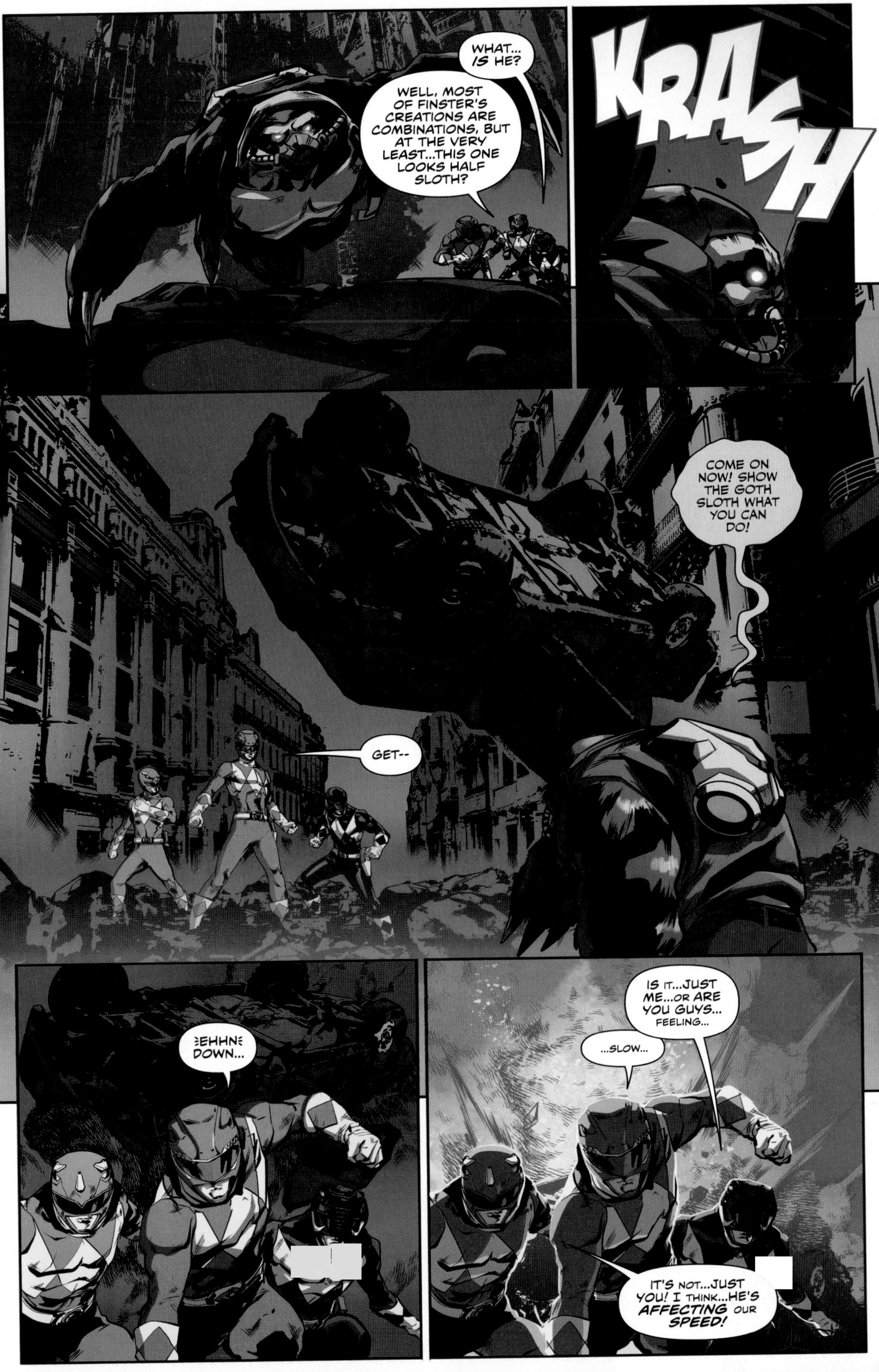
WHAT... IS HE?
WELL, MOST OF FINSTER'S CREATIONS ARE COMBINATIONS, BUT AT THE VERY LEAST...THIS ONE LOOKS HALF SLOTH?
KRASH
COME ON NOW! SHOW THE GOTH SLOTH WHAT YOU CAN DO!
GET--
EHHN DOWN...
IS IT...JUST ME...OR ARE YOU GUYS... FEELING...
...SLOW...
IT'S NOT...JUST YOU! I THINK...HE'S AFFECTING OUR SPEED!

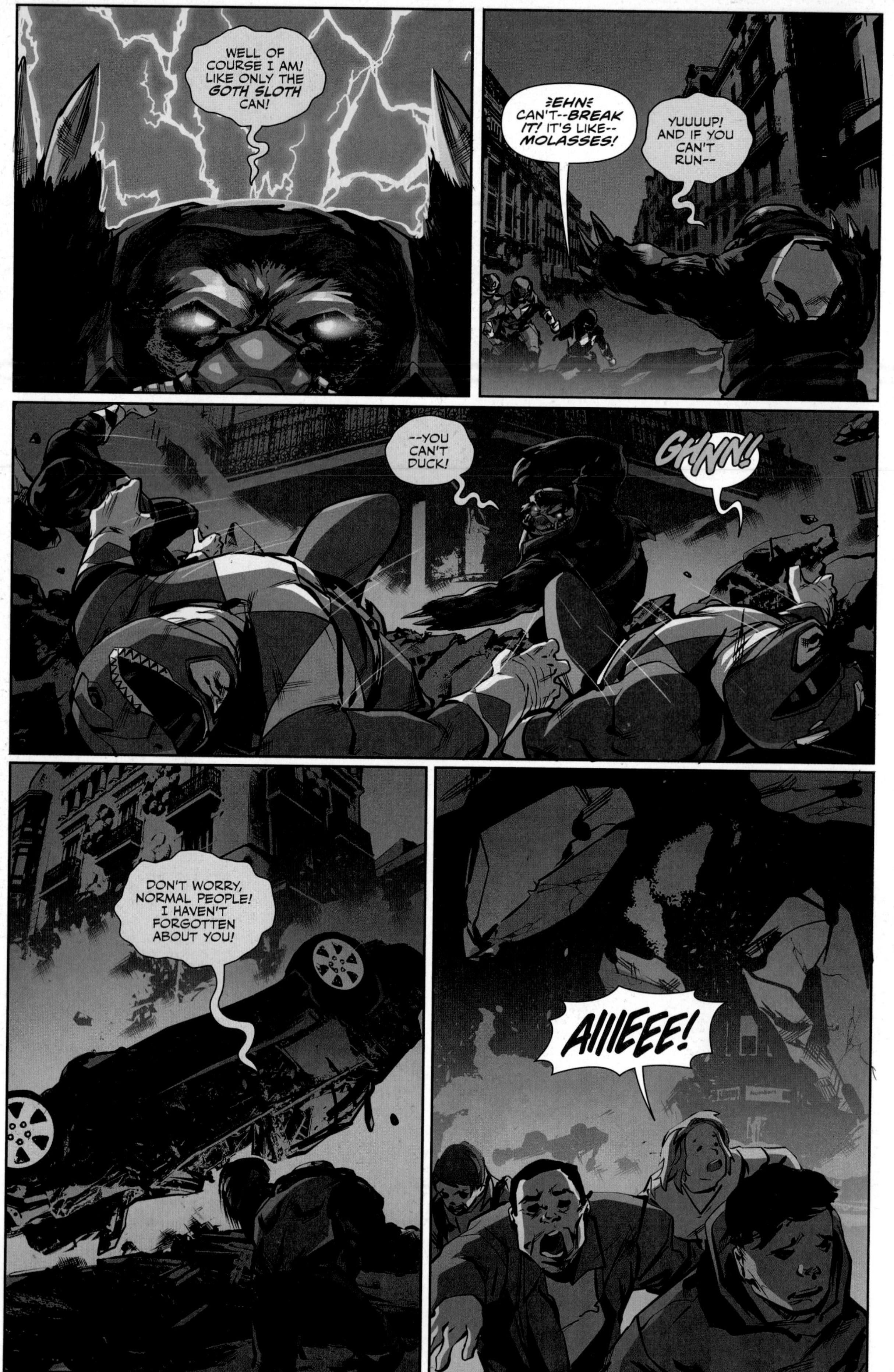

WELL OF COURSE I AM! LIKE ONLY THE GOTH SLOTH CAN!
EHN CAN'T--BREAK IT! IT'S LIKE--MOLASSES!
YUUUUP! AND IF YOU CAN'T RUN--
--YOU CAN'T DUCK!
GHNN!
DON'T WORRY, NORMAL PEOPLE! I HAVEN'T FORGOTTEN ABOUT YOU!
AIIIEEE!

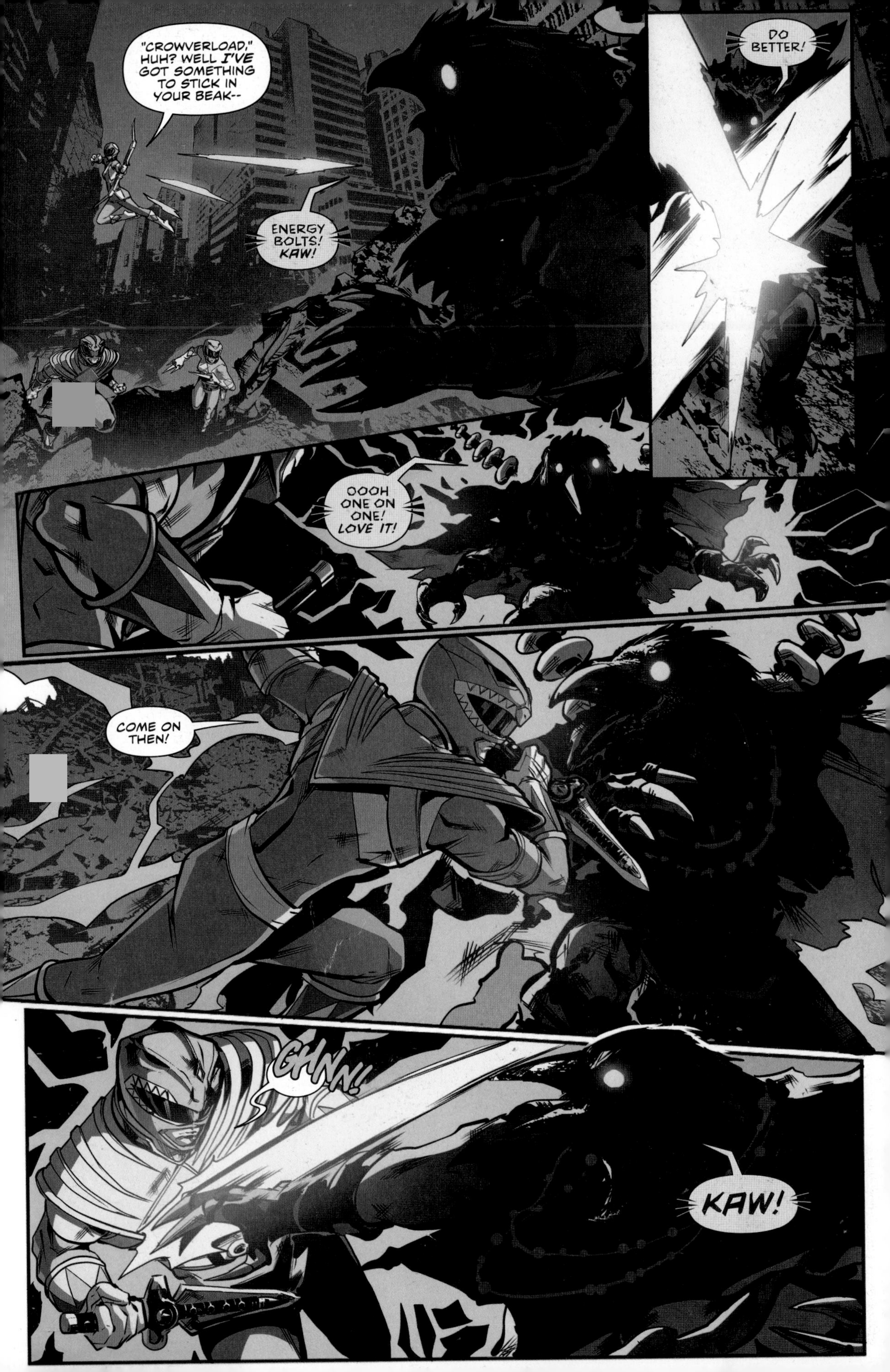
"CROWVERLOAD," HUH? WELL I'VE GOT SOMETHING TO STICK IN YOUR BEAK--
ENERGY BOLTS! KAW!
DO BETTER!
OOOH ONE ON ONE! LOVE IT!
COME ON THEN!
GHNN!
KAW!

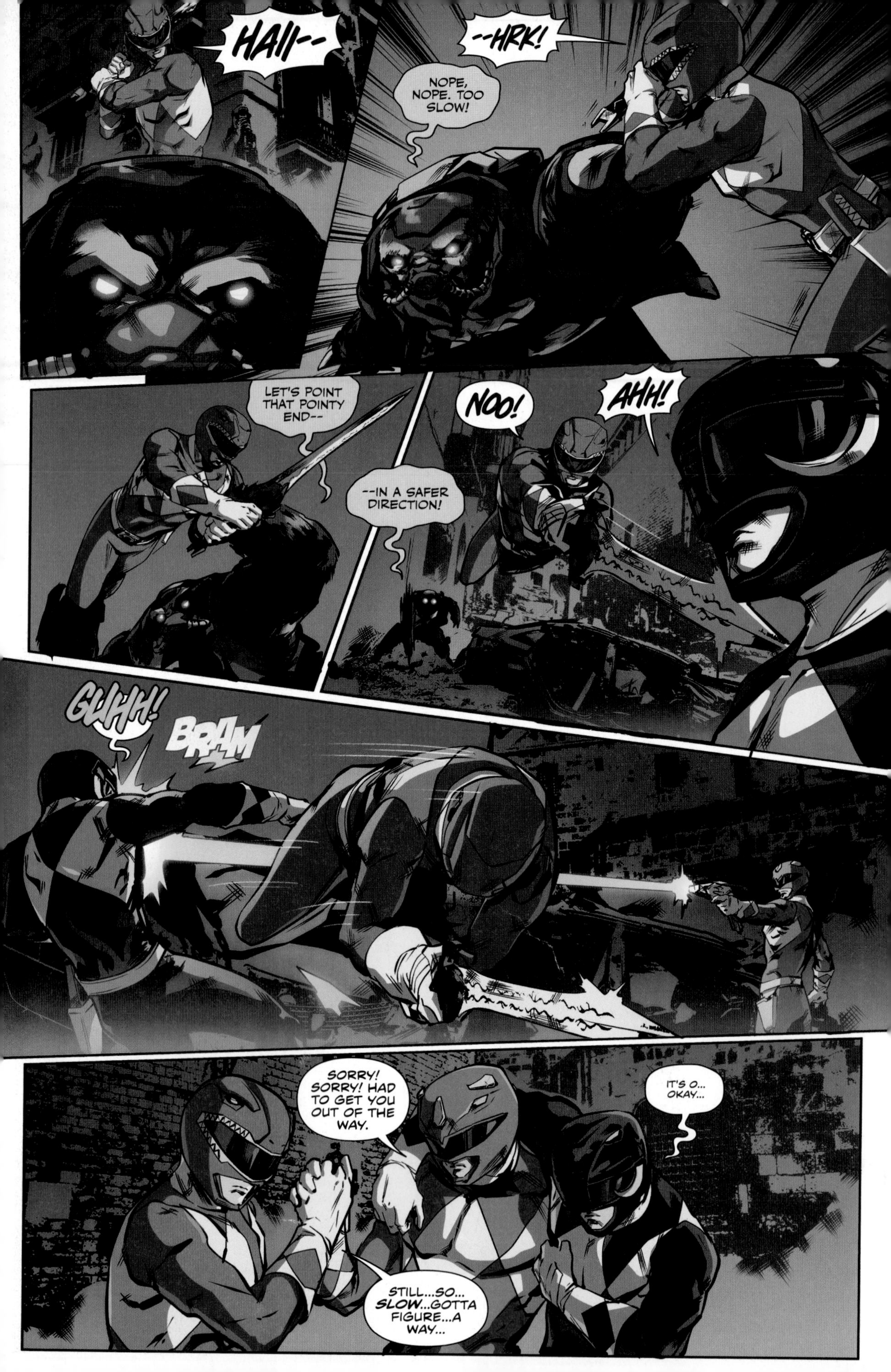
HAI!--
--HRK!
NOPE, NOPE. TOO SLOW!
LET'S POINT THAT POINTY END--
--IN A SAFER DIRECTION!
NOO!
AHH!
GUHH!
BRAM
SORRY! SORRY! HAD TO GET YOU OUT OF THE WAY.
IT'S O... OKAY...
STILL...SO... SLOW...GOTTA FIGURE...A WAY...

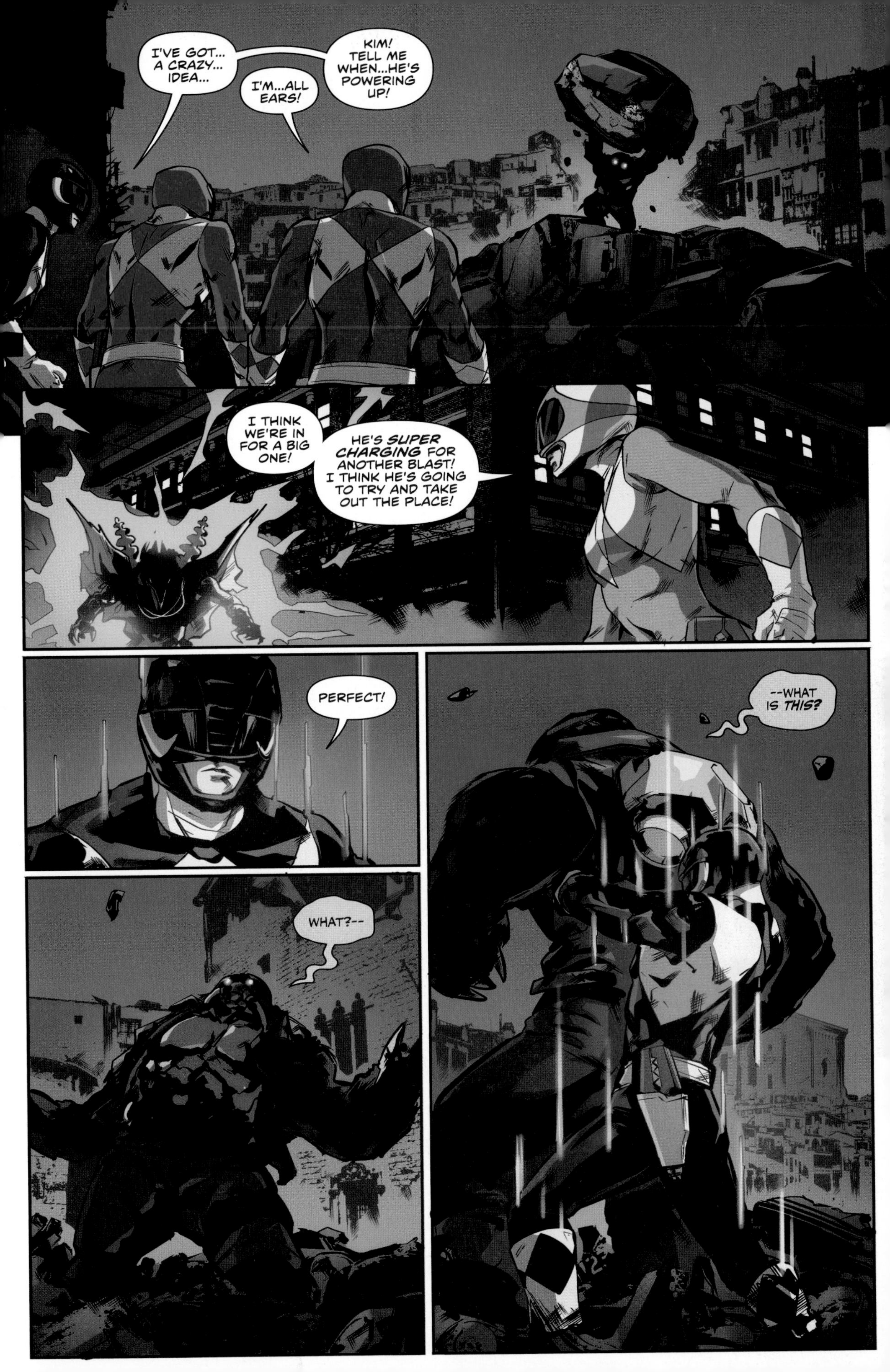
I'VE GOT... A CRAZY... IDEA...
I'M...ALL EARS!
KIM! TELL ME WHEN...HE'S POWERING UP!
I THINK WE'RE IN FOR A BIG ONE!
HE'S SUPER CHARGING FOR ANOTHER BLAST! I THINK HE'S GOING TO TRY AND TAKE OUT THE PLACE!
PERFECT!
WHAT?--
--WHAT IS THIS?

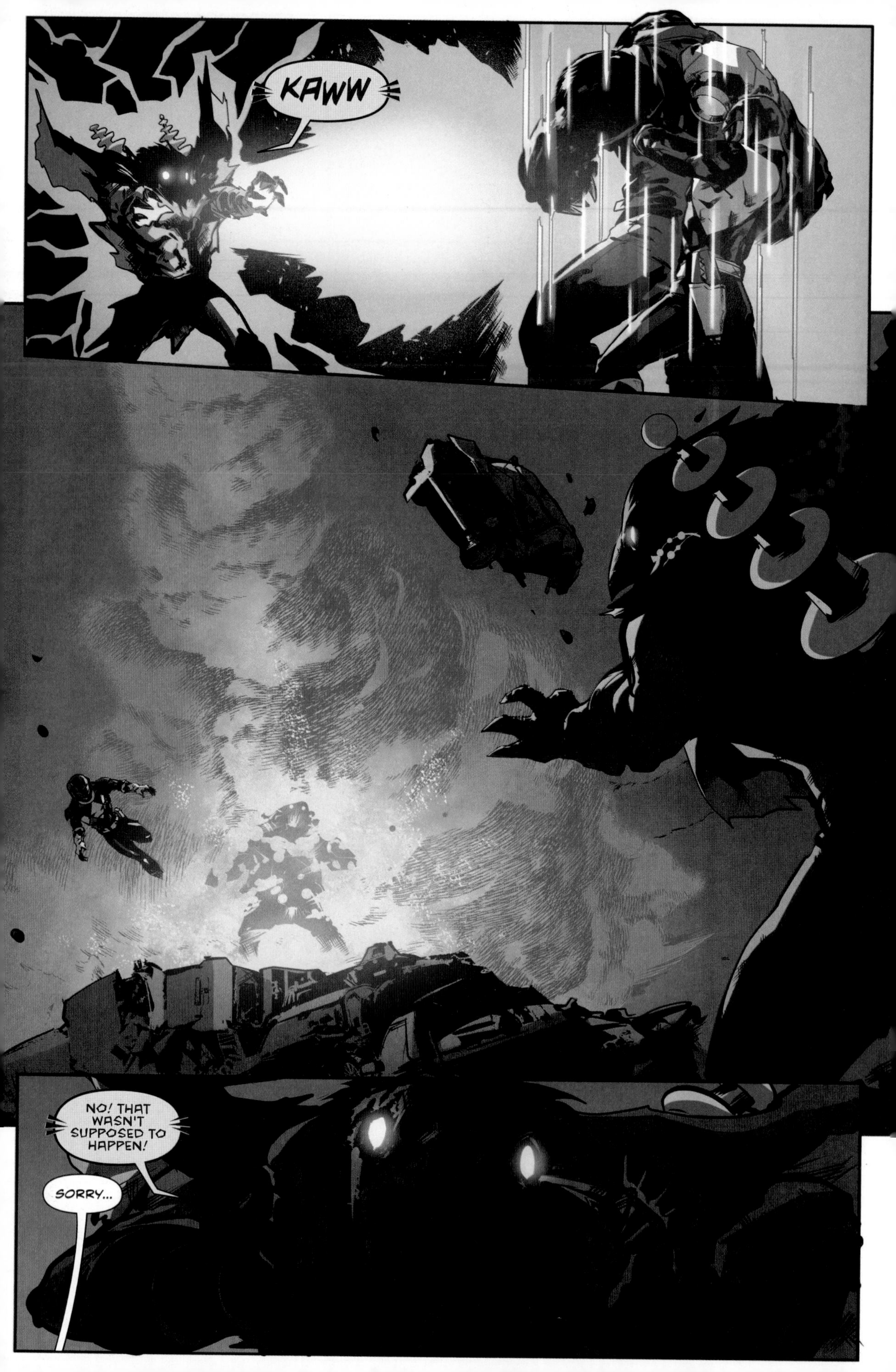
KAWW
NO! THAT WASN'T SUPPOSED TO HAPPEN!
SORRY...

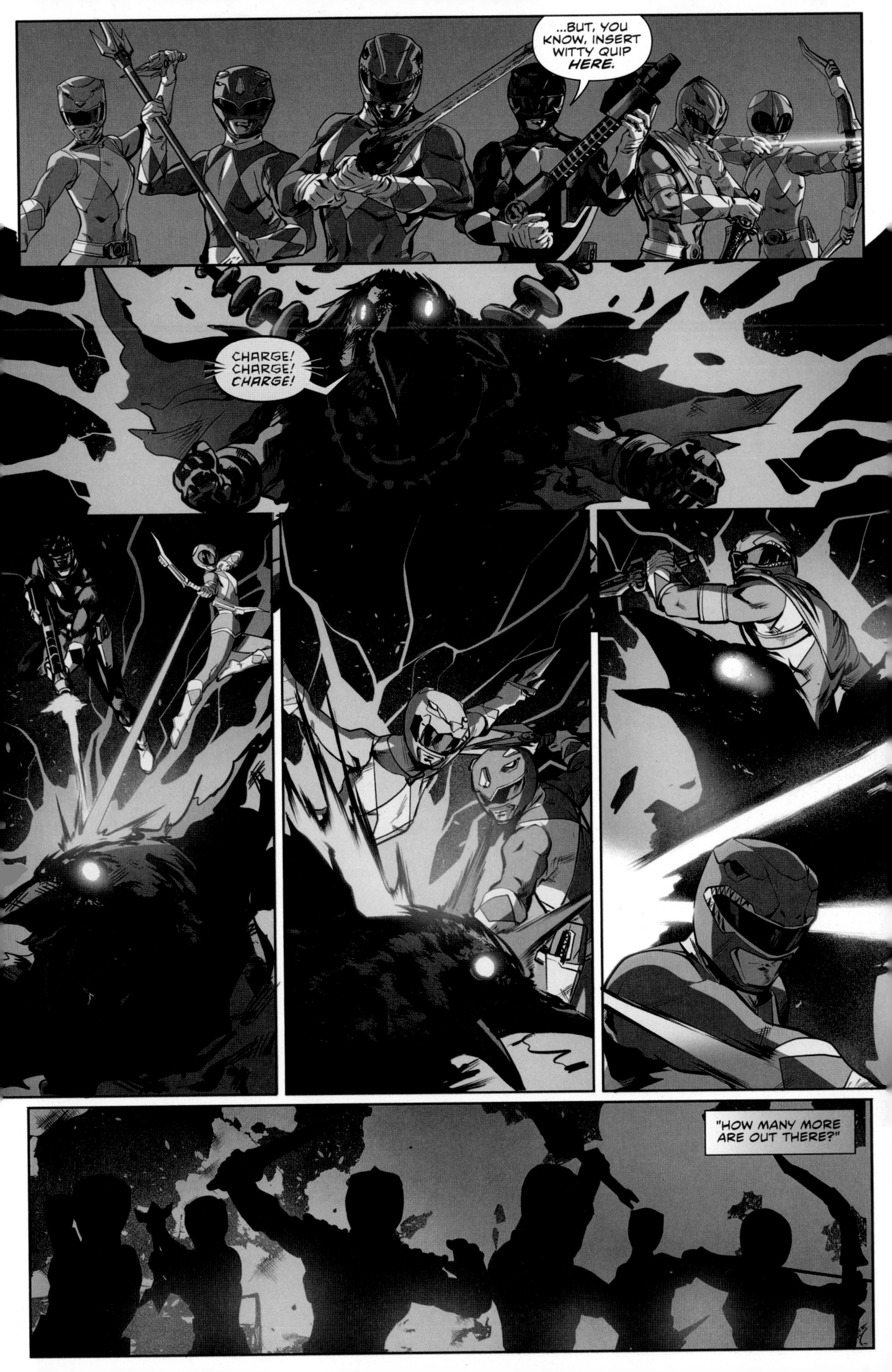
...BUT, YOU KNOW, INSERT WITTY QUIP HERE.
CHARGE! CHARGE! CHARGE!
"HOW MANY MORE ARE OUT THERE?"

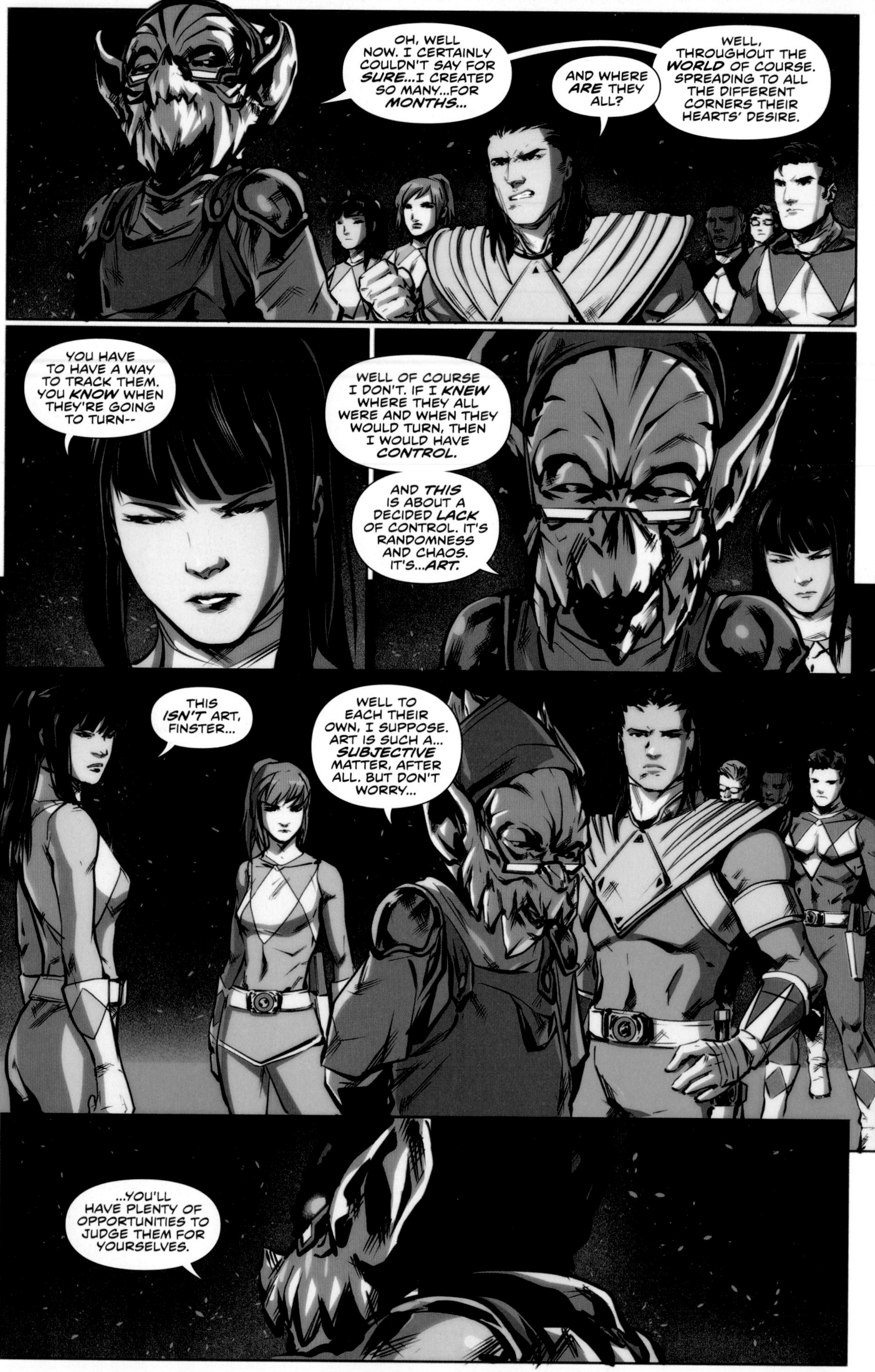
OH, WELL NOW. I CERTAINLY COULDN'T SAY FOR SURE...I CREATED SO MANY...FOR MONTHS...
AND WHERE ARE THEY ALL?
WELL, THROUGHOUT THE WORLD OF COURSE. SPREADING TO ALL THE DIFFERENT CORNERS THEIR HEARTS' DESIRE.
YOU HAVE TO HAVE A WAY TO TRACK THEM. YOU KNOW WHEN THEY'RE GOING TO TURN--
WELL OF COURSE I DON'T. IF I KNEW WHERE THEY ALL WERE AND WHEN THEY WOULD TURN, THEN I WOULD HAVE CONTROL.
AND THIS IS ABOUT A DECIDED LACK OF CONTROL. IT'S RANDOMNESS AND CHAOS. IT'S...ART.
THIS ISN'T ART, FINSTER...
WELL TO EACH THEIR OWN, I SUPPOSE. ART IS SUCH A... SUBJECTIVE MATTER, AFTER ALL. BUT DON'T WORRY...
...YOU'LL HAVE PLENTY OF OPPORTUNITIES TO JUDGE THEM FOR YOURSELVES.

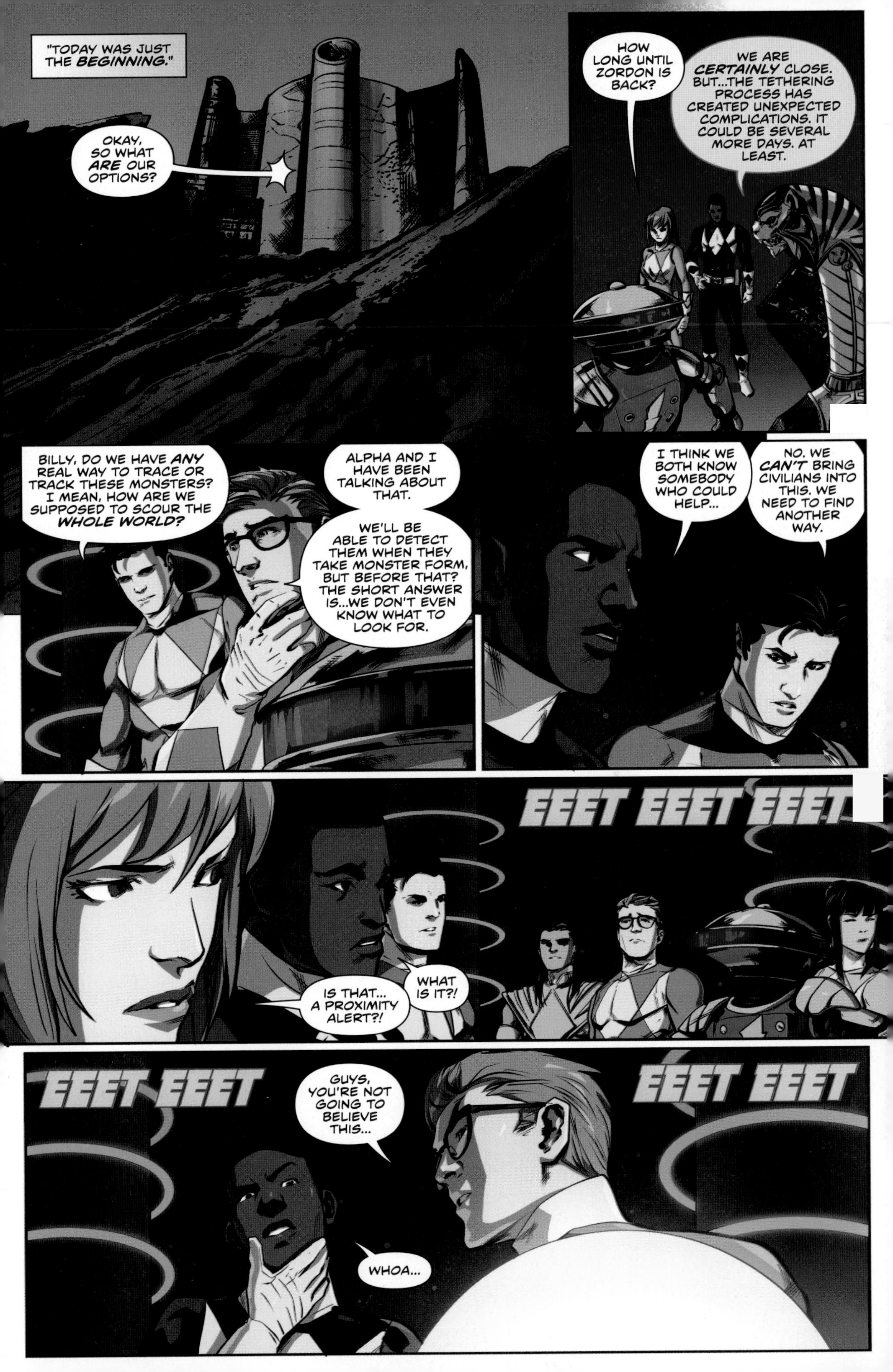
"TODAY WAS JUST THE BEGINNING."
OKAY, SO WHAT ARE OUR OPTIONS?
HOW LONG UNTIL ZORDON IS BACK?
WE ARE CERTAINLY CLOSE. BUT...THE TETHERING PROCESS HAS CREATED UNEXPECTED COMPLICATIONS. IT COULD BE SEVERAL MORE DAYS. AT LEAST.
BILLY, DO WE HAVE ANY REAL WAY TO TRACE OR TRACK THESE MONSTERS? I MEAN, HOW ARE WE SUPPOSED TO SCOUR THE WHOLE WORLD?
ALPHA AND I HAVE BEEN TALKING ABOUT THAT.
WE'LL BE ABLE TO DETECT THEM WHEN THEY TAKE MONSTER FORM, BUT BEFORE THAT? THE SHORT ANSWER IS...WE DON'T EVEN KNOW WHAT TO LOOK FOR.
I THINK WE BOTH KNOW SOMEBODY WHO COULD HELP...
NO. WE CAN'T BRING CIVILIANS INTO THIS. WE NEED TO FIND ANOTHER WAY.
EEET EEET EEET
IS THAT... A PROXIMITY ALERT?!
WHAT IS IT?!
EEET EEET
GUYS, YOU'RE NOT GOING TO BELIEVE THIS...
EEET EEET
WHOA...

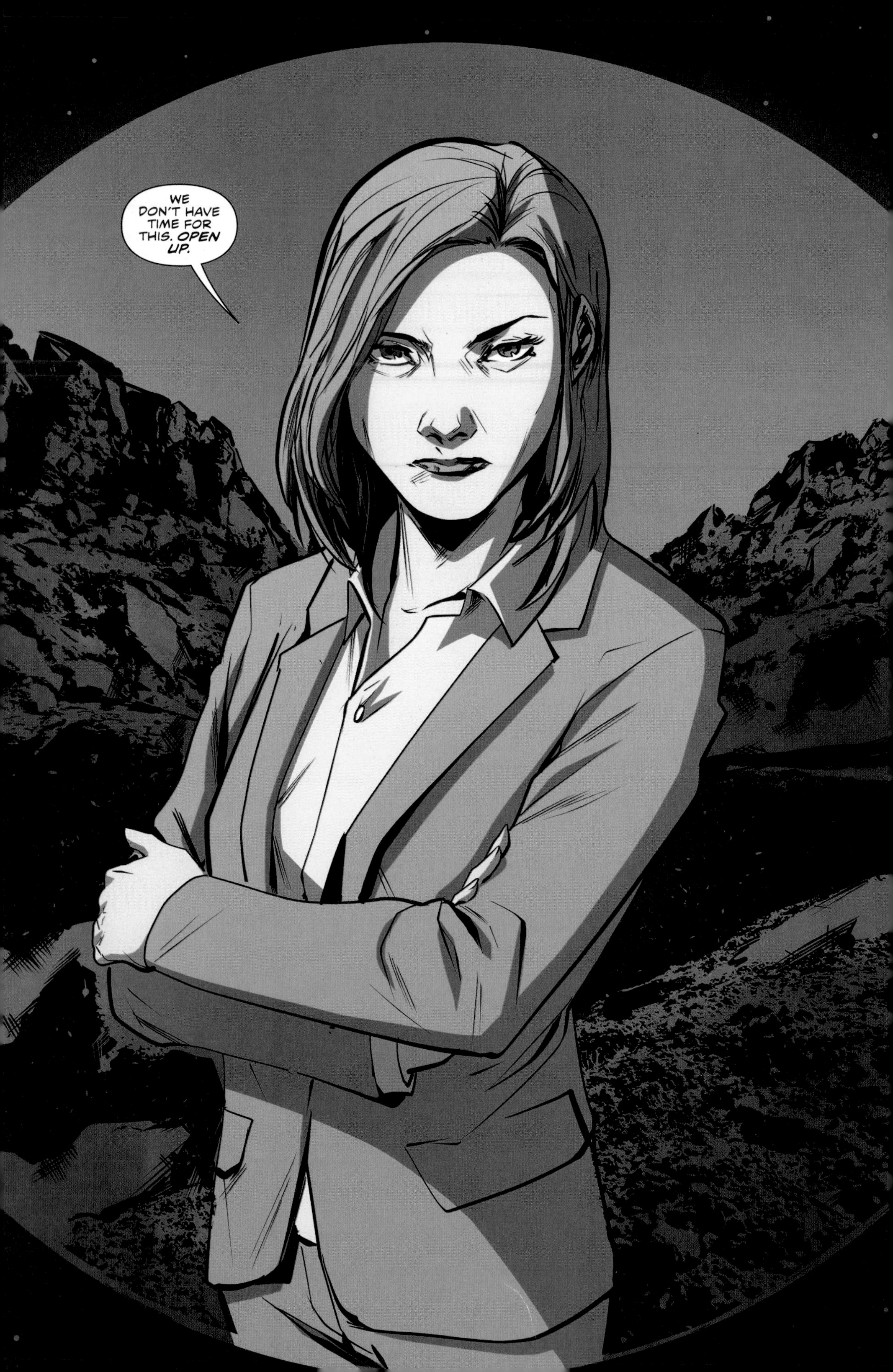
WE DON'T HAVE TIME FOR THIS. OPEN UP.

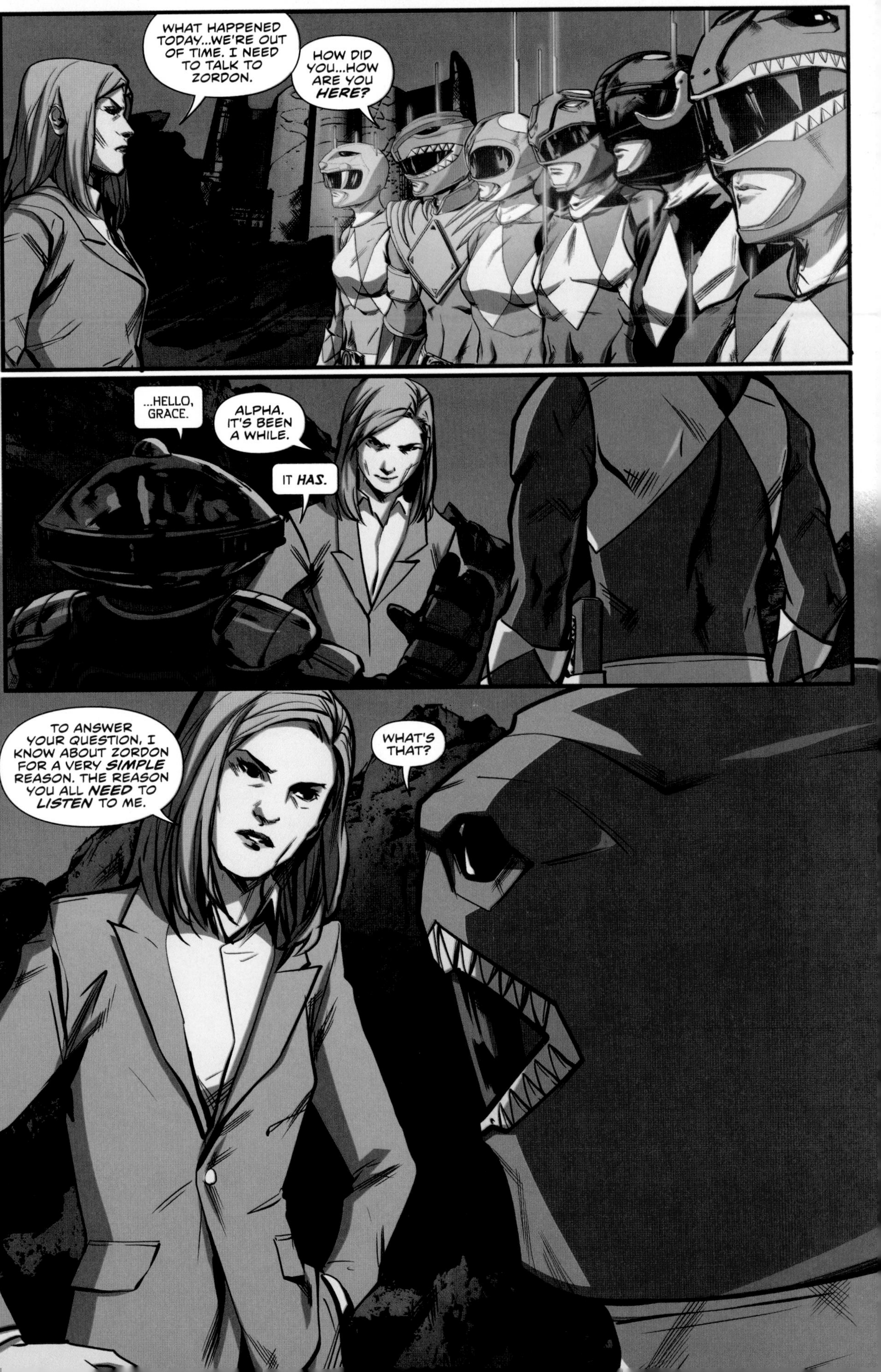
WHAT HAPPENED TODAY...WE'RE OUT OF TIME. I NEED TO TALK TO ZORDON.
HOW DID YOU...HOW ARE YOU *HERE?*
...HELLO, GRACE.
ALPHA. IT'S BEEN A WHILE.
IT *HAS.*
TO ANSWER YOUR QUESTION, I KNOW ABOUT ZORDON FOR A VERY *SIMPLE* REASON. THE REASON YOU ALL *NEED* TO *LISTEN* TO ME.
WHAT'S THAT?

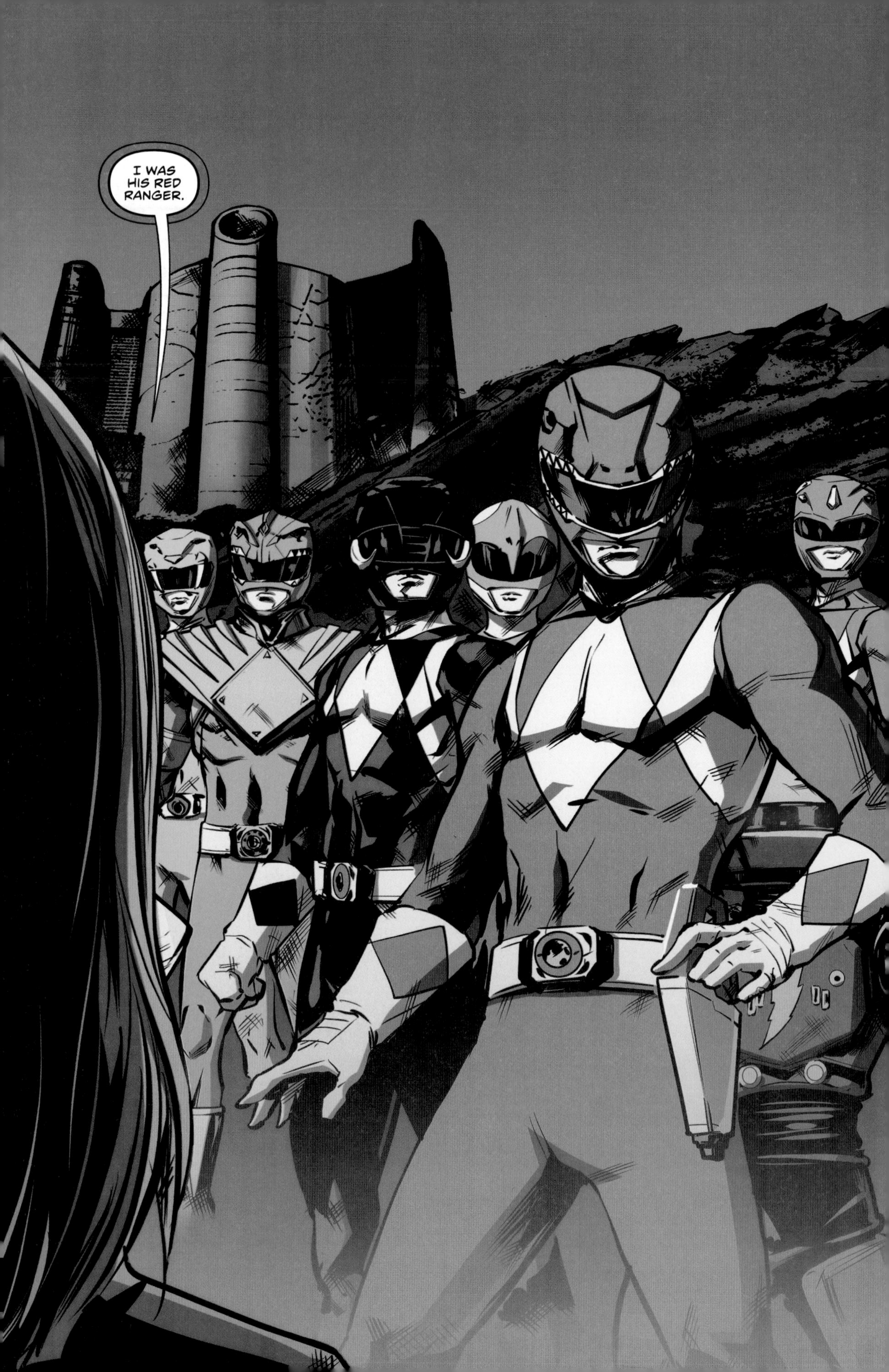
I WAS HIS RED RANGER.

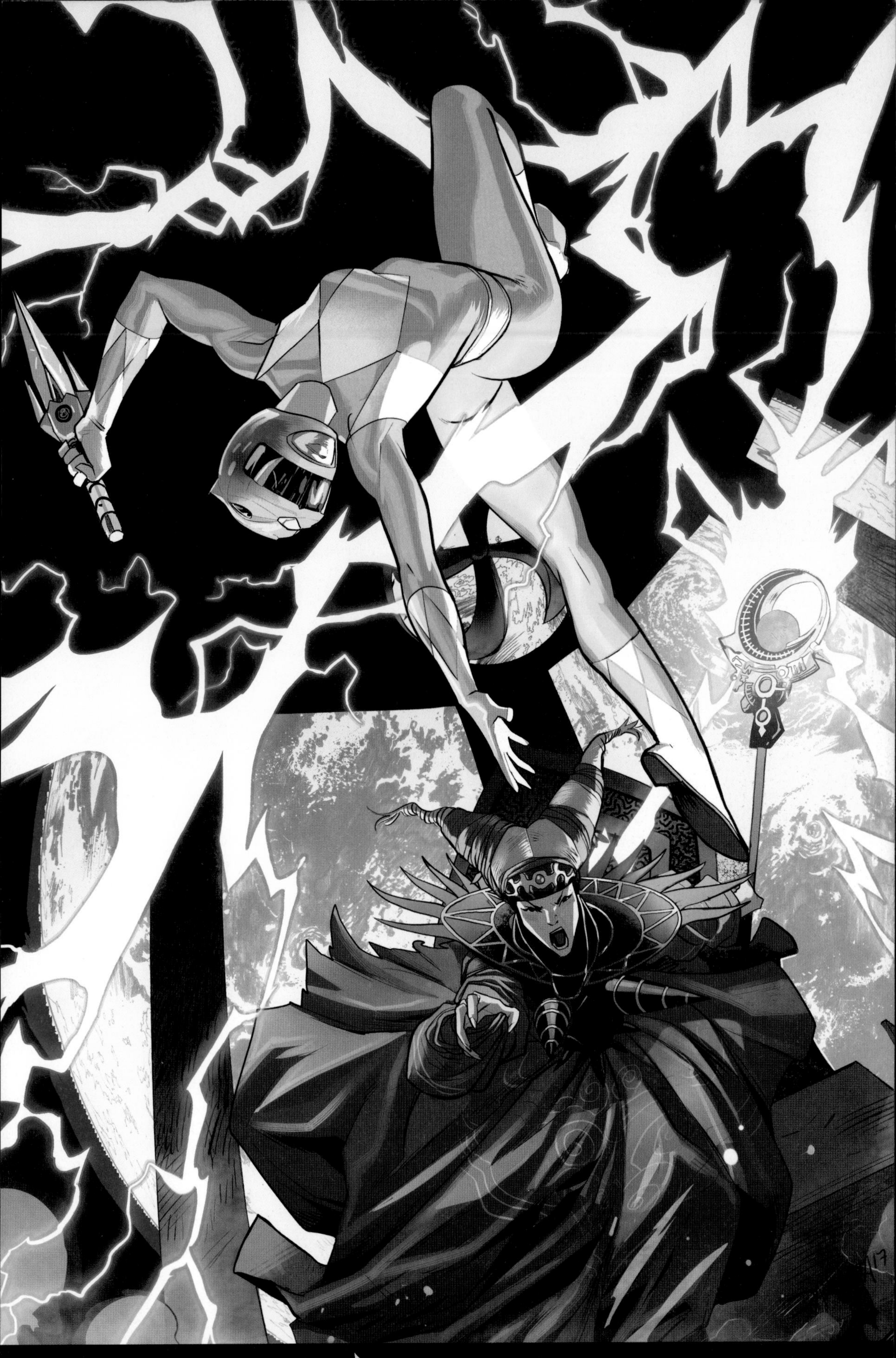

DAN MORA ISSUE NINETEEN VERSUS VARIANT COVER

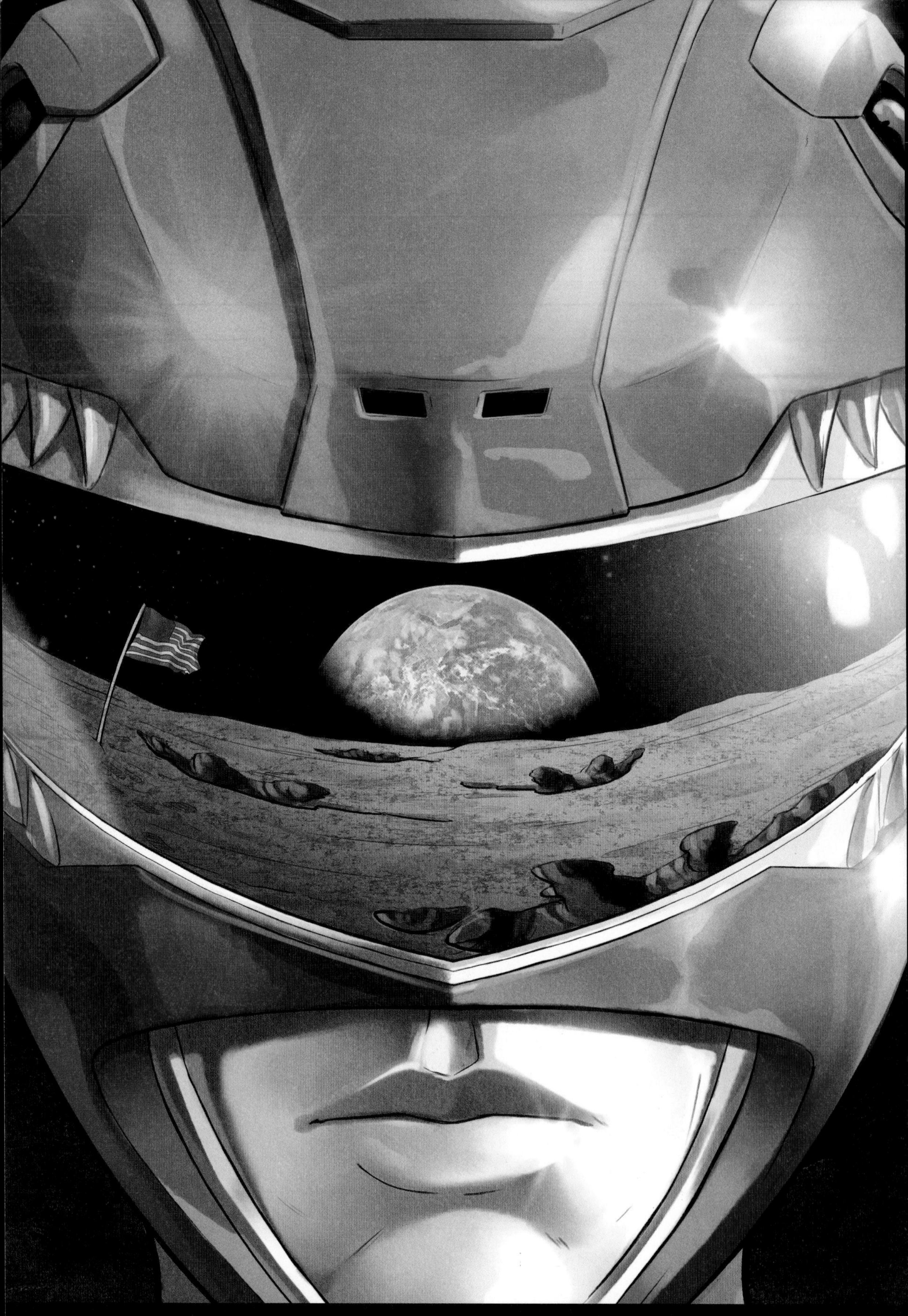

CHAPTER **TWENTY**

JAMAL CAMPBELL | ISSUE TWENTY COVER

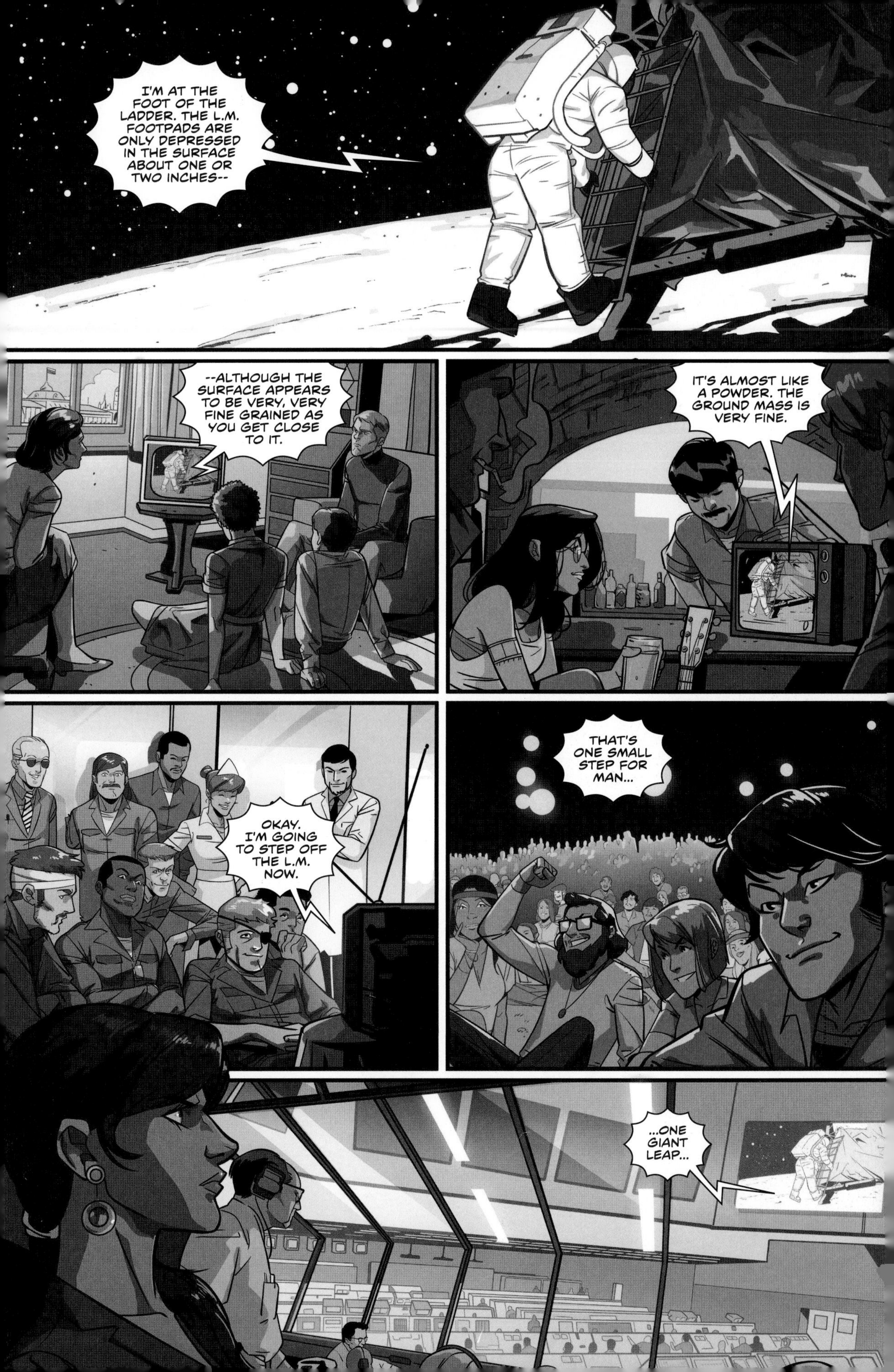
I'M AT THE FOOT OF THE LADDER. THE L.M. FOOTPADS ARE ONLY DEPRESSED IN THE SURFACE ABOUT ONE OR TWO INCHES--
--ALTHOUGH THE SURFACE APPEARS TO BE VERY, VERY FINE GRAINED AS YOU GET CLOSE TO IT.
IT'S ALMOST LIKE A POWDER. THE GROUND MASS IS VERY FINE.
OKAY. I'M GOING TO STEP OFF THE L.M. NOW.
THAT'S ONE SMALL STEP FOR MAN...
...ONE GIANT LEAP...

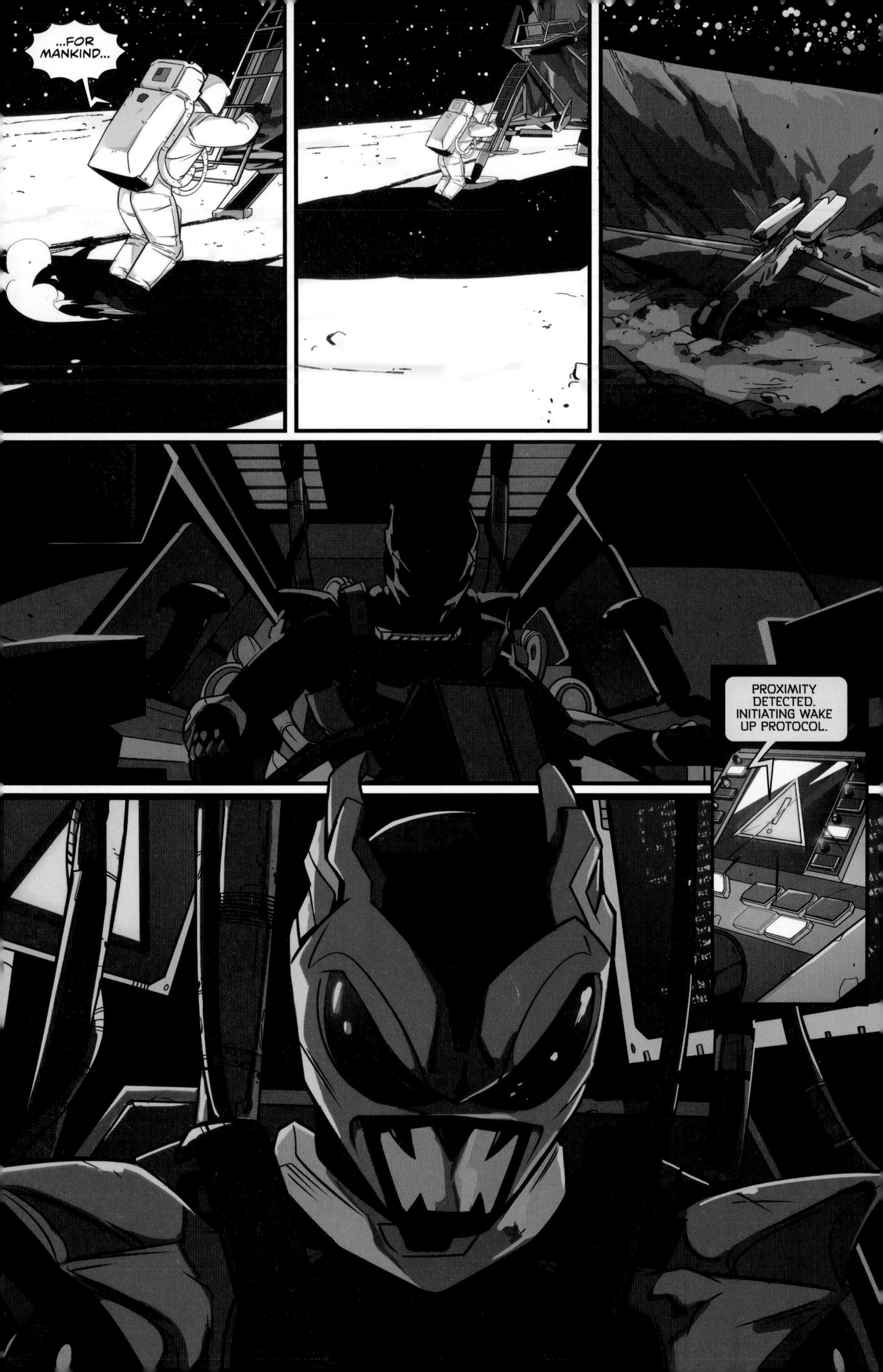
...FOR MANKIND...
PROXIMITY DETECTED. INITIATING WAKE UP PROTOCOL.

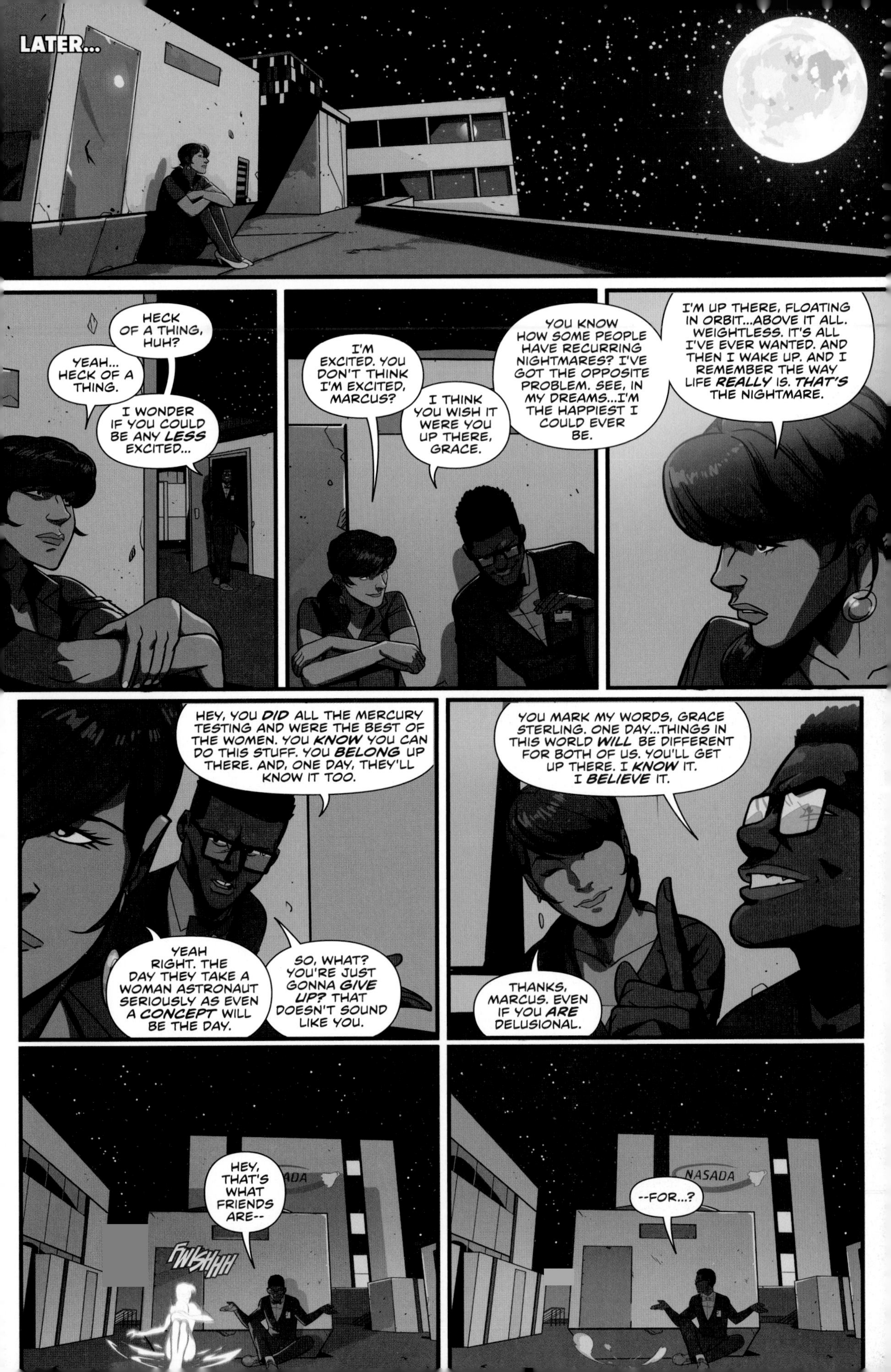
LATER...
HECK OF A THING, HUH?
YEAH... HECK OF A THING.
I WONDER IF YOU COULD BE ANY LESS EXCITED...
I'M EXCITED. YOU DON'T THINK I'M EXCITED, MARCUS?
I THINK YOU WISH IT WERE YOU UP THERE, GRACE.
YOU KNOW HOW SOME PEOPLE HAVE RECURRING NIGHTMARES? I'VE GOT THE OPPOSITE PROBLEM. SEE, IN MY DREAMS...I'M THE HAPPIEST I COULD EVER BE.
I'M UP THERE, FLOATING IN ORBIT...ABOVE IT ALL. WEIGHTLESS. IT'S ALL I'VE EVER WANTED. AND THEN I WAKE UP. AND I REMEMBER THE WAY LIFE REALLY IS. THAT'S THE NIGHTMARE.
HEY, YOU DID ALL THE MERCURY TESTING AND WERE THE BEST OF THE WOMEN. YOU KNOW YOU CAN DO THIS STUFF. YOU BELONG UP THERE. AND, ONE DAY, THEY'LL KNOW IT TOO.
YEAH RIGHT. THE DAY THEY TAKE A WOMAN ASTRONAUT SERIOUSLY AS EVEN A CONCEPT WILL BE THE DAY.
SO, WHAT? YOU'RE JUST GONNA GIVE UP? THAT DOESN'T SOUND LIKE YOU.
YOU MARK MY WORDS, GRACE STERLING. ONE DAY...THINGS IN THIS WORLD WILL BE DIFFERENT FOR BOTH OF US. YOU'LL GET UP THERE. I KNOW IT. I BELIEVE IT.
THANKS, MARCUS. EVEN IF YOU ARE DELUSIONAL.
HEY, THAT'S WHAT FRIENDS ARE--
FWISHHH
NASADA
--FOR...?

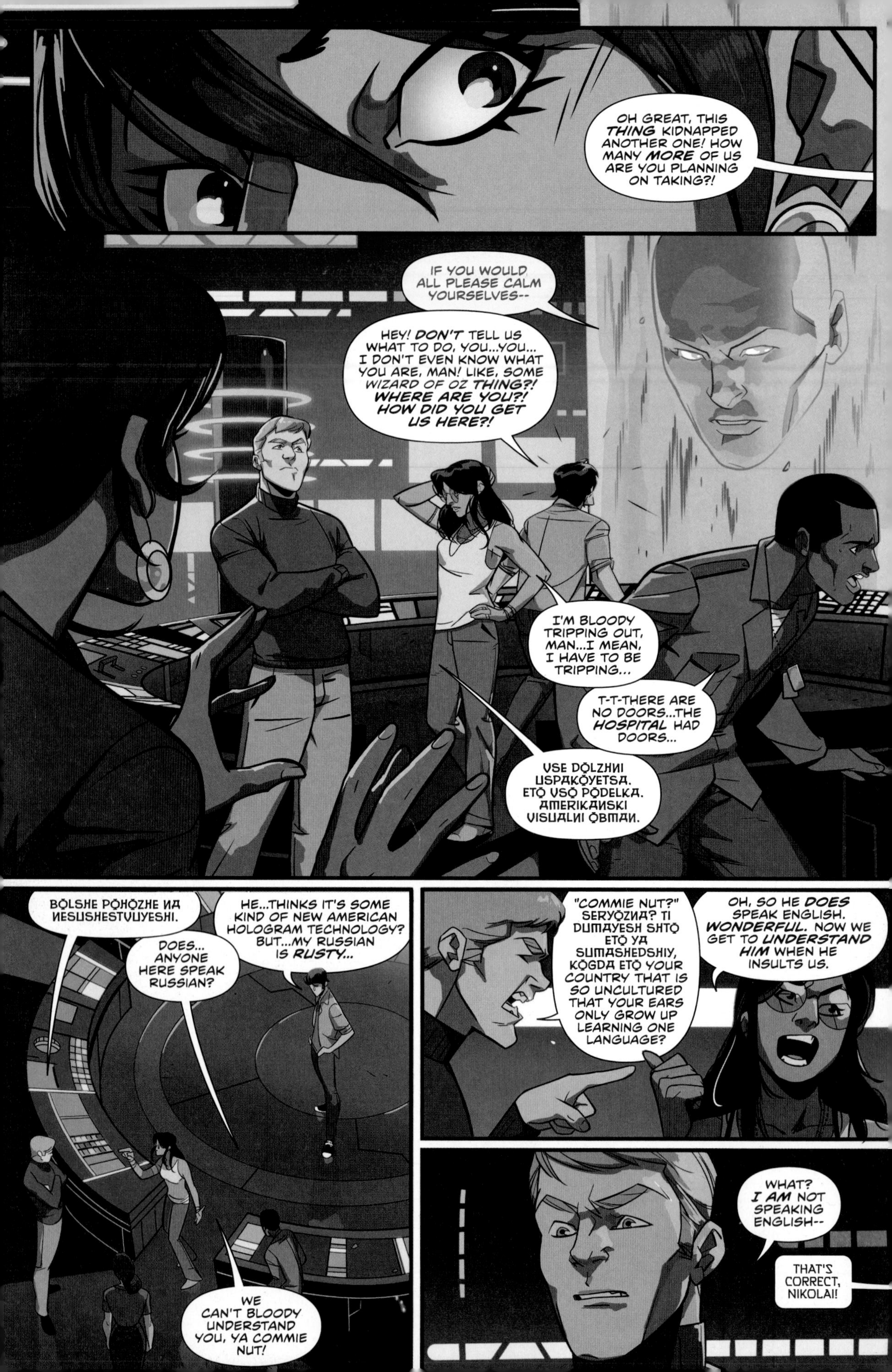
OH GREAT, THIS THING KIDNAPPED ANOTHER ONE! HOW MANY MORE OF US ARE YOU PLANNING ON TAKING?!
IF YOU WOULD ALL PLEASE CALM YOURSELVES--
HEY! DON'T TELL US WHAT TO DO, YOU...YOU... I DON'T EVEN KNOW WHAT YOU ARE, MAN! LIKE, SOME WIZARD OF OZ THING?! WHERE ARE YOU?! HOW DID YOU GET US HERE?!
I'M BLOODY TRIPPING OUT, MAN...I MEAN, I HAVE TO BE TRIPPING...
T-T-THERE ARE NO DOORS...THE HOSPITAL HAD DOORS...
VSE DÖLZHNI USPAKÖYETSA. ETÖ VSÖ PÖDELKA. AMERIKANSKI VISUALNI ÖBMAN.
BÖLSHE PÖHÖZHE NA NESUSHESTVUYESHI.
DOES... ANYONE HERE SPEAK RUSSIAN?
HE...THINKS IT'S SOME KIND OF NEW AMERICAN HOLOGRAM TECHNOLOGY? BUT...MY RUSSIAN IS RUSTY...
WE CAN'T BLOODY UNDERSTAND YOU, YA COMMIE NUT!
"COMMIE NUT?" SERYÖZNA? TI DUMAYESH SHTÖ ETÖ YA SUMASHEDSHIY, KÖGDA ETÖ YOUR COUNTRY THAT IS SO UNCULTURED THAT YOUR EARS ONLY GROW UP LEARNING ONE LANGUAGE?
OH, SO HE DOES SPEAK ENGLISH. WONDERFUL. NOW WE GET TO UNDERSTAND HIM WHEN HE INSULTS US.
WHAT? I AM NOT SPEAKING ENGLISH--
THAT'S CORRECT, NIKOLAI!

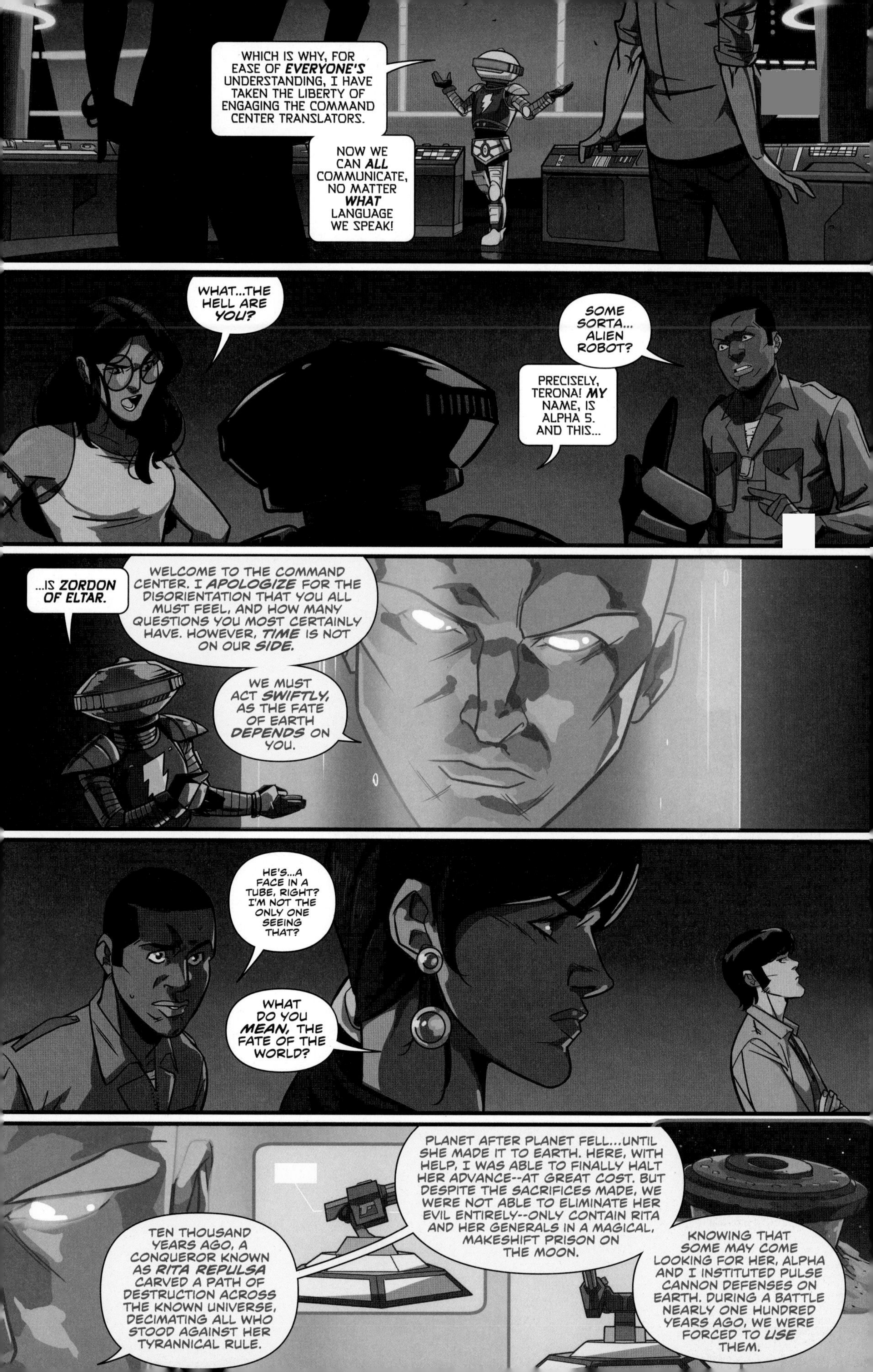
WHICH IS WHY, FOR EASE OF EVERYONE'S UNDERSTANDING, I HAVE TAKEN THE LIBERTY OF ENGAGING THE COMMAND CENTER TRANSLATORS.
NOW WE CAN ALL COMMUNICATE, NO MATTER WHAT LANGUAGE WE SPEAK!
WHAT...THE HELL ARE YOU?
SOME SORTA... ALIEN ROBOT?
PRECISELY, TERONA! MY NAME, IS ALPHA 5. AND THIS...
...IS ZORDON OF ELTAR.
WELCOME TO THE COMMAND CENTER. I APOLOGIZE FOR THE DISORIENTATION THAT YOU ALL MUST FEEL, AND HOW MANY QUESTIONS YOU MOST CERTAINLY HAVE. HOWEVER, TIME IS NOT ON OUR SIDE.
WE MUST ACT SWIFTLY, AS THE FATE OF EARTH DEPENDS ON YOU.
HE'S...A FACE IN A TUBE, RIGHT? I'M NOT THE ONLY ONE SEEING THAT?
WHAT DO YOU MEAN, THE FATE OF THE WORLD?
TEN THOUSAND YEARS AGO, A CONQUEROR KNOWN AS RITA REPULSA CARVED A PATH OF DESTRUCTION ACROSS THE KNOWN UNIVERSE, DECIMATING ALL WHO STOOD AGAINST HER TYRANNICAL RULE.
PLANET AFTER PLANET FELL...UNTIL SHE MADE IT TO EARTH. HERE, WITH HELP, I WAS ABLE TO FINALLY HALT HER ADVANCE--AT GREAT COST. BUT DESPITE THE SACRIFICES MADE, WE WERE NOT ABLE TO ELIMINATE HER EVIL ENTIRELY--ONLY CONTAIN RITA AND HER GENERALS IN A MAGICAL, MAKESHIFT PRISON ON THE MOON.
KNOWING THAT SOME MAY COME LOOKING FOR HER, ALPHA AND I INSTITUTED PULSE CANNON DEFENSES ON EARTH. DURING A BATTLE NEARLY ONE HUNDRED YEARS AGO, WE WERE FORCED TO USE THEM.

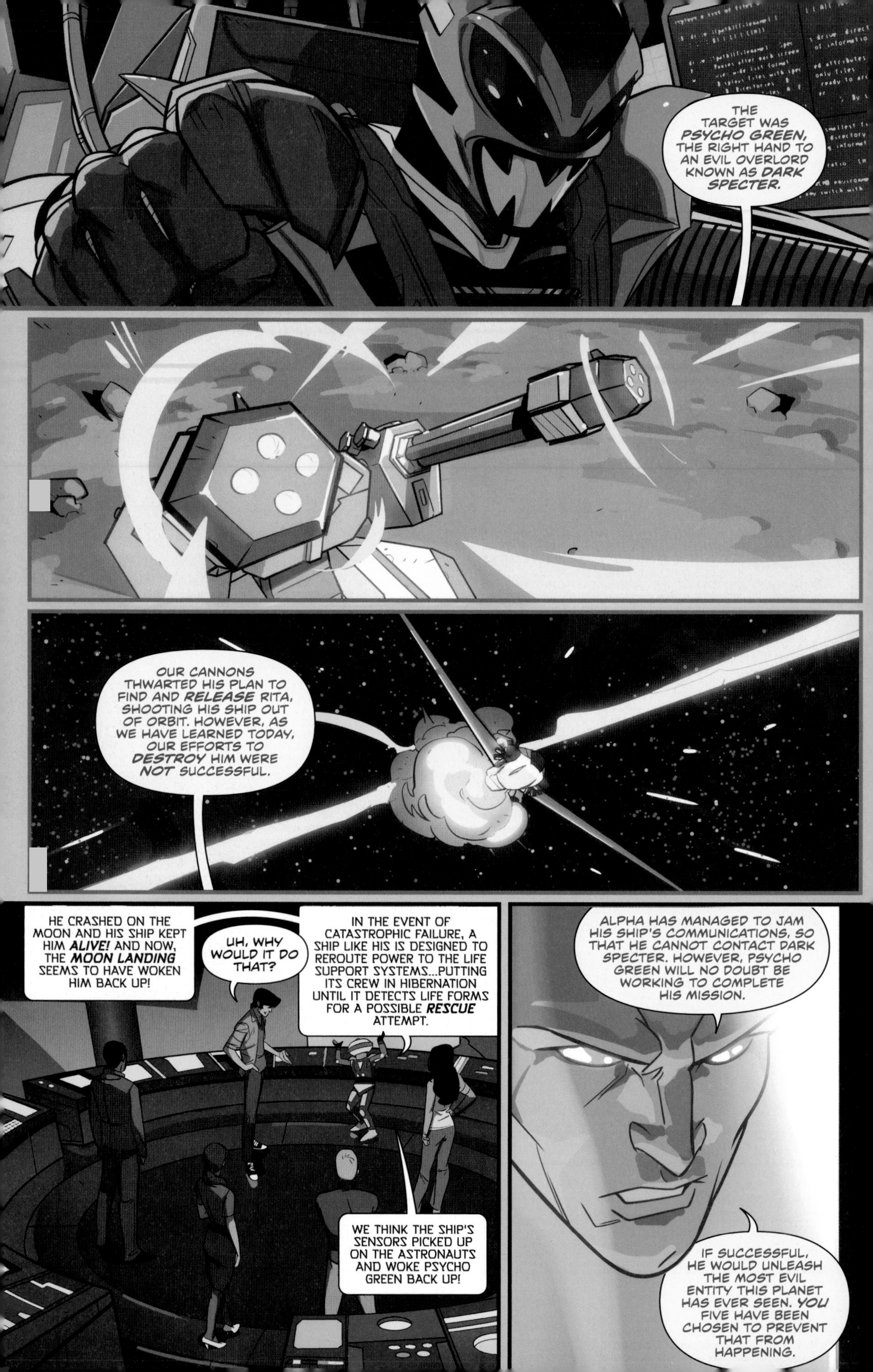

THE TARGET WAS PSYCHO GREEN, THE RIGHT HAND TO AN EVIL OVERLORD KNOWN AS DARK SPECTER.
OUR CANNONS THWARTED HIS PLAN TO FIND AND RELEASE RITA, SHOOTING HIS SHIP OUT OF ORBIT. HOWEVER, AS WE HAVE LEARNED TODAY, OUR EFFORTS TO DESTROY HIM WERE NOT SUCCESSFUL.
HE CRASHED ON THE MOON AND HIS SHIP KEPT HIM ALIVE! AND NOW, THE MOON LANDING SEEMS TO HAVE WOKEN HIM BACK UP!
UH, WHY WOULD IT DO THAT?
IN THE EVENT OF CATASTROPHIC FAILURE, A SHIP LIKE HIS IS DESIGNED TO REROUTE POWER TO THE LIFE SUPPORT SYSTEMS...PUTTING ITS CREW IN HIBERNATION UNTIL IT DETECTS LIFE FORMS FOR A POSSIBLE RESCUE ATTEMPT.
WE THINK THE SHIP'S SENSORS PICKED UP ON THE ASTRONAUTS AND WOKE PSYCHO GREEN BACK UP!
ALPHA HAS MANAGED TO JAM HIS SHIP'S COMMUNICATIONS, SO THAT HE CANNOT CONTACT DARK SPECTER. HOWEVER, PSYCHO GREEN WILL NO DOUBT BE WORKING TO COMPLETE HIS MISSION.
IF SUCCESSFUL, HE WOULD UNLEASH THE MOST EVIL ENTITY THIS PLANET HAS EVER SEEN. YOU FIVE HAVE BEEN CHOSEN TO PREVENT THAT FROM HAPPENING.

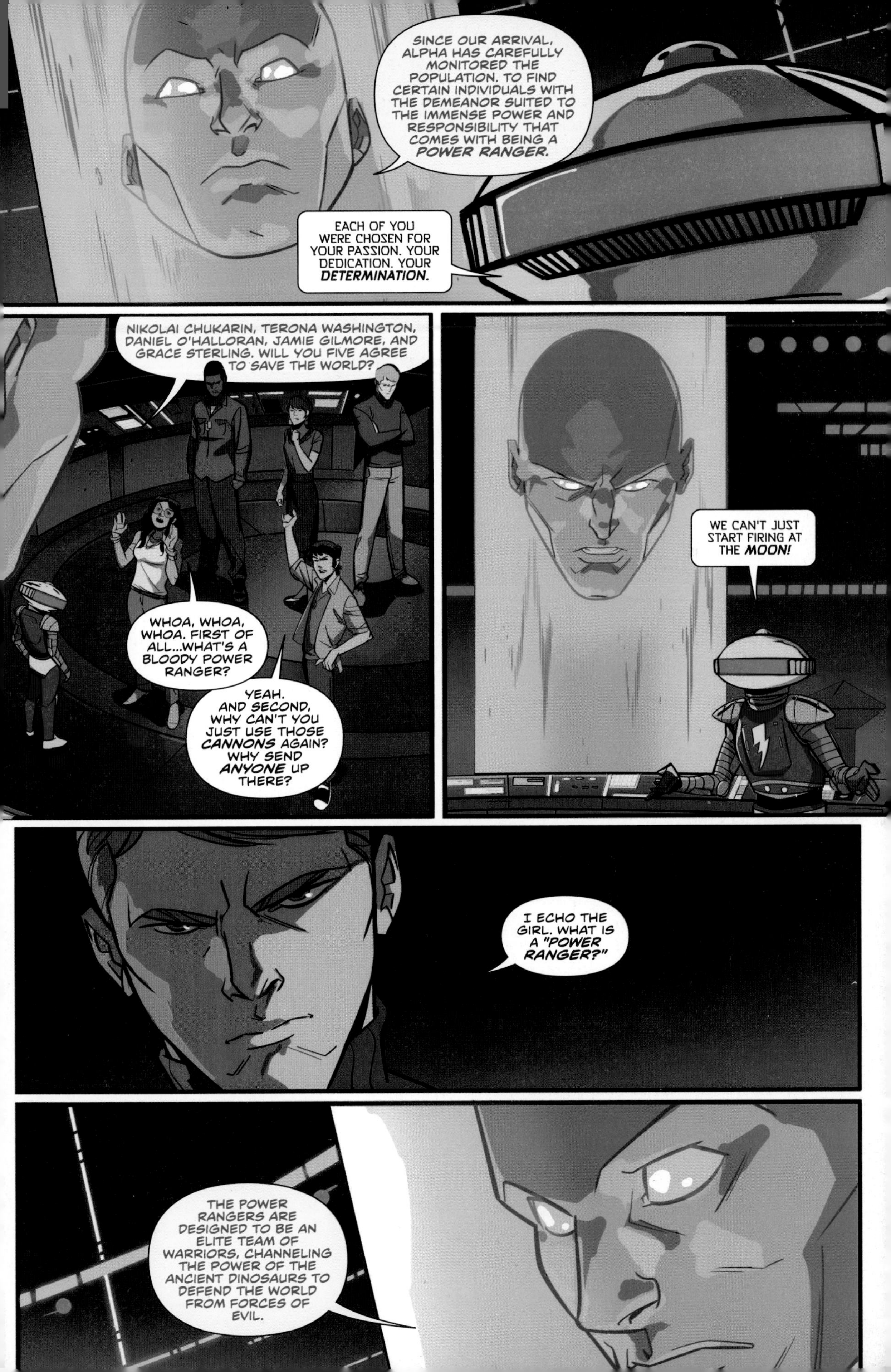
SINCE OUR ARRIVAL, ALPHA HAS CAREFULLY MONITORED THE POPULATION. TO FIND CERTAIN INDIVIDUALS WITH THE DEMEANOR SUITED TO THE IMMENSE POWER AND RESPONSIBILITY THAT COMES WITH BEING A ***POWER RANGER.***
EACH OF YOU WERE CHOSEN FOR YOUR PASSION. YOUR DEDICATION. YOUR ***DETERMINATION.***
NIKOLAI CHUKARIN, TERONA WASHINGTON, DANIEL O'HALLORAN, JAMIE GILMORE, AND GRACE STERLING. WILL YOU FIVE AGREE TO SAVE THE WORLD?
WHOA, WHOA, WHOA. FIRST OF ALL...WHAT'S A BLOODY POWER RANGER?
YEAH. AND SECOND, WHY CAN'T YOU JUST USE THOSE ***CANNONS*** AGAIN? WHY SEND ***ANYONE*** UP THERE?
WE CAN'T JUST START FIRING AT THE ***MOON!***
I ECHO THE GIRL. WHAT IS A ***"POWER RANGER?"***
THE POWER RANGERS ARE DESIGNED TO BE AN ELITE TEAM OF WARRIORS, CHANNELING THE POWER OF THE ANCIENT DINOSAURS TO DEFEND THE WORLD FROM FORCES OF EVIL.

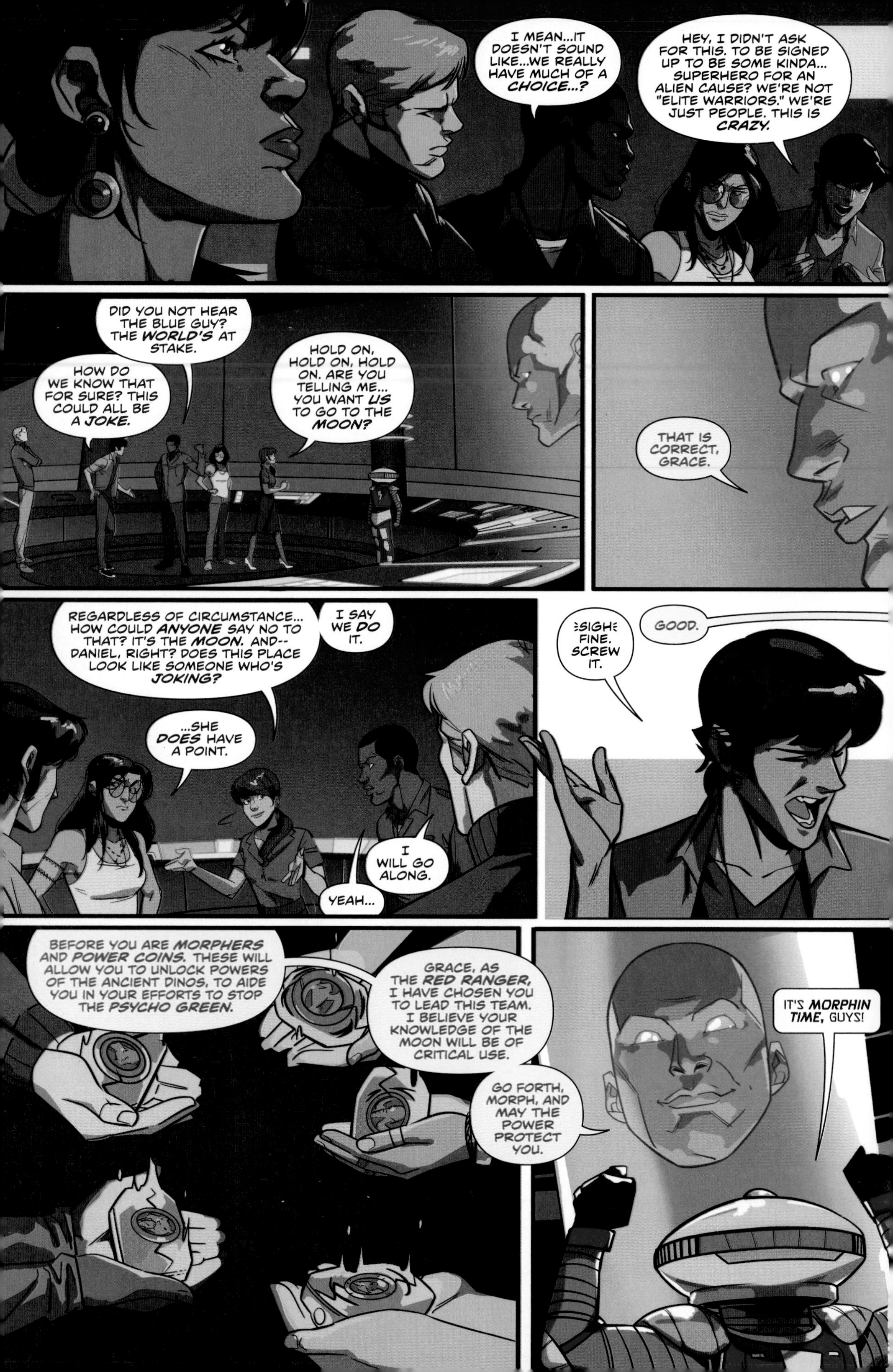
I MEAN...IT DOESN'T SOUND LIKE...WE REALLY HAVE MUCH OF A CHOICE...?
HEY, I DIDN'T ASK FOR THIS. TO BE SIGNED UP TO BE SOME KINDA... SUPERHERO FOR AN ALIEN CAUSE? WE'RE NOT "ELITE WARRIORS." WE'RE JUST PEOPLE. THIS IS CRAZY.
DID YOU NOT HEAR THE BLUE GUY? THE WORLD'S AT STAKE.
HOW DO WE KNOW THAT FOR SURE? THIS COULD ALL BE A JOKE.
HOLD ON, HOLD ON, HOLD ON. ARE YOU TELLING ME... YOU WANT US TO GO TO THE MOON?
THAT IS CORRECT, GRACE.
REGARDLESS OF CIRCUMSTANCE... HOW COULD ANYONE SAY NO TO THAT? IT'S THE MOON. AND-- DANIEL, RIGHT? DOES THIS PLACE LOOK LIKE SOMEONE WHO'S JOKING?
I SAY WE DO IT.
...SHE DOES HAVE A POINT.
I WILL GO ALONG.
YEAH...
SIGH FINE. SCREW IT.
GOOD.
BEFORE YOU ARE MORPHERS AND POWER COINS. THESE WILL ALLOW YOU TO UNLOCK POWERS OF THE ANCIENT DINOS, TO AIDE YOU IN YOUR EFFORTS TO STOP THE PSYCHO GREEN.
GRACE, AS THE RED RANGER, I HAVE CHOSEN YOU TO LEAD THIS TEAM. I BELIEVE YOUR KNOWLEDGE OF THE MOON WILL BE OF CRITICAL USE.
GO FORTH, MORPH, AND MAY THE POWER PROTECT YOU.
IT'S MORPHIN TIME, GUYS!

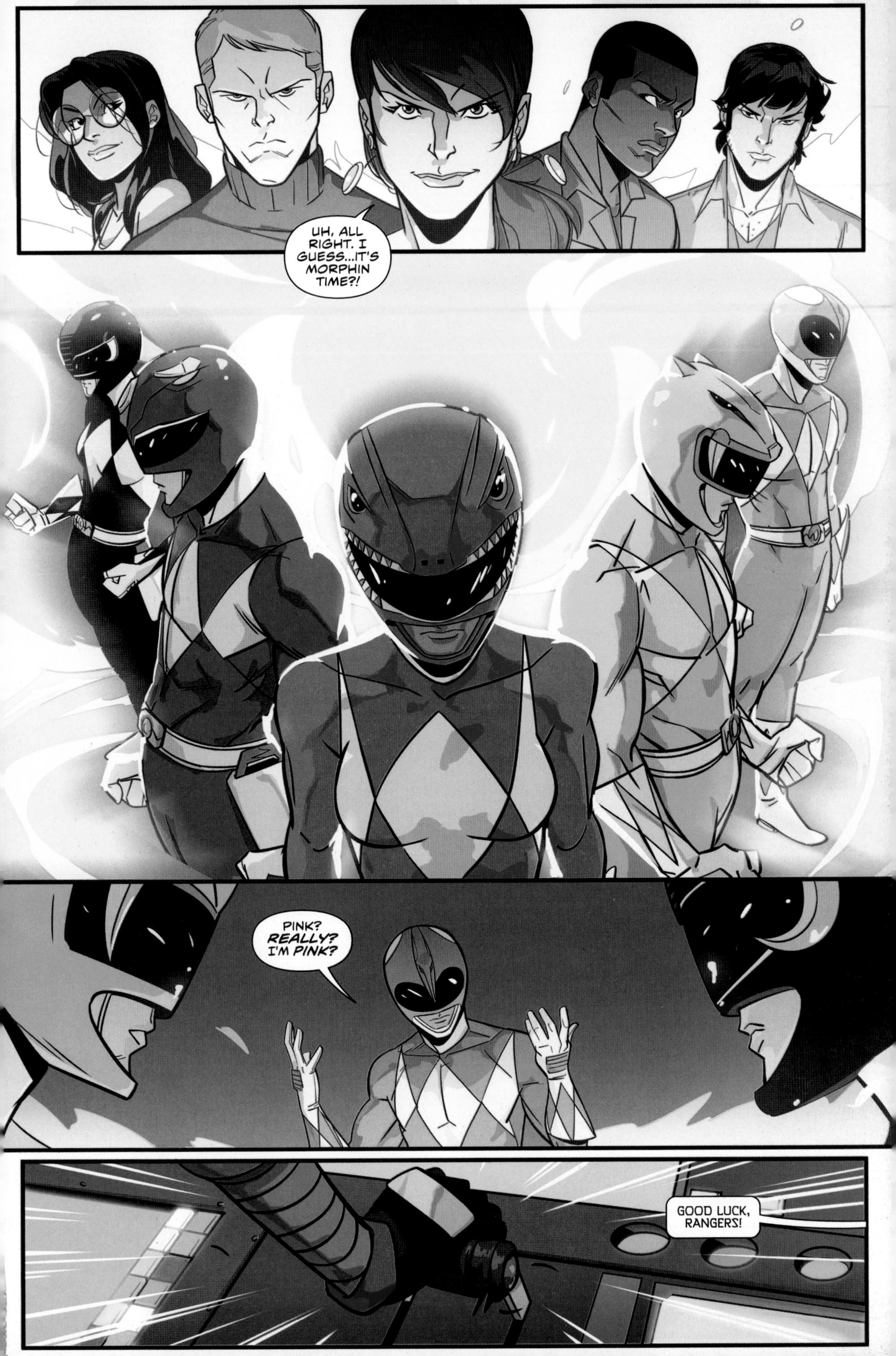
UH, ALL RIGHT. I GUESS...IT'S MORPHIN TIME?!
PINK? *REALLY?* I'M *PINK?*
GOOD LUCK, RANGERS!

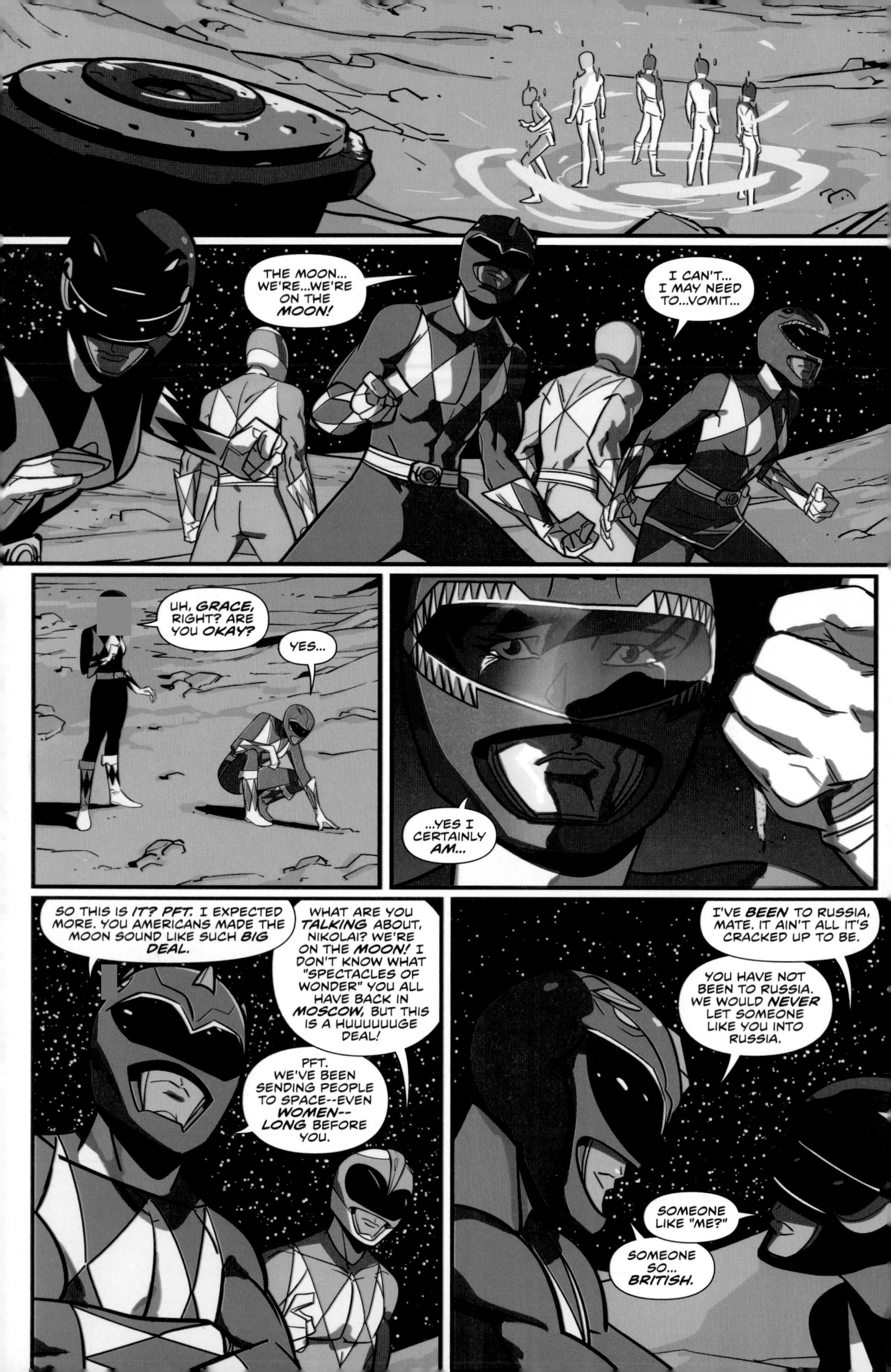
THE MOON... WE'RE...WE'RE ON THE MOON!
I CAN'T... I MAY NEED TO...VOMIT...
UH, GRACE, RIGHT? ARE YOU OKAY?
YES...
...YES I CERTAINLY AM...
SO THIS IS IT? PFT. I EXPECTED MORE. YOU AMERICANS MADE THE MOON SOUND LIKE SUCH BIG DEAL.
WHAT ARE YOU TALKING ABOUT, NIKOLAI? WE'RE ON THE MOON! I DON'T KNOW WHAT "SPECTACLES OF WONDER" YOU ALL HAVE BACK IN MOSCOW, BUT THIS IS A HUUUUUUGE DEAL!
PFT. WE'VE BEEN SENDING PEOPLE TO SPACE--EVEN WOMEN--LONG BEFORE YOU.
I'VE BEEN TO RUSSIA, MATE. IT AIN'T ALL IT'S CRACKED UP TO BE.
YOU HAVE NOT BEEN TO RUSSIA. WE WOULD NEVER LET SOMEONE LIKE YOU INTO RUSSIA.
SOMEONE LIKE "ME?"
SOMEONE SO... BRITISH.

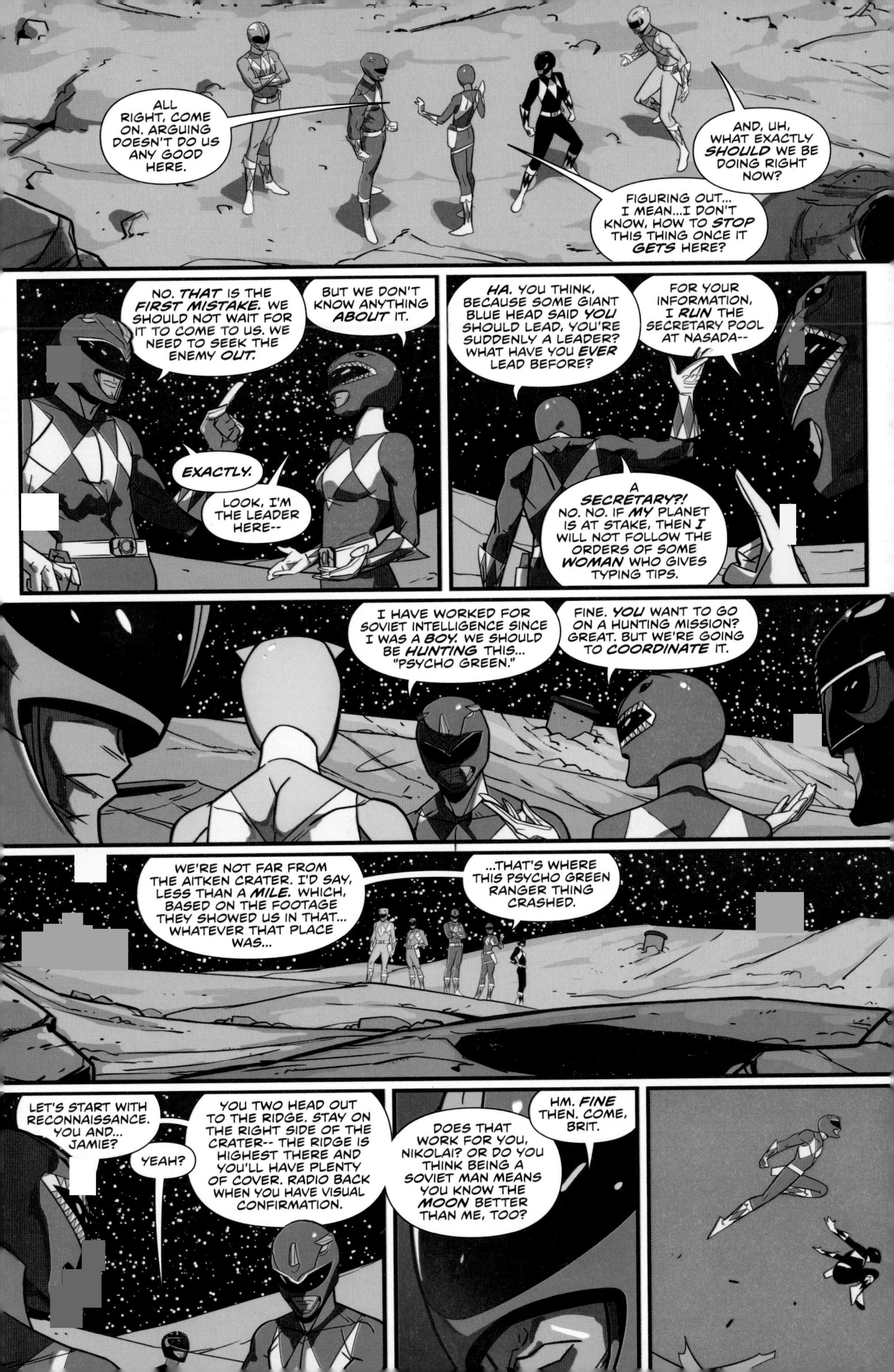
ALL RIGHT, COME ON. ARGUING DOESN'T DO US ANY GOOD HERE.
AND, UH, WHAT EXACTLY *SHOULD* WE BE DOING RIGHT NOW?
FIGURING OUT... I MEAN...I DON'T KNOW, HOW TO *STOP* THIS THING ONCE IT *GETS* HERE?
NO. *THAT* IS THE *FIRST MISTAKE.* WE SHOULD NOT WAIT FOR IT TO COME TO US. WE NEED TO SEEK THE ENEMY *OUT.*
BUT WE DON'T KNOW ANYTHING *ABOUT* IT.
EXACTLY.
LOOK, I'M THE LEADER HERE--
HA. YOU THINK, BECAUSE SOME GIANT BLUE HEAD SAID *YOU* SHOULD LEAD, YOU'RE SUDDENLY A LEADER? WHAT HAVE YOU *EVER* LEAD BEFORE?
FOR YOUR INFORMATION, I *RUN* THE SECRETARY POOL AT NASADA--
A *SECRETARY?!* NO. NO. IF *MY* PLANET IS AT STAKE, THEN *I* WILL NOT FOLLOW THE ORDERS OF SOME *WOMAN* WHO GIVES TYPING TIPS.
I HAVE WORKED FOR SOVIET INTELLIGENCE SINCE I WAS A *BOY.* WE SHOULD BE *HUNTING* THIS... "PSYCHO GREEN."
FINE. *YOU* WANT TO GO ON A HUNTING MISSION? GREAT. BUT WE'RE GOING TO *COORDINATE* IT.
WE'RE NOT FAR FROM THE AITKEN CRATER. I'D SAY, LESS THAN A *MILE.* WHICH, BASED ON THE FOOTAGE THEY SHOWED US IN THAT... WHATEVER THAT PLACE WAS...
...THAT'S WHERE THIS PSYCHO GREEN RANGER THING CRASHED.
LET'S START WITH RECONNAISSANCE. YOU AND... JAMIE?
YEAH?
YOU TWO HEAD OUT TO THE RIDGE. STAY ON THE RIGHT SIDE OF THE CRATER-- THE RIDGE IS HIGHEST THERE AND YOU'LL HAVE PLENTY OF COVER. RADIO BACK WHEN YOU HAVE VISUAL CONFIRMATION.
DOES THAT WORK FOR YOU, NIKOLAI? OR DO YOU THINK BEING A SOVIET MAN MEANS YOU KNOW THE *MOON* BETTER THAN ME, TOO?
HM. *FINE* THEN. COME, BRIT.

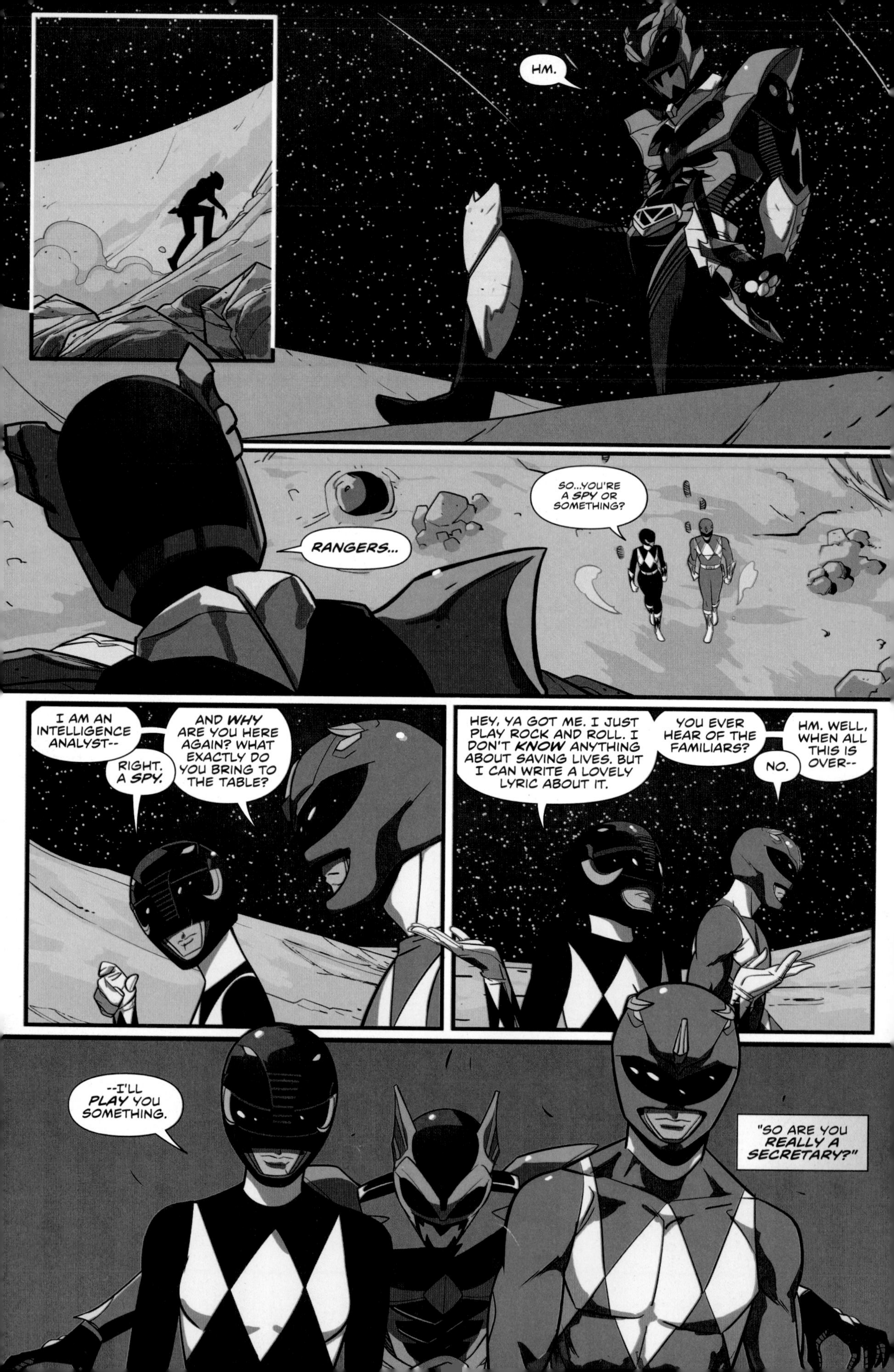
HM.
RANGERS...
SO...YOU'RE A SPY OR SOMETHING?
I AM AN INTELLIGENCE ANALYST--
RIGHT. A SPY.
AND WHY ARE YOU HERE AGAIN? WHAT EXACTLY DO YOU BRING TO THE TABLE?
HEY, YA GOT ME. I JUST PLAY ROCK AND ROLL. I DON'T KNOW ANYTHING ABOUT SAVING LIVES. BUT I CAN WRITE A LOVELY LYRIC ABOUT IT.
YOU EVER HEAR OF THE FAMILIARS?
NO.
HM. WELL, WHEN ALL THIS IS OVER--
--I'LL PLAY YOU SOMETHING.
"SO ARE YOU REALLY A SECRETARY?"

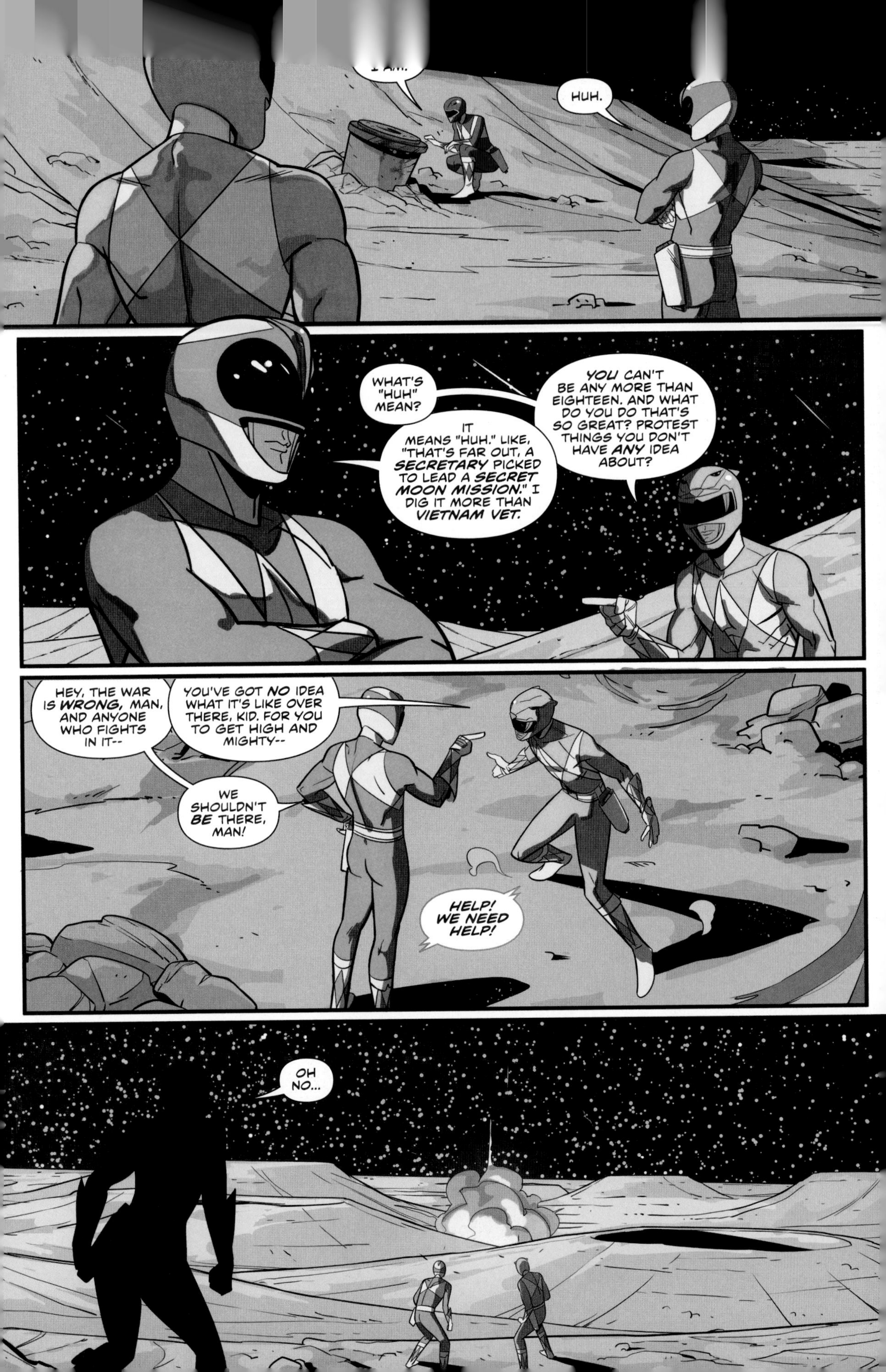
HUH.
WHAT'S "HUH" MEAN?
IT MEANS "HUH." LIKE, "THAT'S FAR OUT, A SECRETARY PICKED TO LEAD A SECRET MOON MISSION." I DIG IT MORE THAN VIETNAM VET.
YOU CAN'T BE ANY MORE THAN EIGHTEEN. AND WHAT DO YOU DO THAT'S SO GREAT? PROTEST THINGS YOU DON'T HAVE ANY IDEA ABOUT?
HEY, THE WAR IS WRONG, MAN, AND ANYONE WHO FIGHTS IN IT--
YOU'VE GOT NO IDEA WHAT IT'S LIKE OVER THERE, KID. FOR YOU TO GET HIGH AND MIGHTY--
WE SHOULDN'T BE THERE, MAN!
HELP! WE NEED HELP!
OH NO...

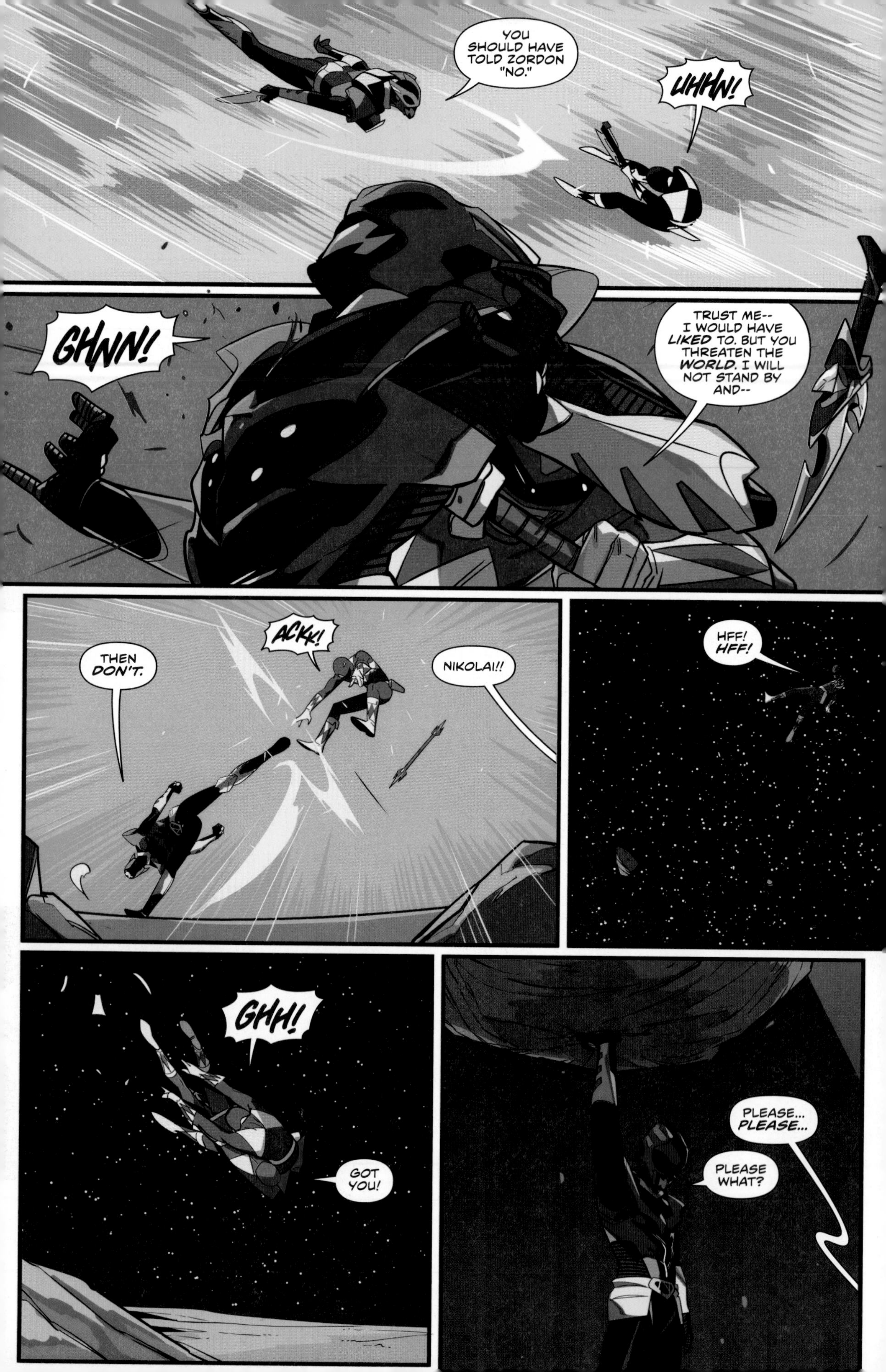
YOU SHOULD HAVE TOLD ZORDON "NO."
UHHN!
GHNN!
TRUST ME-- I WOULD HAVE LIKED TO. BUT YOU THREATEN THE WORLD. I WILL NOT STAND BY AND--
ACKK!
THEN DON'T.
NIKOLAI!!
HFF! HFF!
GHH!
GOT YOU!
PLEASE... PLEASE...
PLEASE WHAT?

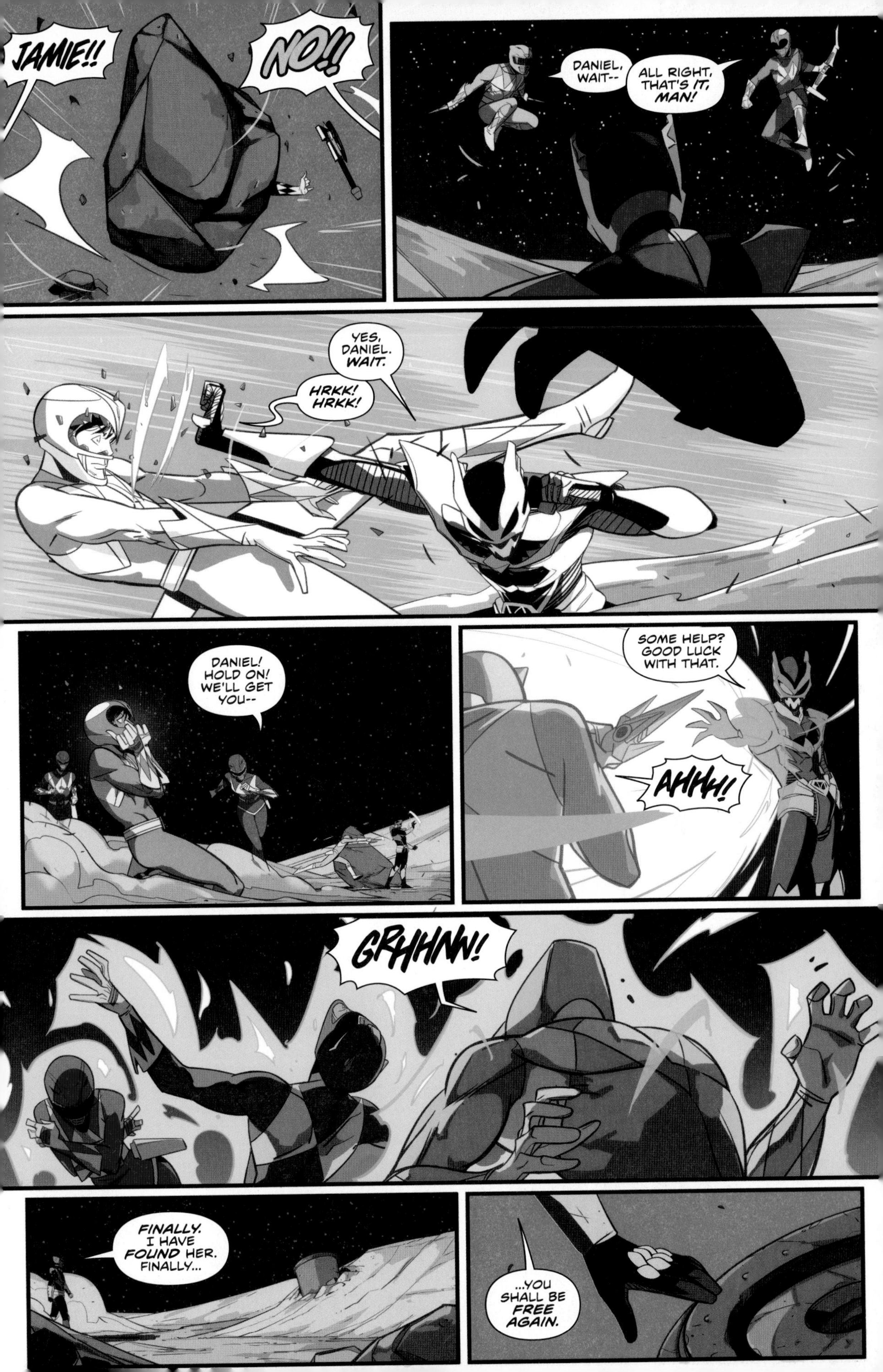
JAMIE!!
NO!!
DANIEL, WAIT--
ALL RIGHT, THAT'S IT, MAN!
YES, DANIEL. WAIT.
HRKK! HRKK!
DANIEL! HOLD ON! WE'LL GET YOU--
SOME HELP? GOOD LUCK WITH THAT.
AHHH!
GRHHNN!
FINALLY. I HAVE FOUND HER. FINALLY...
...YOU SHALL BE FREE AGAIN.

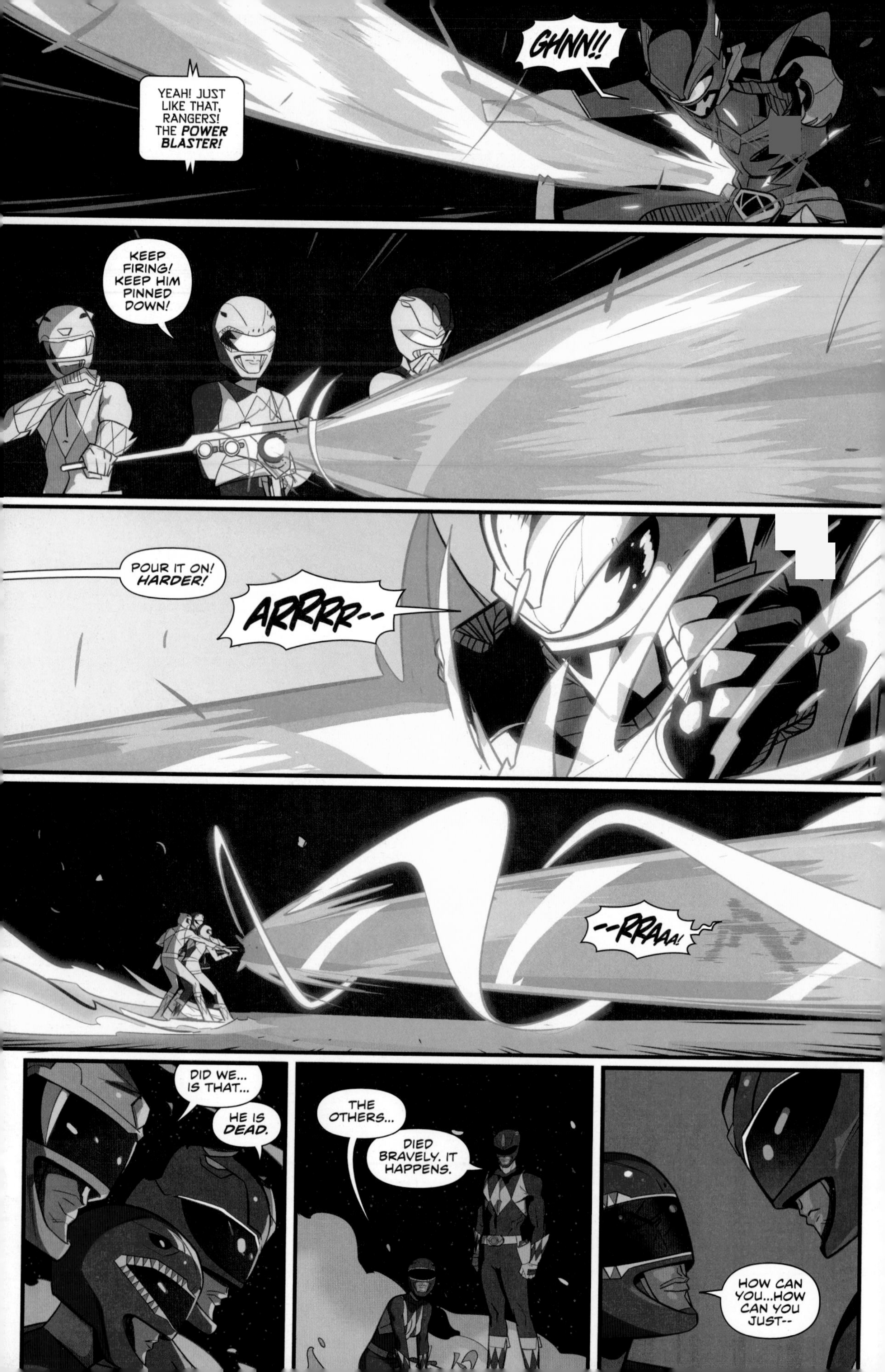
GHNN!!
YEAH! JUST LIKE THAT, RANGERS! THE POWER BLASTER!
KEEP FIRING! KEEP HIM PINNED DOWN!
POUR IT ON! HARDER!
ARRRR--
--RRAAA!
DID WE... IS THAT...
HE IS DEAD.
THE OTHERS...
DIED BRAVELY. IT HAPPENS.
HOW CAN YOU...HOW CAN YOU JUST--

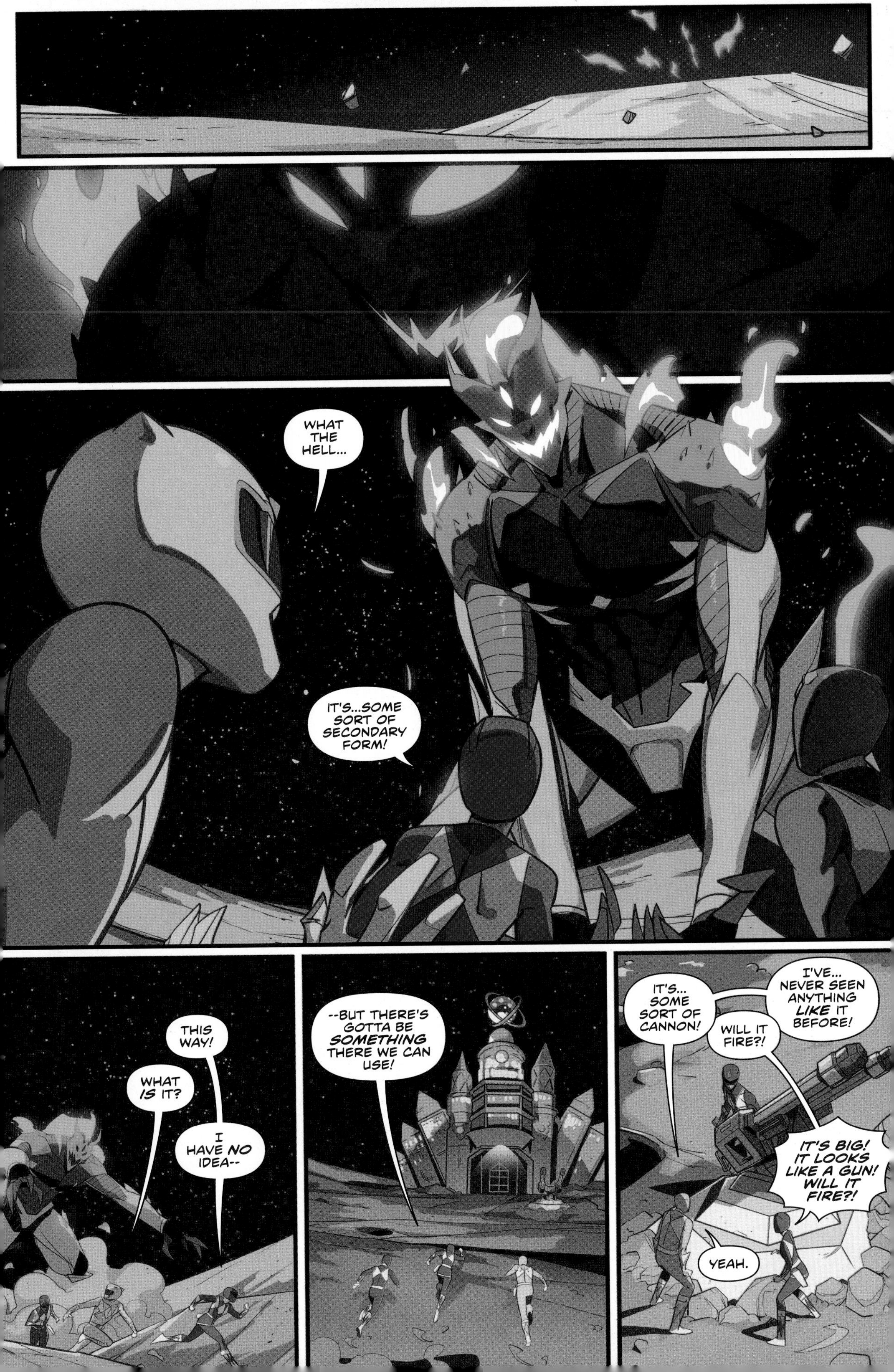

WHAT THE HELL...
IT'S...SOME SORT OF SECONDARY FORM!
THIS WAY!
WHAT IS IT?
I HAVE NO IDEA--
--BUT THERE'S GOTTA BE SOMETHING THERE WE CAN USE!
IT'S... SOME SORT OF CANNON!
I'VE... NEVER SEEN ANYTHING LIKE IT BEFORE!
WILL IT FIRE?!
IT'S BIG! IT LOOKS LIKE A GUN! WILL IT FIRE?!
YEAH.

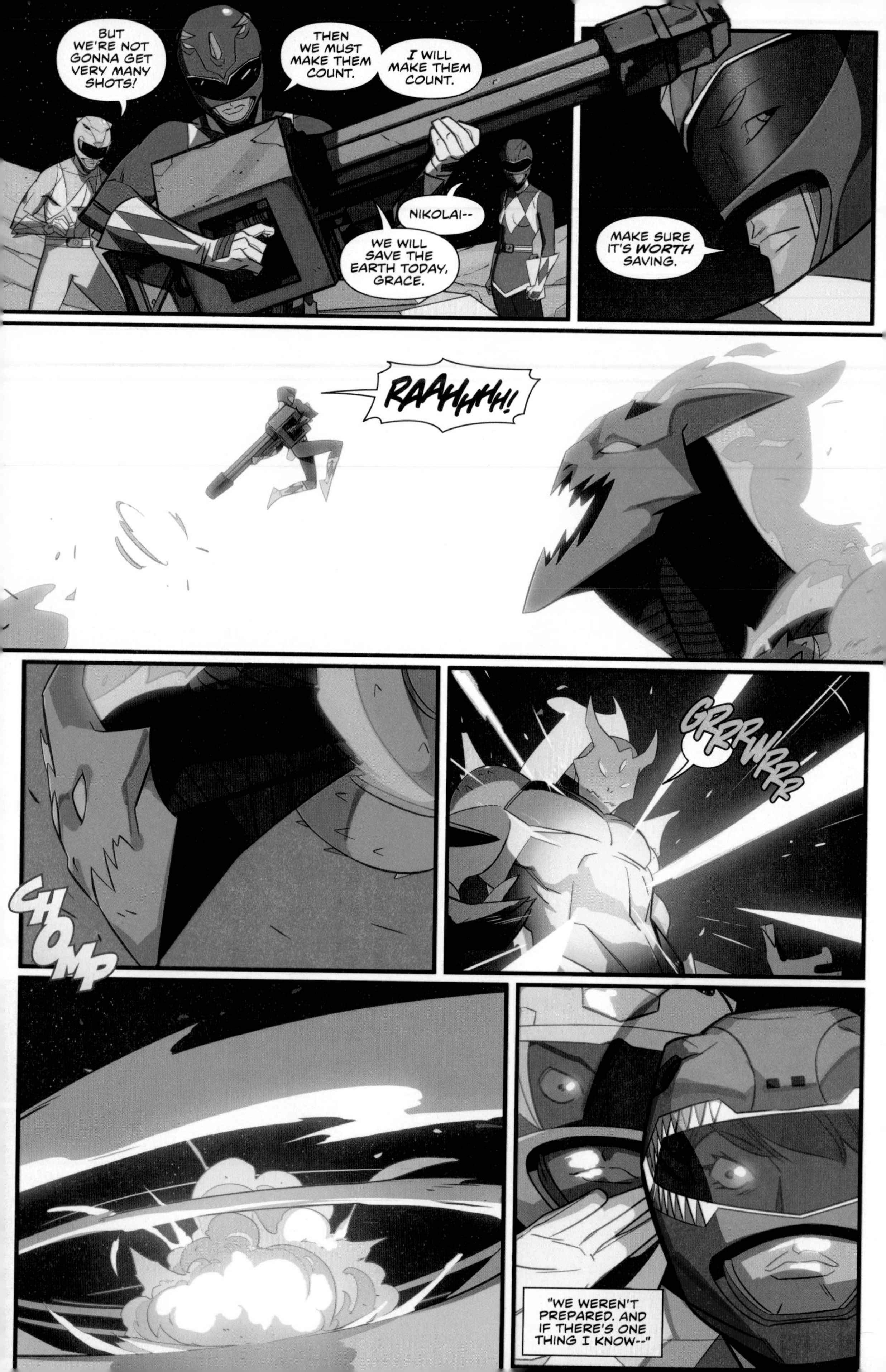

BUT WE'RE NOT GONNA GET VERY MANY SHOTS!
THEN WE MUST MAKE THEM COUNT.
I WILL MAKE THEM COUNT.
NIKOLAI--
WE WILL SAVE THE EARTH TODAY, GRACE.
MAKE SURE IT'S **WORTH** SAVING.
RAAHHHH!
CHOMP
GRRRWRRR
"WE WEREN'T PREPARED. AND IF THERE'S ONE THING I KNOW--"

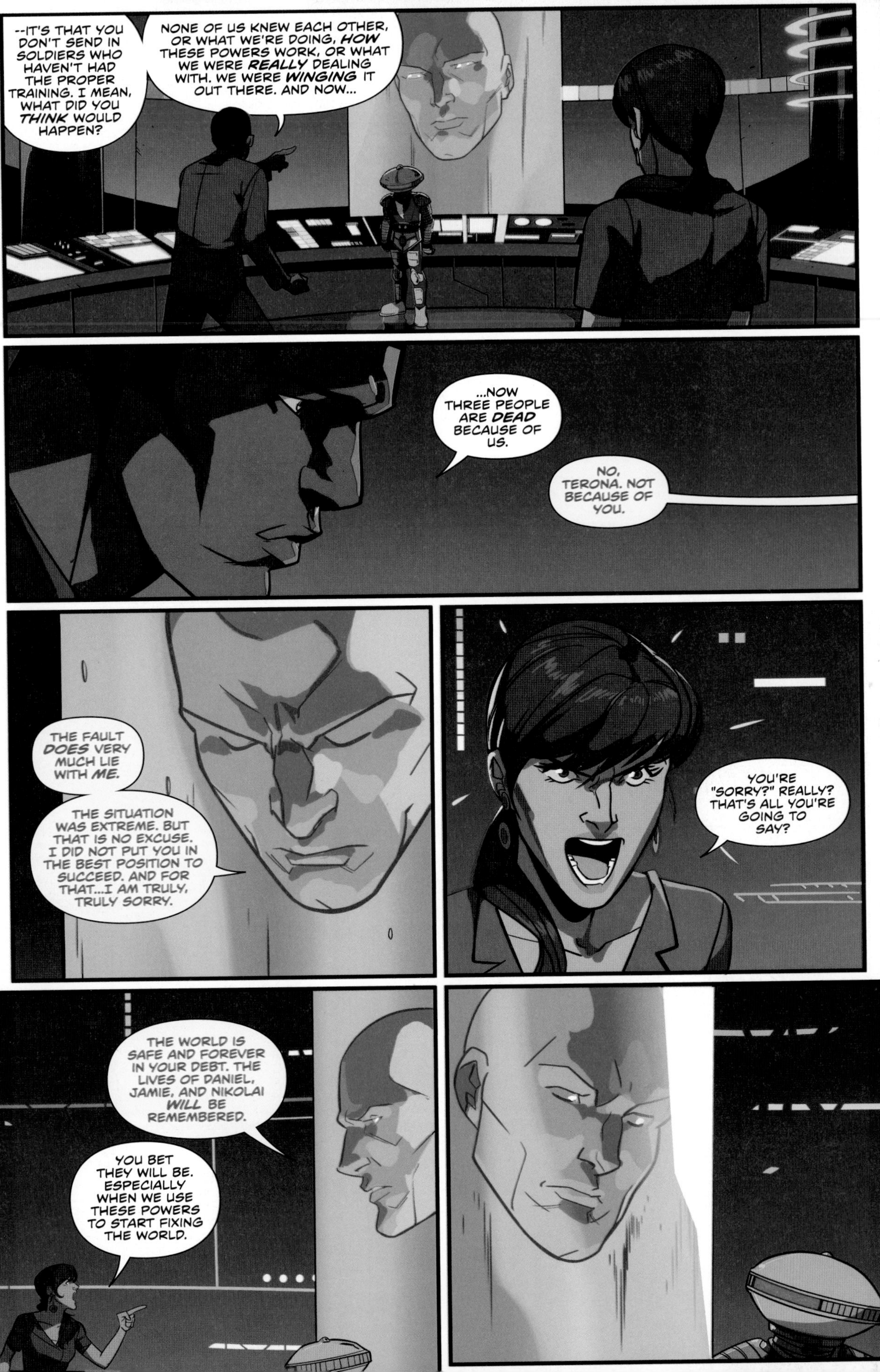
--IT'S THAT YOU DON'T SEND IN SOLDIERS WHO HAVEN'T HAD THE PROPER TRAINING. I MEAN, WHAT DID YOU THINK WOULD HAPPEN?
NONE OF US KNEW EACH OTHER, OR WHAT WE'RE DOING, HOW THESE POWERS WORK, OR WHAT WE WERE REALLY DEALING WITH. WE WERE WINGING IT OUT THERE. AND NOW...
...NOW THREE PEOPLE ARE DEAD BECAUSE OF US.
NO, TERONA. NOT BECAUSE OF YOU.
THE FAULT DOES VERY MUCH LIE WITH ME.
THE SITUATION WAS EXTREME. BUT THAT IS NO EXCUSE. I DID NOT PUT YOU IN THE BEST POSITION TO SUCCEED. AND FOR THAT...I AM TRULY, TRULY SORRY.
YOU'RE "SORRY?" REALLY? THAT'S ALL YOU'RE GOING TO SAY?
THE WORLD IS SAFE AND FOREVER IN YOUR DEBT. THE LIVES OF DANIEL, JAMIE, AND NIKOLAI WILL BE REMEMBERED.
YOU BET THEY WILL BE. ESPECIALLY WHEN WE USE THESE POWERS TO START FIXING THE WORLD.

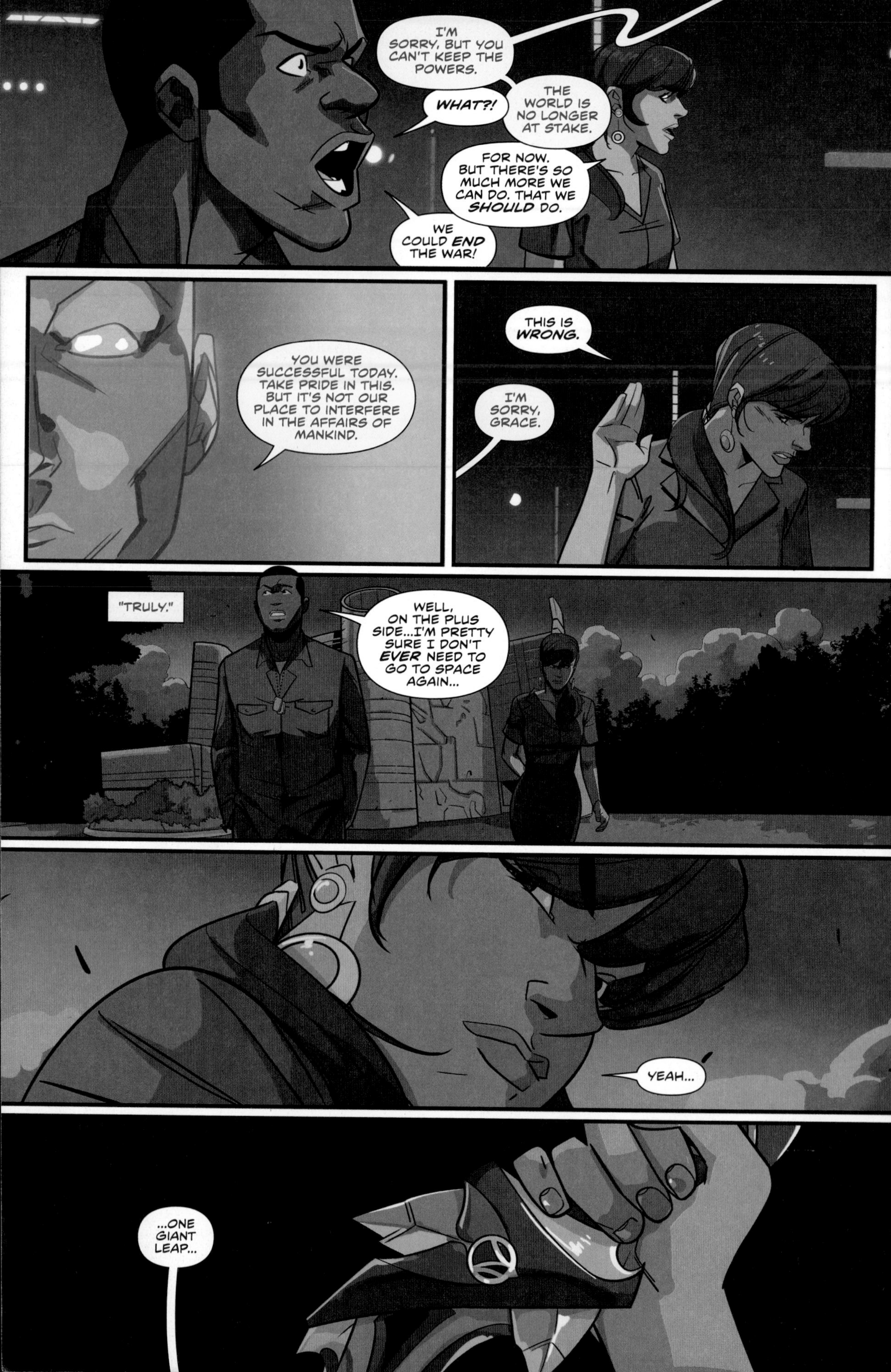
I'M SORRY, BUT YOU CAN'T KEEP THE POWERS.
WHAT?!
THE WORLD IS NO LONGER AT STAKE.
FOR NOW. BUT THERE'S SO MUCH MORE WE CAN DO. THAT WE SHOULD DO.
WE COULD END THE WAR!
YOU WERE SUCCESSFUL TODAY. TAKE PRIDE IN THIS. BUT IT'S NOT OUR PLACE TO INTERFERE IN THE AFFAIRS OF MANKIND.
THIS IS WRONG.
I'M SORRY, GRACE.
"TRULY."
WELL, ON THE PLUS SIDE...I'M PRETTY SURE I DON'T EVER NEED TO GO TO SPACE AGAIN...
YEAH...
...ONE GIANT LEAP...

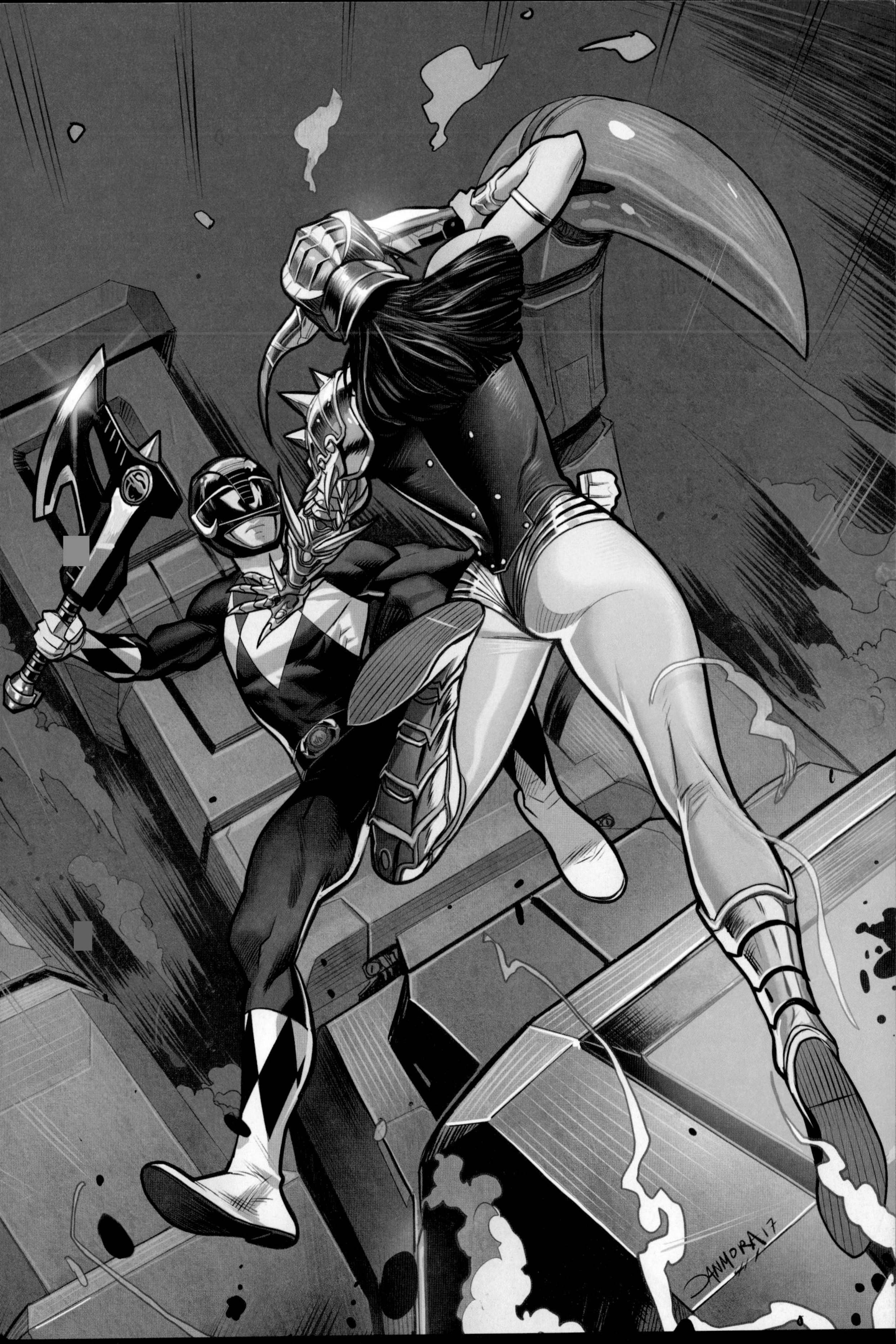
DANMORA 17

DAN MORA ISSUE TWENTY VERSUS VARIANT COVER

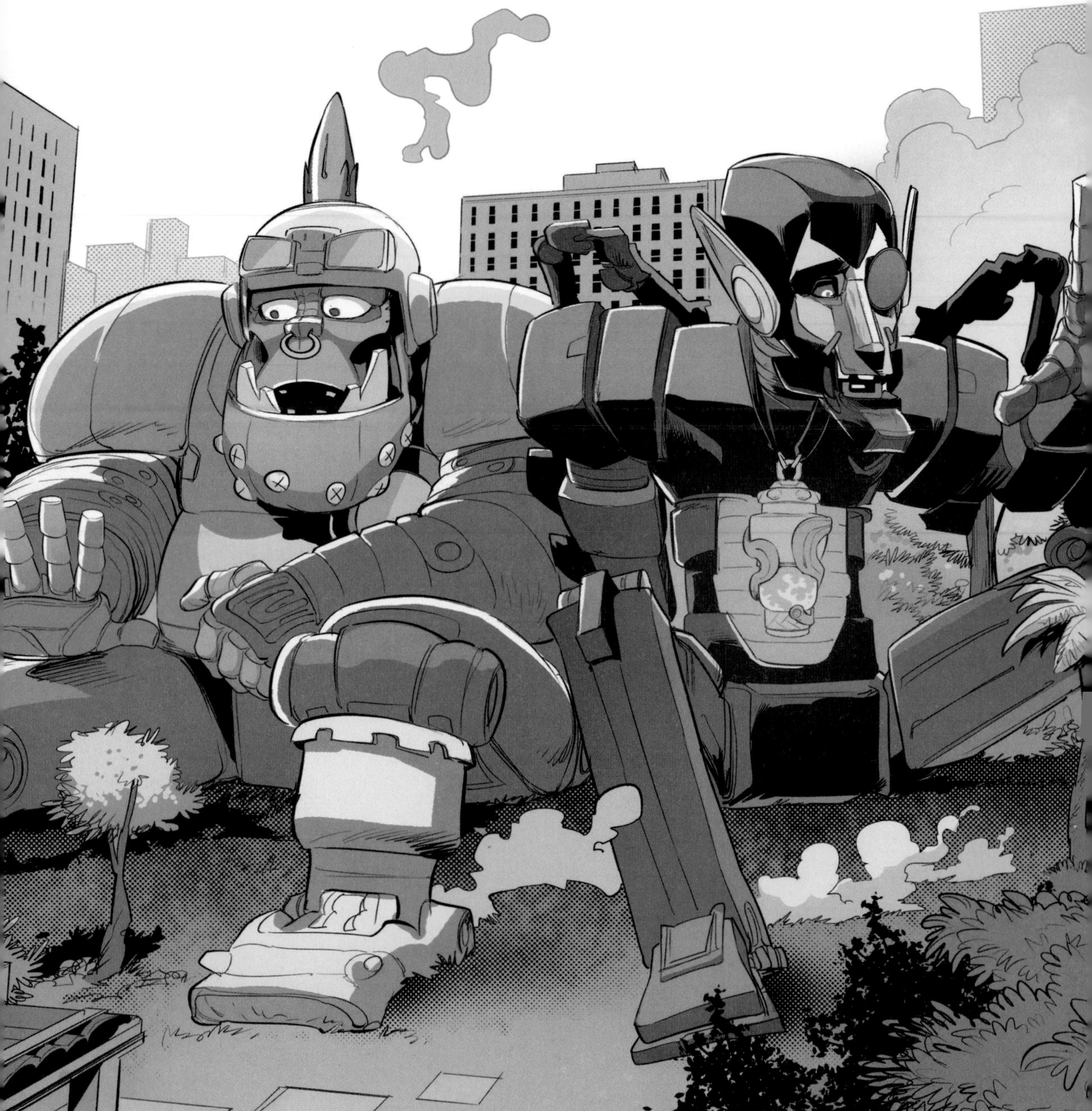

THE ONGOING MISADVENTURES OF
SQUATT & BABOO

WRITTEN BY
RYAN FERRIER

ILLUSTRATED BY
BACHAN

COLORS BY
TRIONA FARRELL

LETTERS BY
JIM CAMPBELL

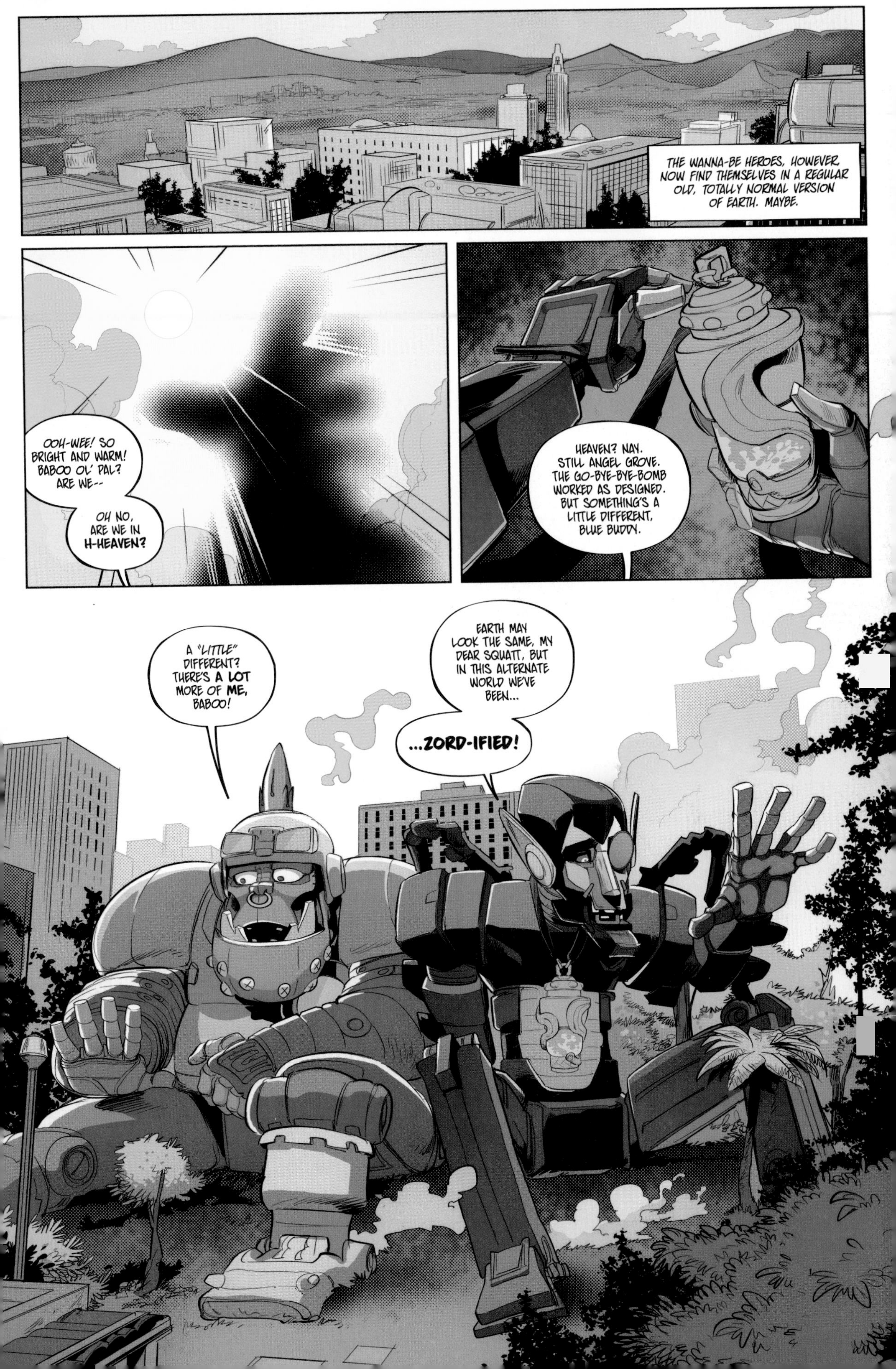
THE WANNA-BE HEROES, HOWEVER NOW FIND THEMSELVES IN A REGULAR OLD, TOTALLY NORMAL VERSION OF EARTH. MAYBE.
OOH-WEE! SO BRIGHT AND WARM! BABOO OL' PAL? ARE WE--
OH NO, ARE WE IN H-HEAVEN?
HEAVEN? NAY. STILL ANGEL GROVE. THE GO-BYE-BYE-BOMB WORKED AS DESIGNED. BUT SOMETHING'S A LITTLE DIFFERENT, BLUE BUDDY.
A "LITTLE" DIFFERENT? THERE'S A LOT MORE OF ME, BABOO!
EARTH MAY LOOK THE SAME, MY DEAR SQUATT, BUT IN THIS ALTERNATE WORLD WE'VE BEEN...
...ZORD-IFIED!

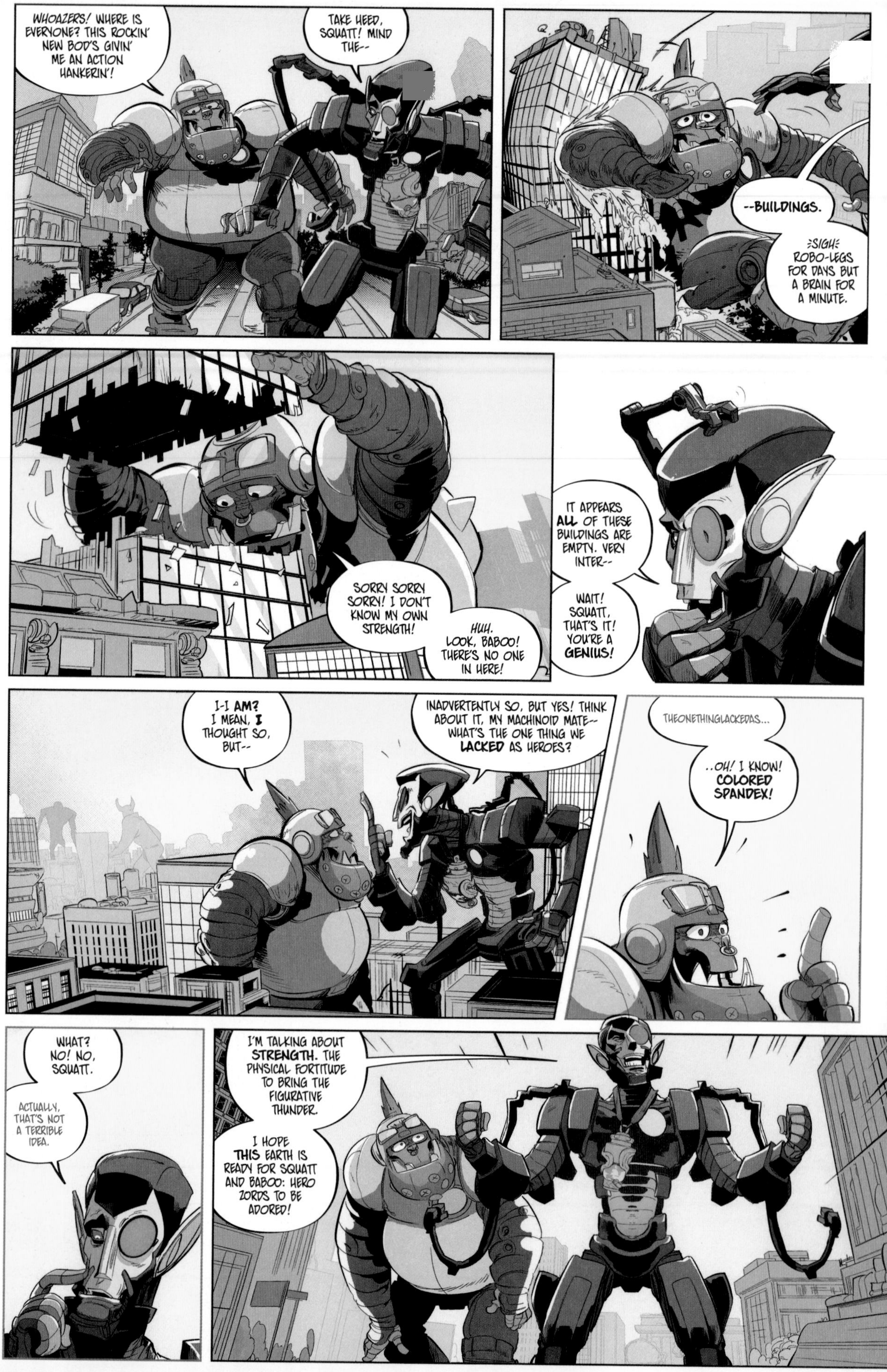
WHOAZERS! WHERE IS EVERYONE? THIS ROCKIN' NEW BOD'S GIVIN' ME AN ACTION HANKERIN'!
TAKE HEED, SQUATT! MIND THE--
--BUILDINGS.
SIGH
ROBO-LEGS FOR DAYS BUT A BRAIN FOR A MINUTE.
SORRY SORRY SORRY! I DON'T KNOW MY OWN STRENGTH!
HUH. LOOK, BABOO! THERE'S NO ONE IN HERE!
IT APPEARS ALL OF THESE BUILDINGS ARE EMPTY. VERY INTER--
WAIT! SQUATT, THAT'S IT! YOU'RE A GENIUS!
I-I AM? I MEAN, I THOUGHT SO, BUT--
INADVERTENTLY SO, BUT YES! THINK ABOUT IT, MY MACHINOID MATE-- WHAT'S THE ONE THING WE LACKED AS HEROES?
THEONETHINGLACKEDAS...
..OH! I KNOW! COLORED SPANDEX!
WHAT? NO! NO, SQUATT.
ACTUALLY, THAT'S NOT A TERRIBLE IDEA.
I'M TALKING ABOUT STRENGTH. THE PHYSICAL FORTITUDE TO BRING THE FIGURATIVE THUNDER.
I HOPE THIS EARTH IS READY FOR SQUATT AND BABOO: HERO ZORDS TO BE ADORED!

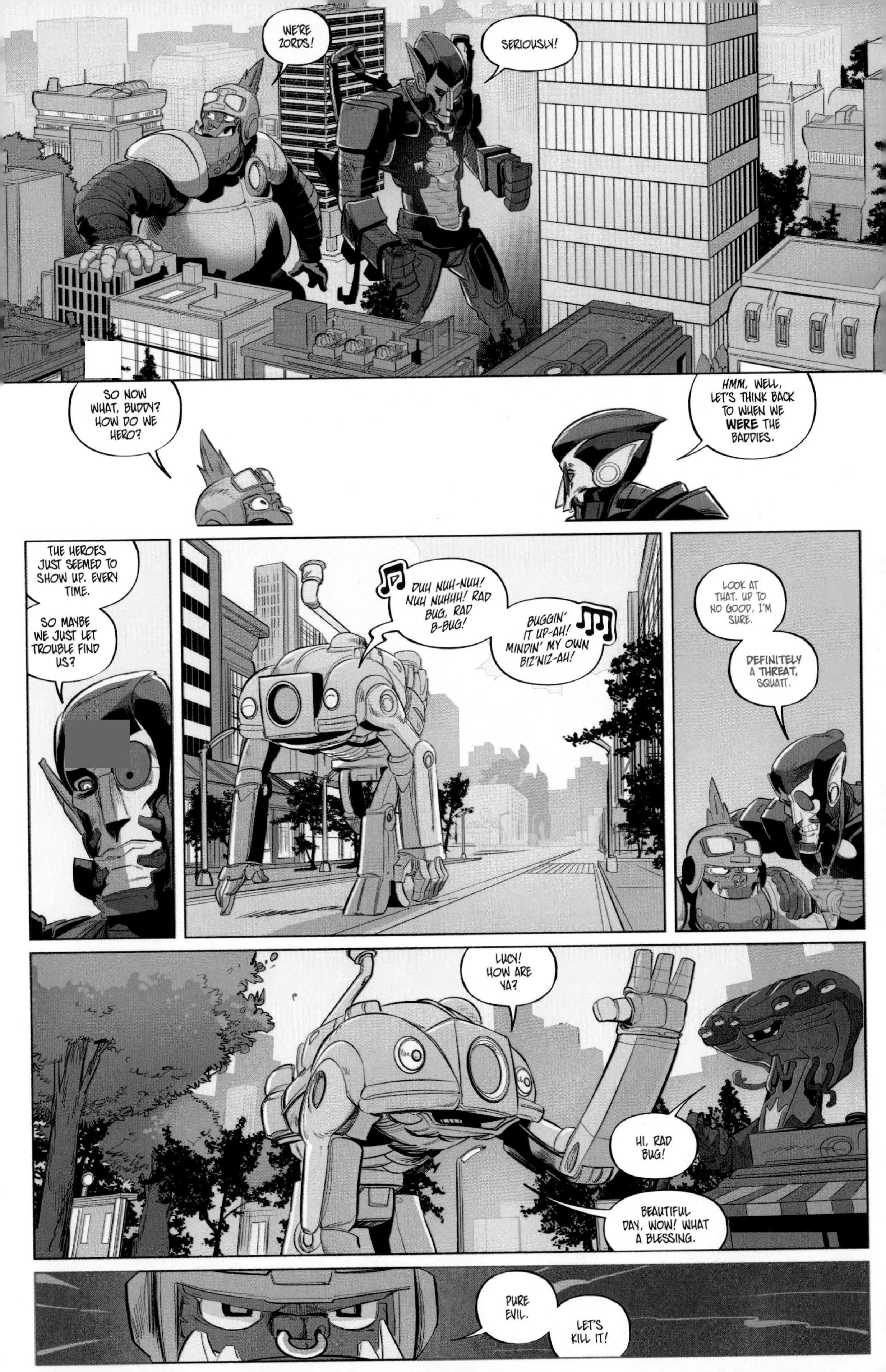
WE'RE ZORDS!
SERIOUSLY!
SO NOW WHAT, BUDDY? HOW DO WE HERO?
HMM, WELL, LET'S THINK BACK TO WHEN WE **WERE** THE BADDIES.
THE HEROES JUST SEEMED TO SHOW UP. EVERY TIME.
SO MAYBE WE JUST LET TROUBLE FIND US?
DUH NUH-NUH! NUH NUHHH! RAD BUG, RAD B-BUG!
BUGGIN' IT UP-AH! MINDIN' MY OWN BIZ'NIZ-AH!
LOOK AT THAT. UP TO NO GOOD, I'M SURE.
DEFINITELY A THREAT, SQUATT.
LUCY! HOW ARE YA?
HI, RAD BUG!
BEAUTIFUL DAY, WOW! WHAT A BLESSING.
PURE EVIL.
LET'S KILL IT!

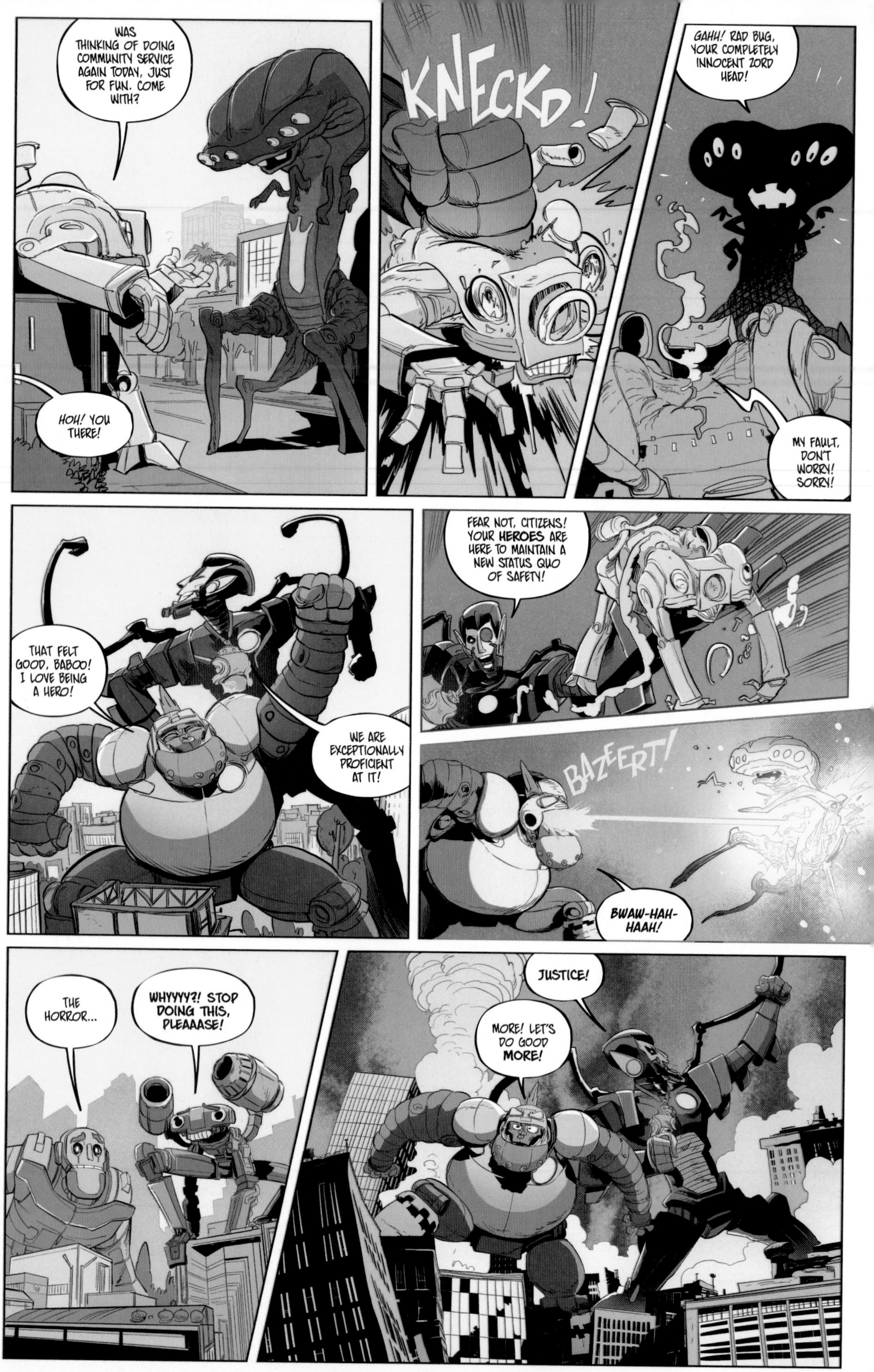
WAS THINKING OF DOING COMMUNITY SERVICE AGAIN TODAY, JUST FOR FUN. COME WITH?
HOH! YOU THERE!
KNECKD!
GAHH! RAD BUG, YOUR COMPLETELY INNOCENT ZORD HEAD!
MY FAULT, DON'T WORRY! SORRY!
THAT FELT GOOD, BABOO! I LOVE BEING A HERO!
WE ARE EXCEPTIONALLY PROFICIENT AT IT!
FEAR NOT, CITIZENS! YOUR HEROES ARE HERE TO MAINTAIN A NEW STATUS QUO OF SAFETY!
BAZEERT!
BWAW-HAH-HAAH!
THE HORROR...
WHYYYY?! STOP DOING THIS, PLEAAASE!
JUSTICE!
MORE! LET'S DO GOOD MORE!

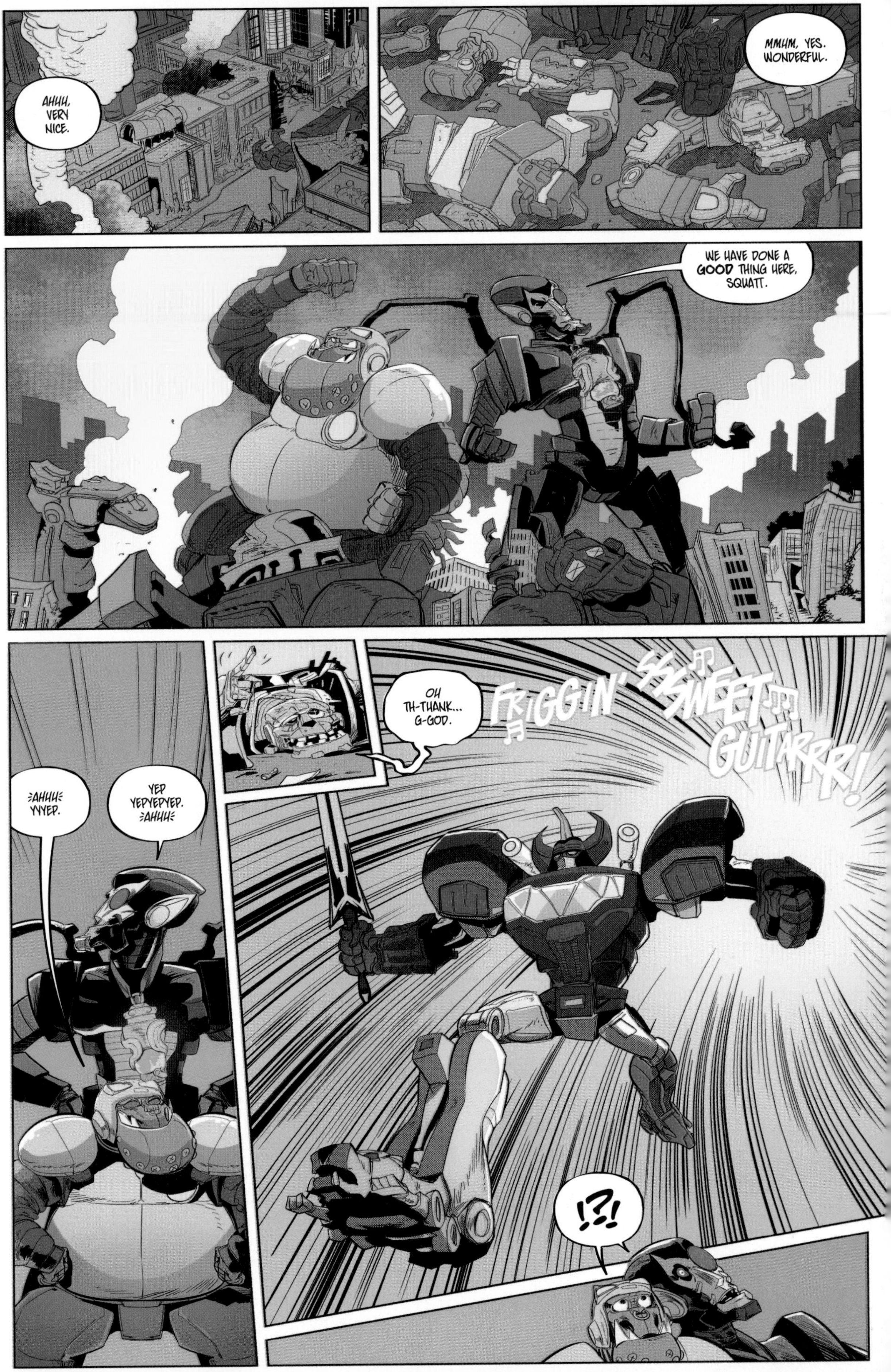
AHHH, VERY NICE.
MMHM, YES. WONDERFUL.
WE HAVE DONE A GOOD THING HERE, SQUATT.
≈AHHH≈ YYYEP.
YEP YEPYEPYEP. ≈AHHH≈
OH TH-THANK... G-GOD.
FRIGGIN' SWEET GUITARRR!
!?!

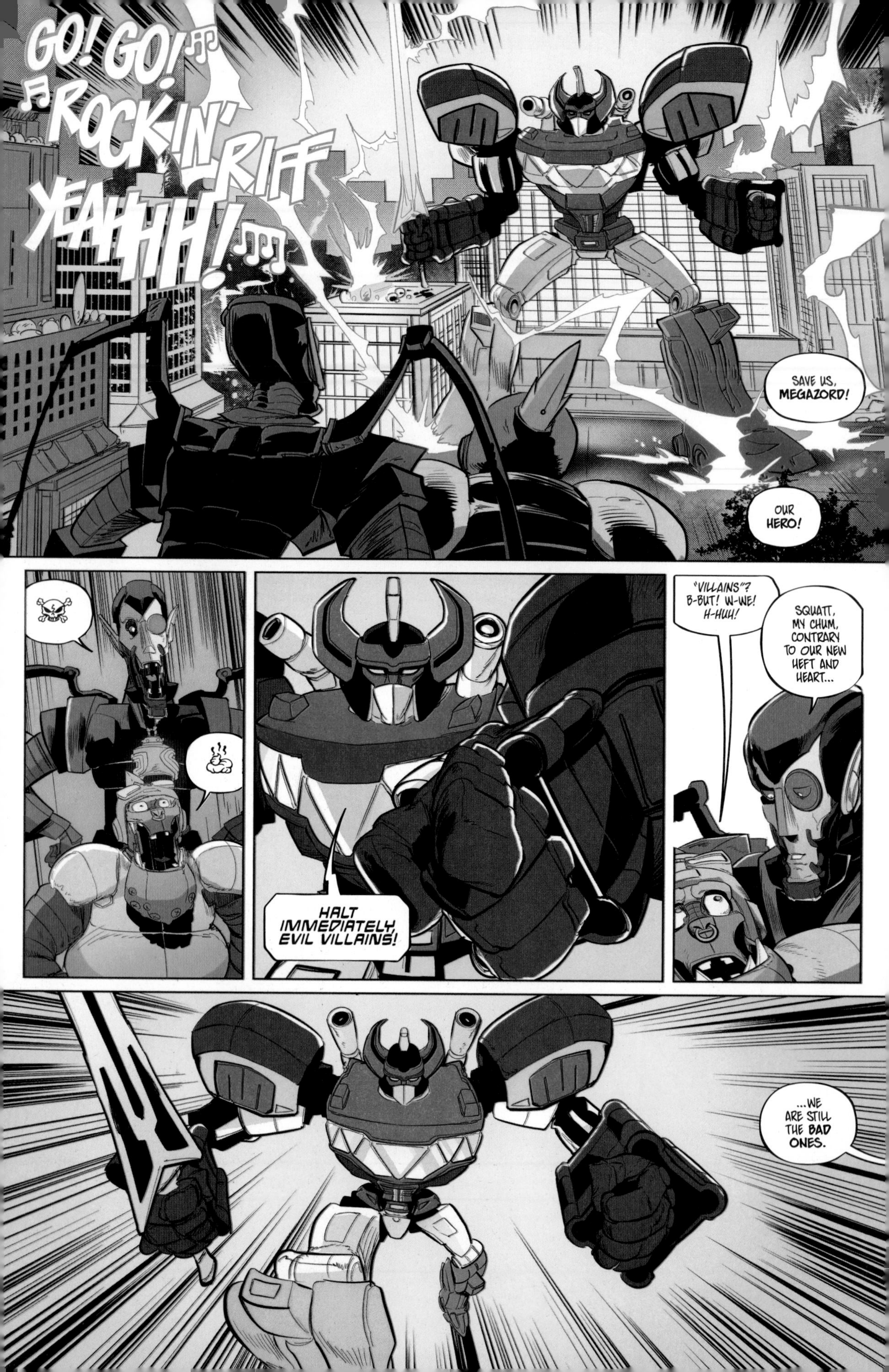
GO! GO! ROCKIN' RIFF YEAHHHH!
SAVE US, MEGAZORD!
OUR HERO!
HALT IMMEDIATELY, EVIL VILLAINS!
"VILLAINS"? B-BUT! W-WE! H-HUH!
SQUATT, MY CHUM, CONTRARY TO OUR NEW HEFT AND HEART...
...WE ARE STILL THE BAD ONES.

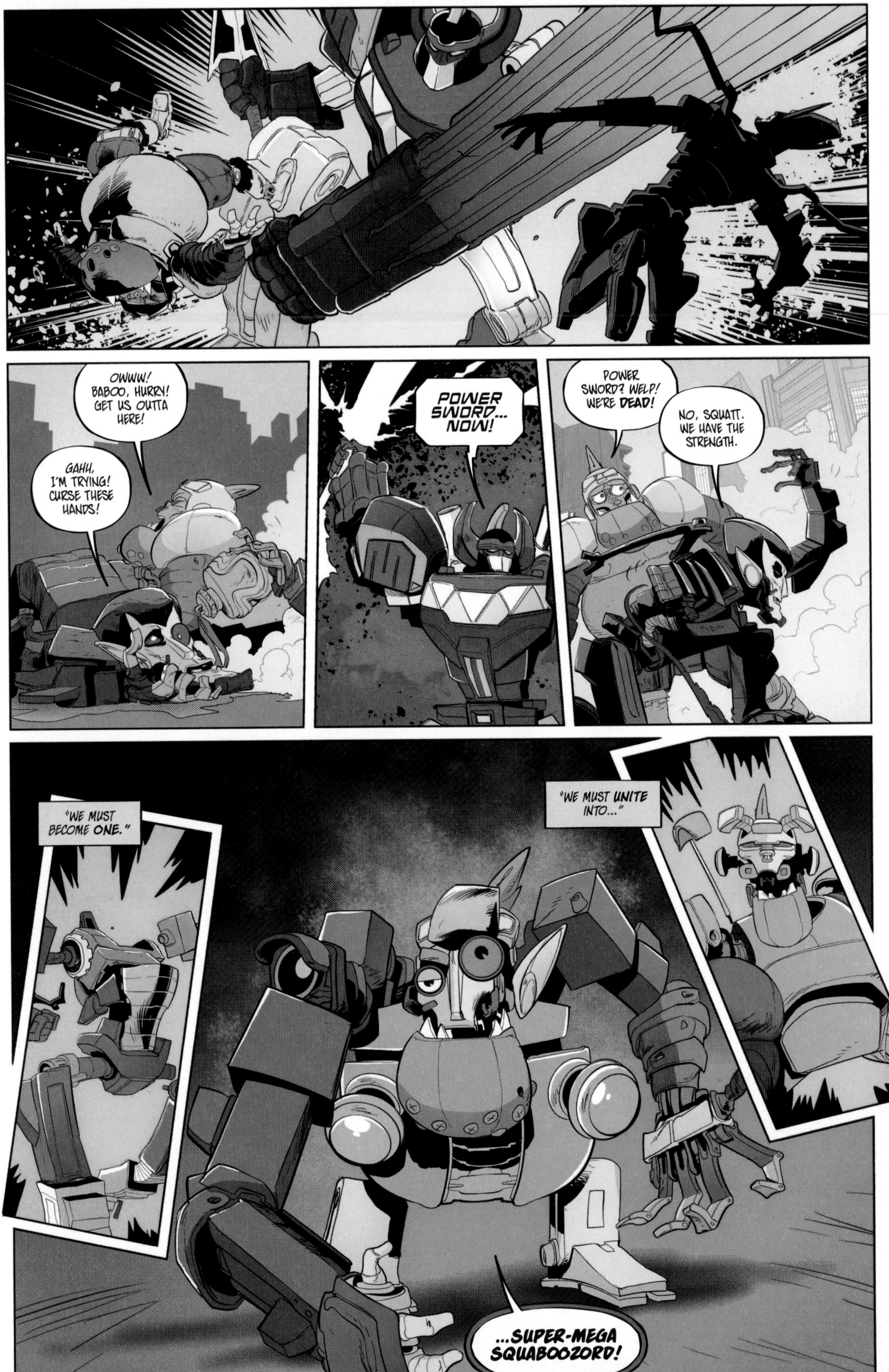
OWWW! BABOO, HURRY! GET US OUTTA HERE!
GAHH, I'M TRYING! CURSE THESE HANDS!
POWER SWORD... NOW!
POWER SWORD? WELP! WE'RE DEAD!
NO, SQUATT. WE HAVE THE STRENGTH.
"WE MUST BECOME ONE."
"WE MUST UNITE INTO..."
...SUPER-MEGA SQUABOOZORD!

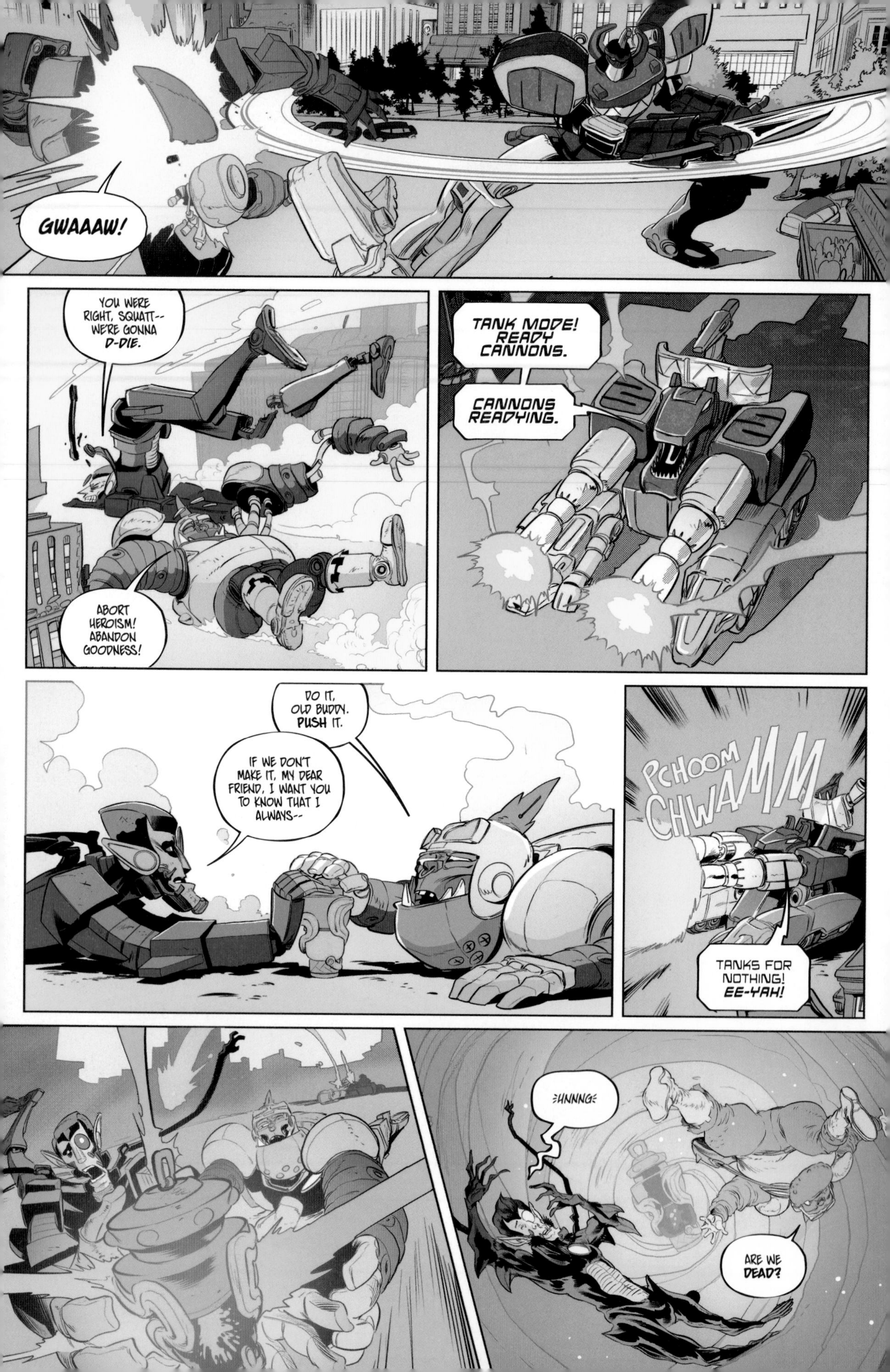
GWAAAW!
YOU WERE RIGHT, SQUATT-- WE'RE GONNA D-DIE.
ABORT HEROISM! ABANDON GOODNESS!
TANK MODE! READY CANNONS.
CANNONS READYING.
DO IT, OLD BUDDY. PUSH IT.
IF WE DON'T MAKE IT, MY DEAR FRIEND, I WANT YOU TO KNOW THAT I ALWAYS--
PCHOOM
CHWAMM
TANKS FOR NOTHING! EE-YAH!
UNNNG
ARE WE DEAD?

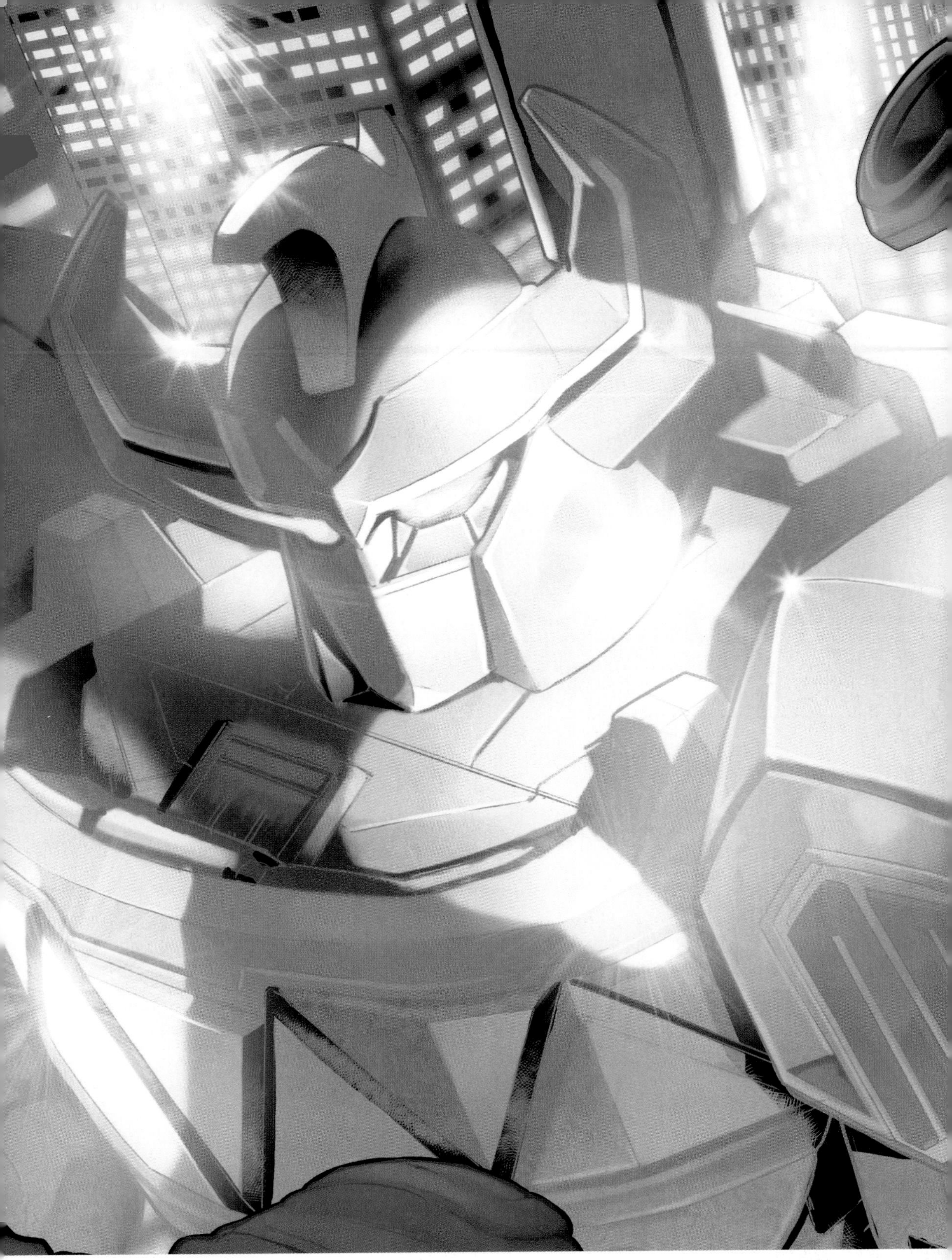

COVER GALLERY

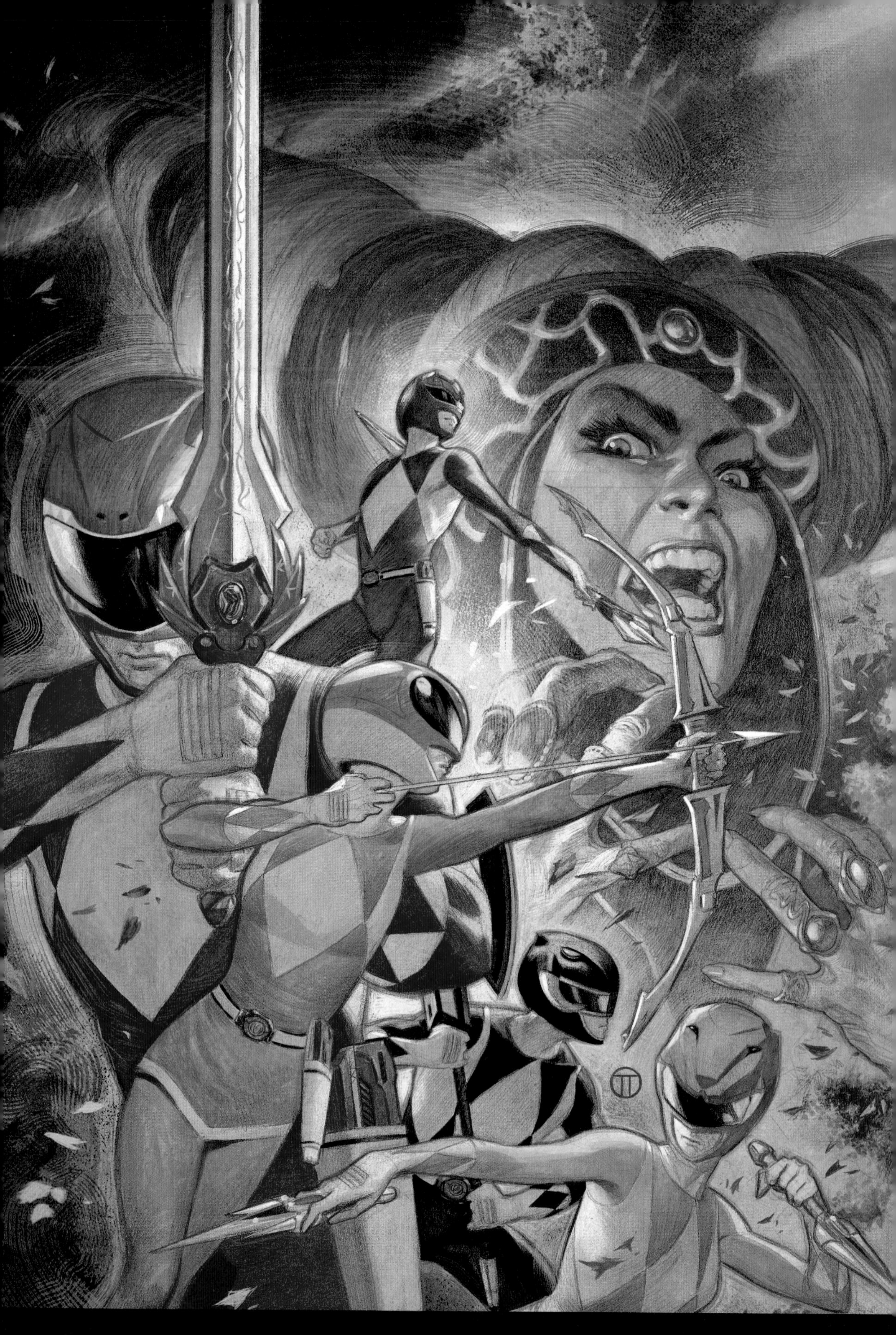

JULIAN TOTINO TEDESCO ISSUE SEVENTEEN UNLOCKED RETAILER CONNECTING VARIANT COVER

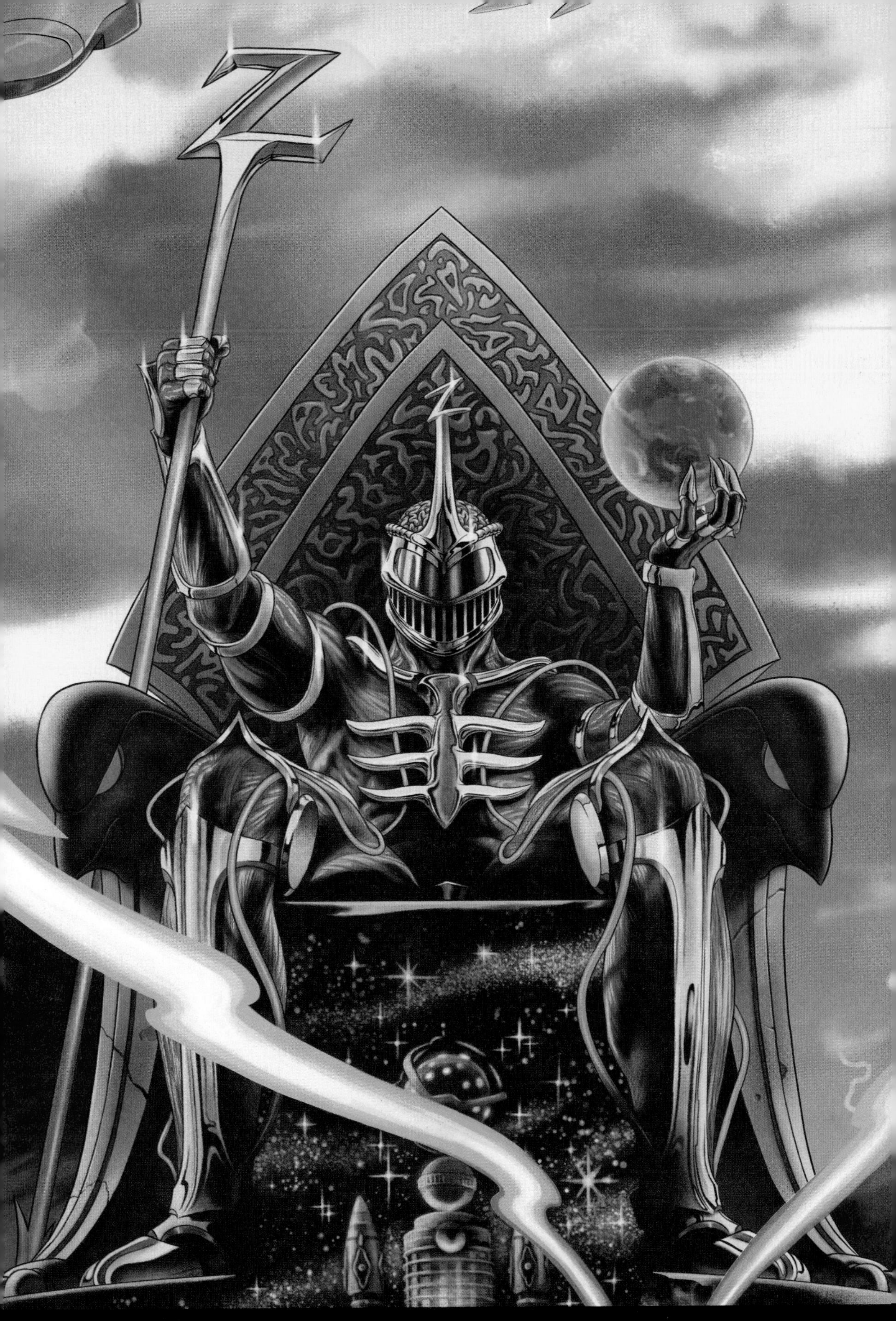

STEVE MORRIS | ISSUE SEVENTEEN CONNECTING VARIANT COVER

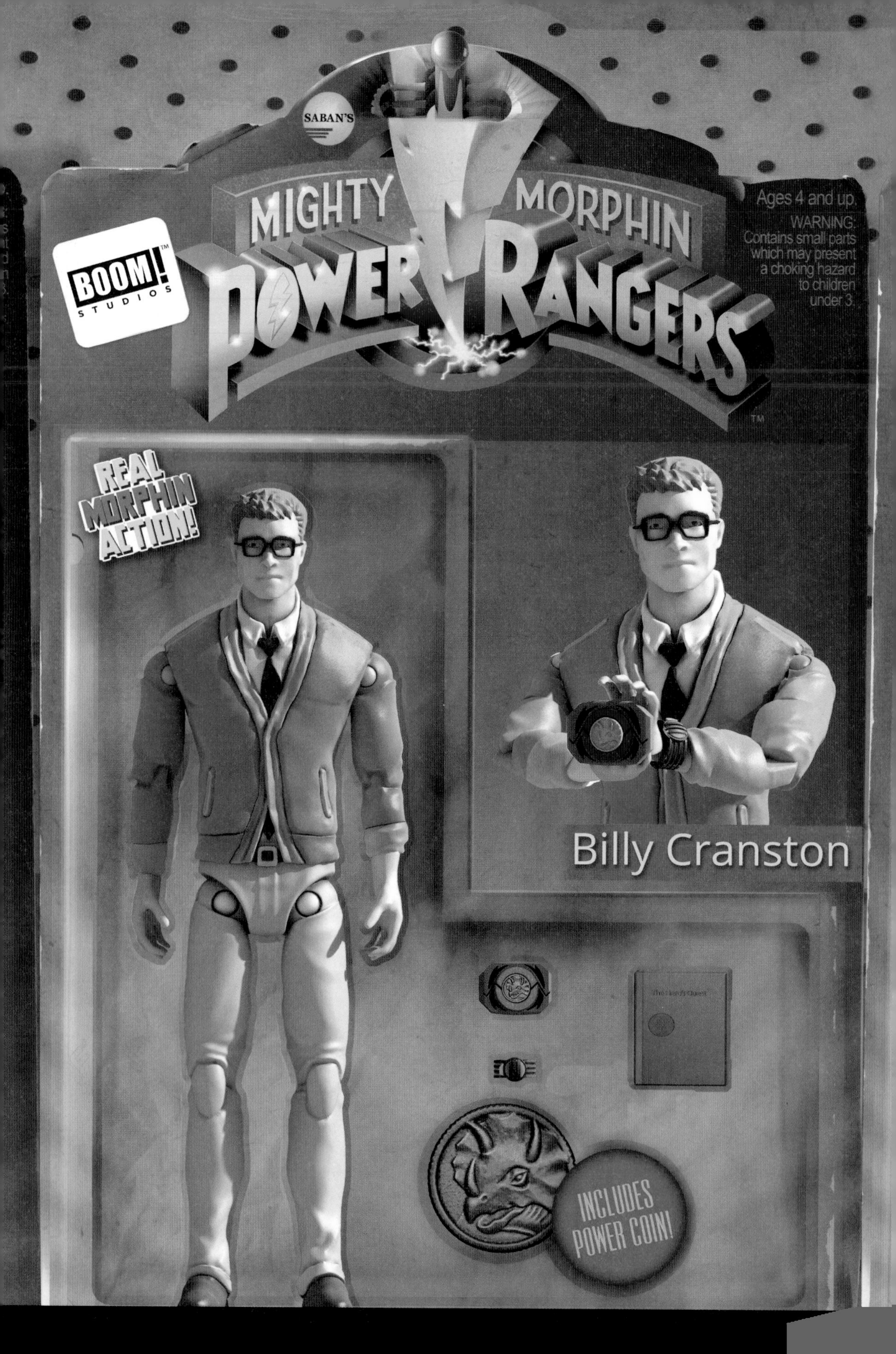
SABAN'S
MIGHTY MORPHIN
POWER RANGERS
TM
BOOM! STUDIOS
Ages 4 and up.
WARNING:
Contains small parts
which may present
a choking hazard
to children
under 3.
REAL MORPHIN ACTION!
Billy Cranston
INCLUDES POWER COIN!

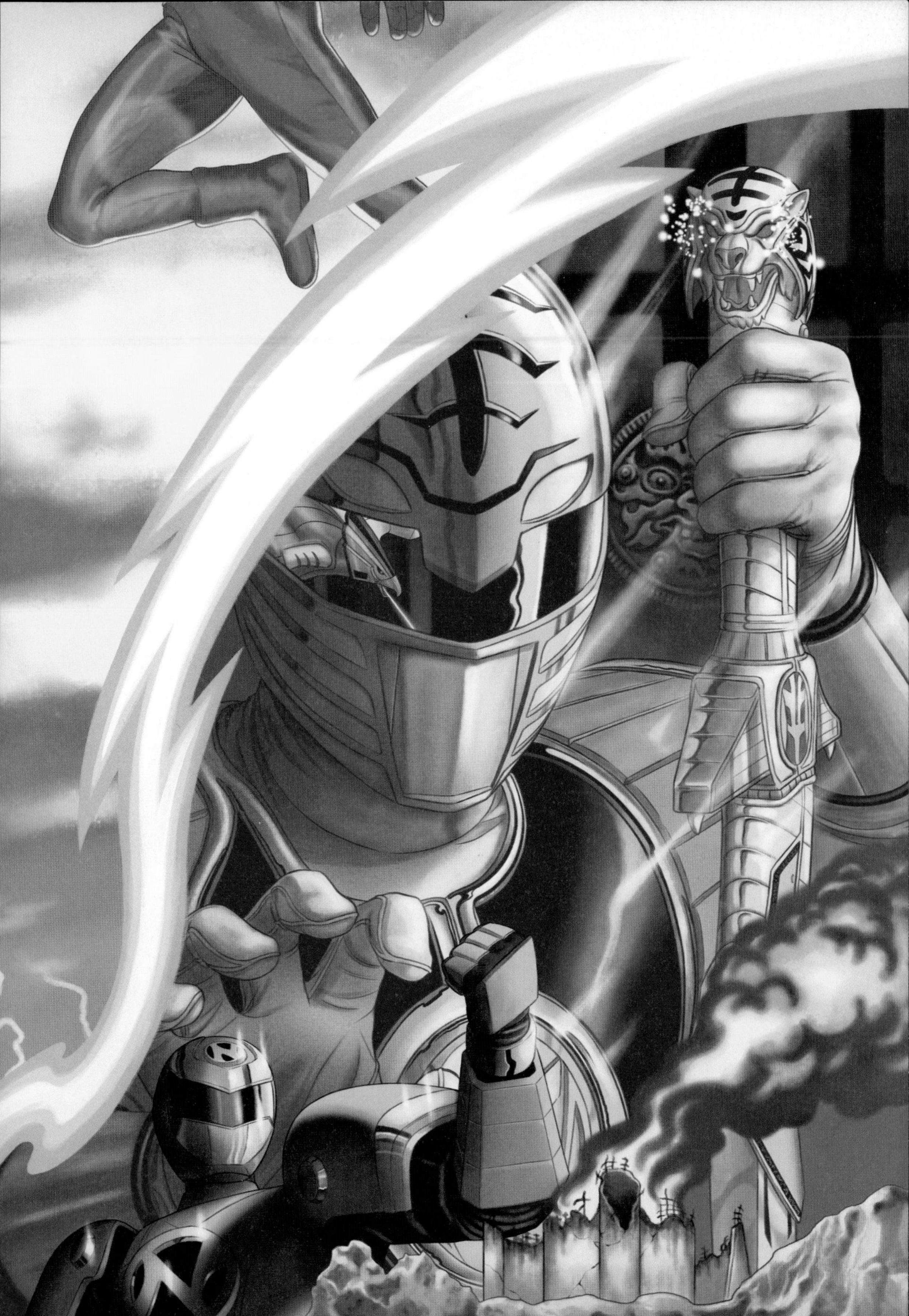

STEVE MORRIS ISSUE EIGHTTEEN CONNECTING VARIANT COVER

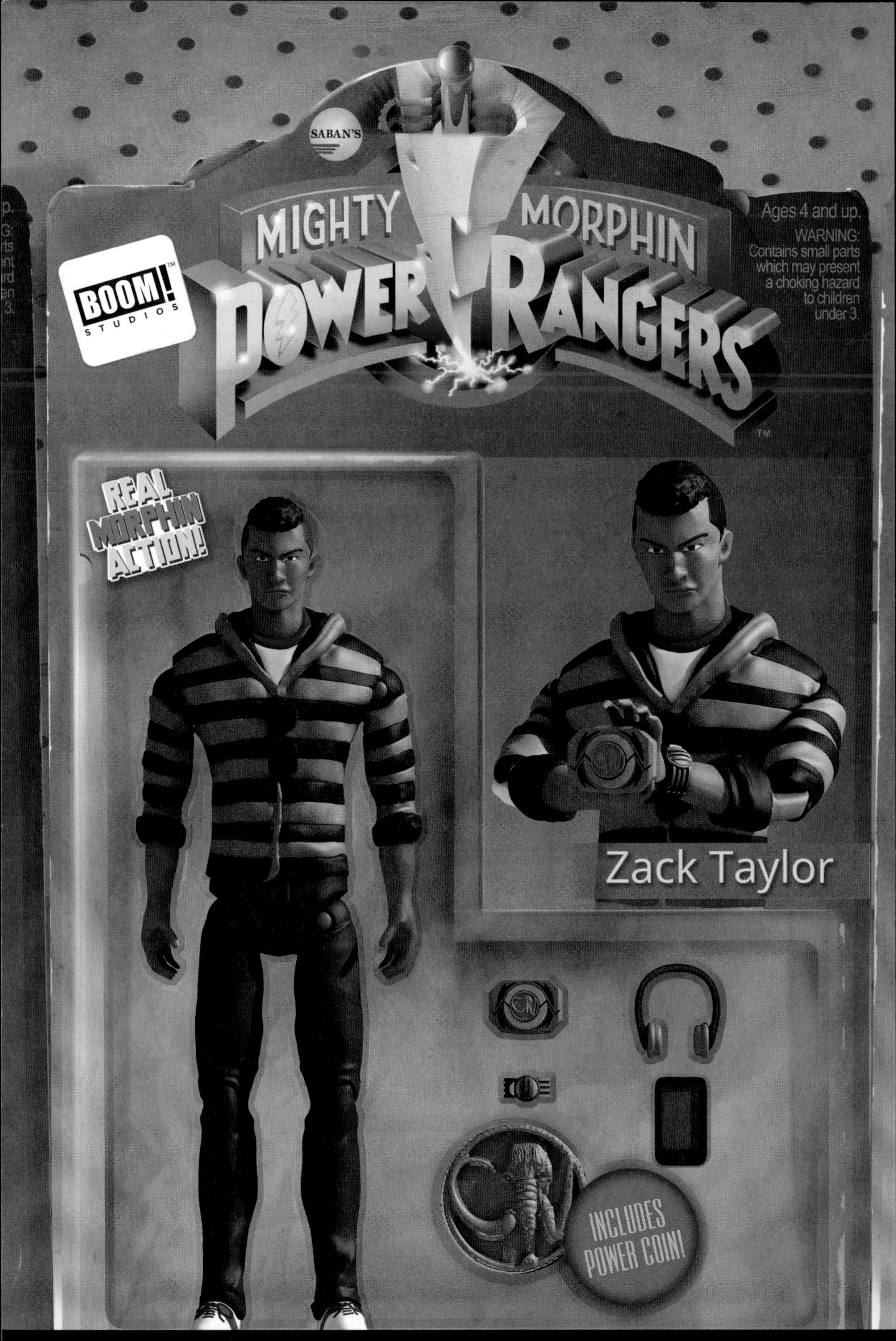
SABAN'S
MIGHTY MORPHIN
POWER RANGERS
TM
BOOM! STUDIOS
TM
Ages 4 and up.
WARNING:
Contains small parts
which may present
a choking hazard
to children
under 3.
REAL MORPHIN ACTION!
Zack Taylor
INCLUDES POWER COIN!

HASKELL MACKOWSKI WITH PACKAGING DESIGN BY **DAVID RYAN ROBINSON**
ISSUE EIGHTEEN ACTION FIGURE VARIANT COVER

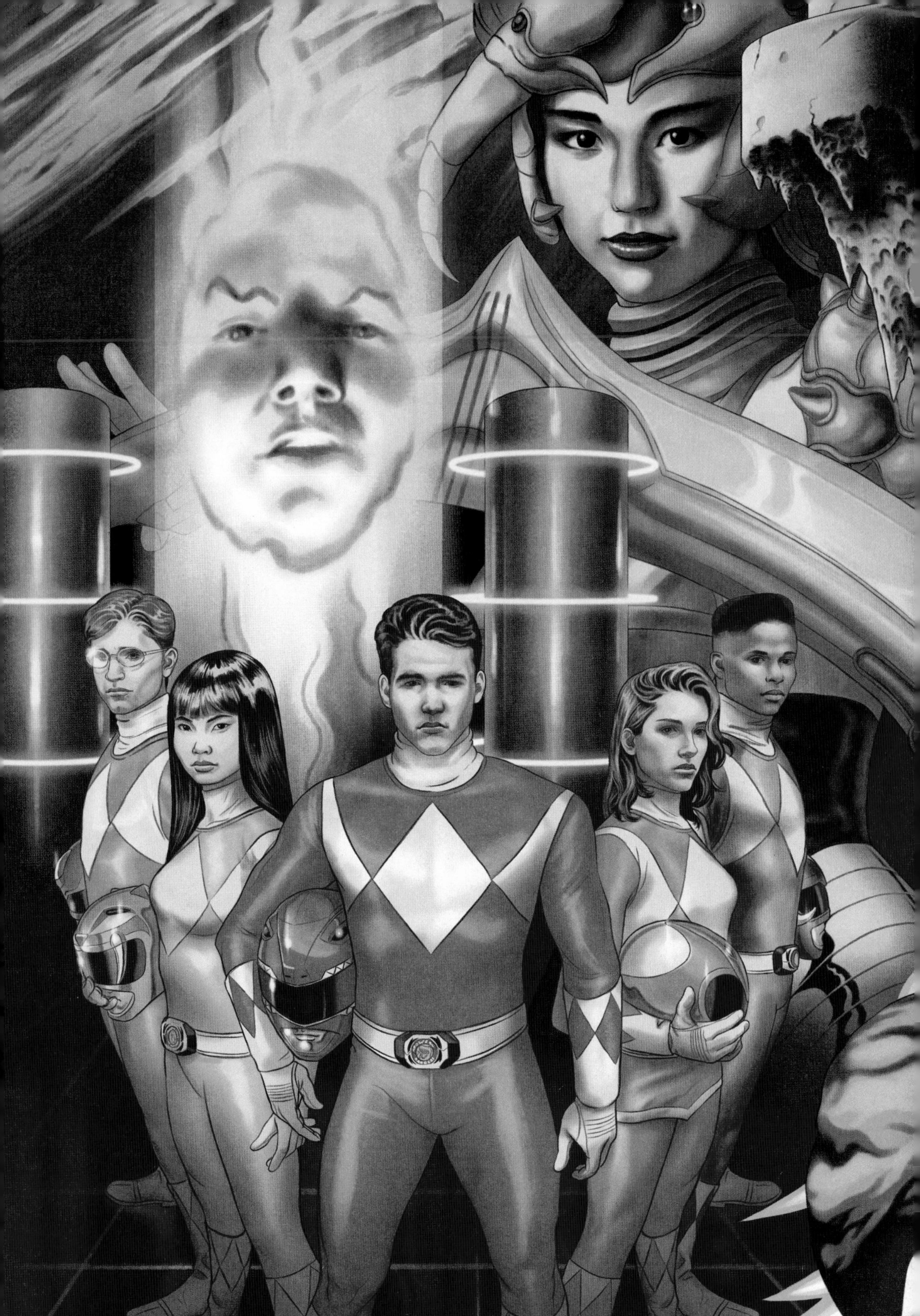

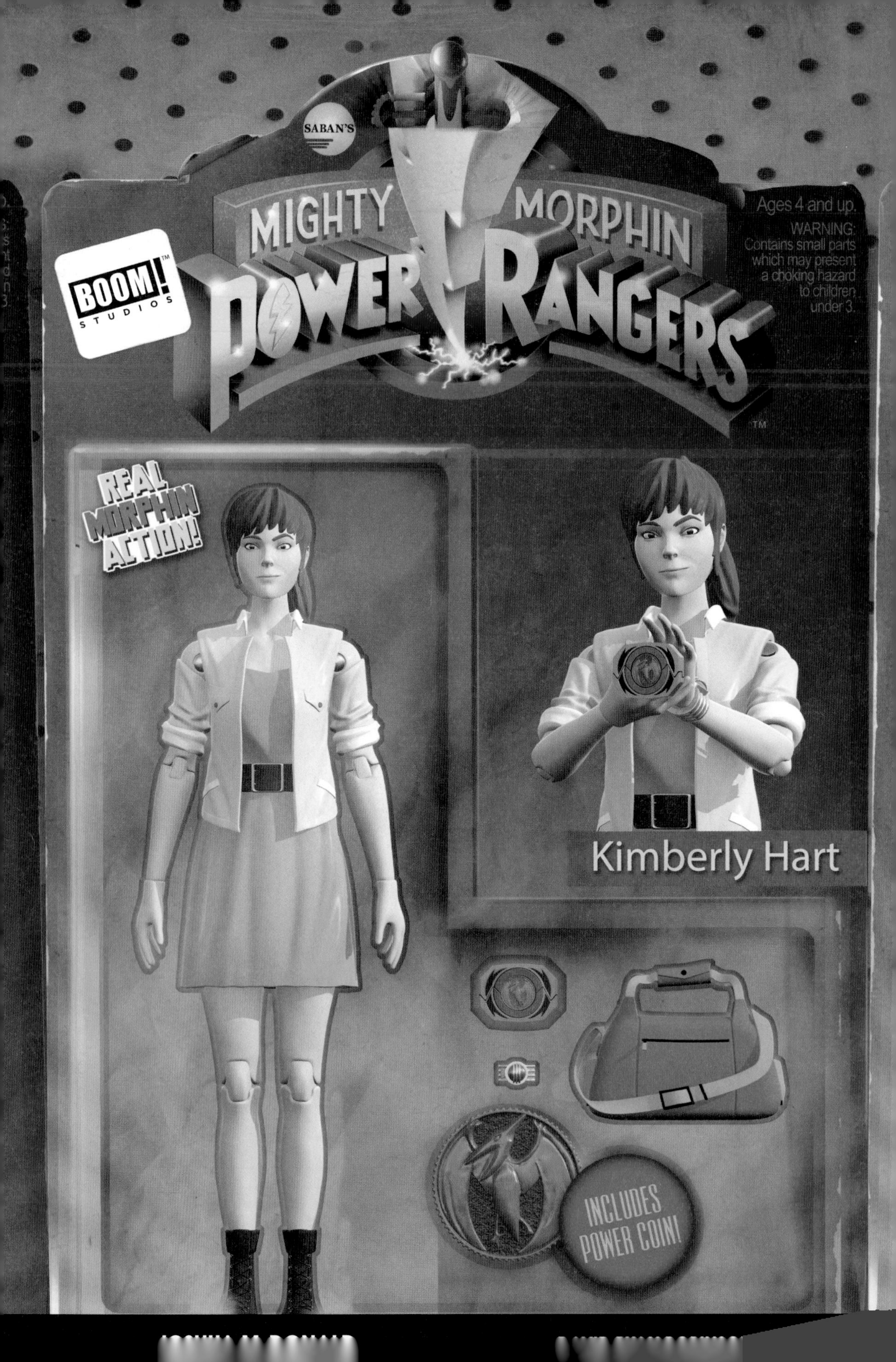
SABAN'S
MIGHTY MORPHIN
POWER RANGERS
TM
BOOM! STUDIOS
Ages 4 and up.
WARNING:
Contains small parts
which may present
a choking hazard
to children
under 3.
REAL MORPHIN ACTION!
Kimberly Hart
INCLUDES POWER COIN!

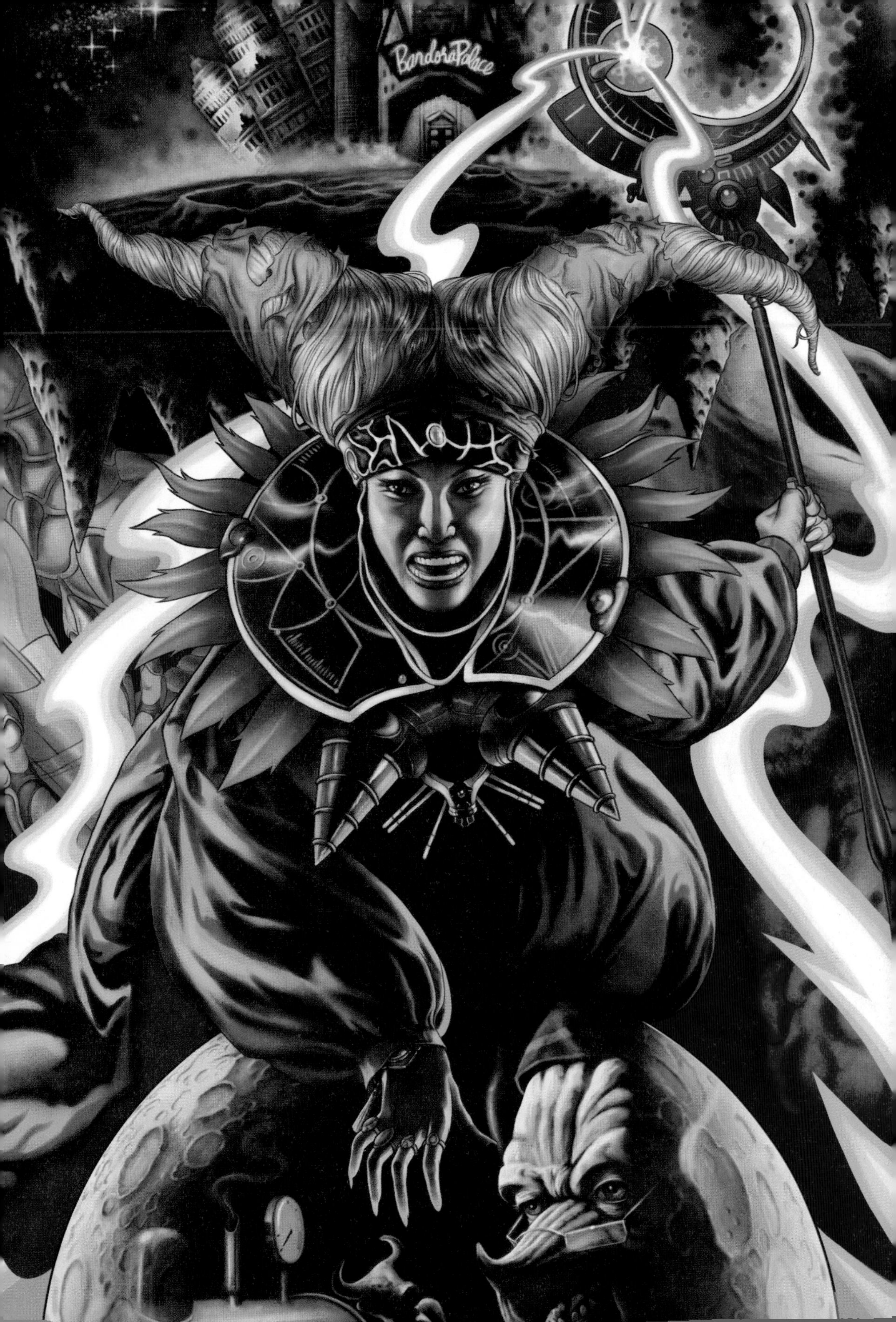
Bandora Palace

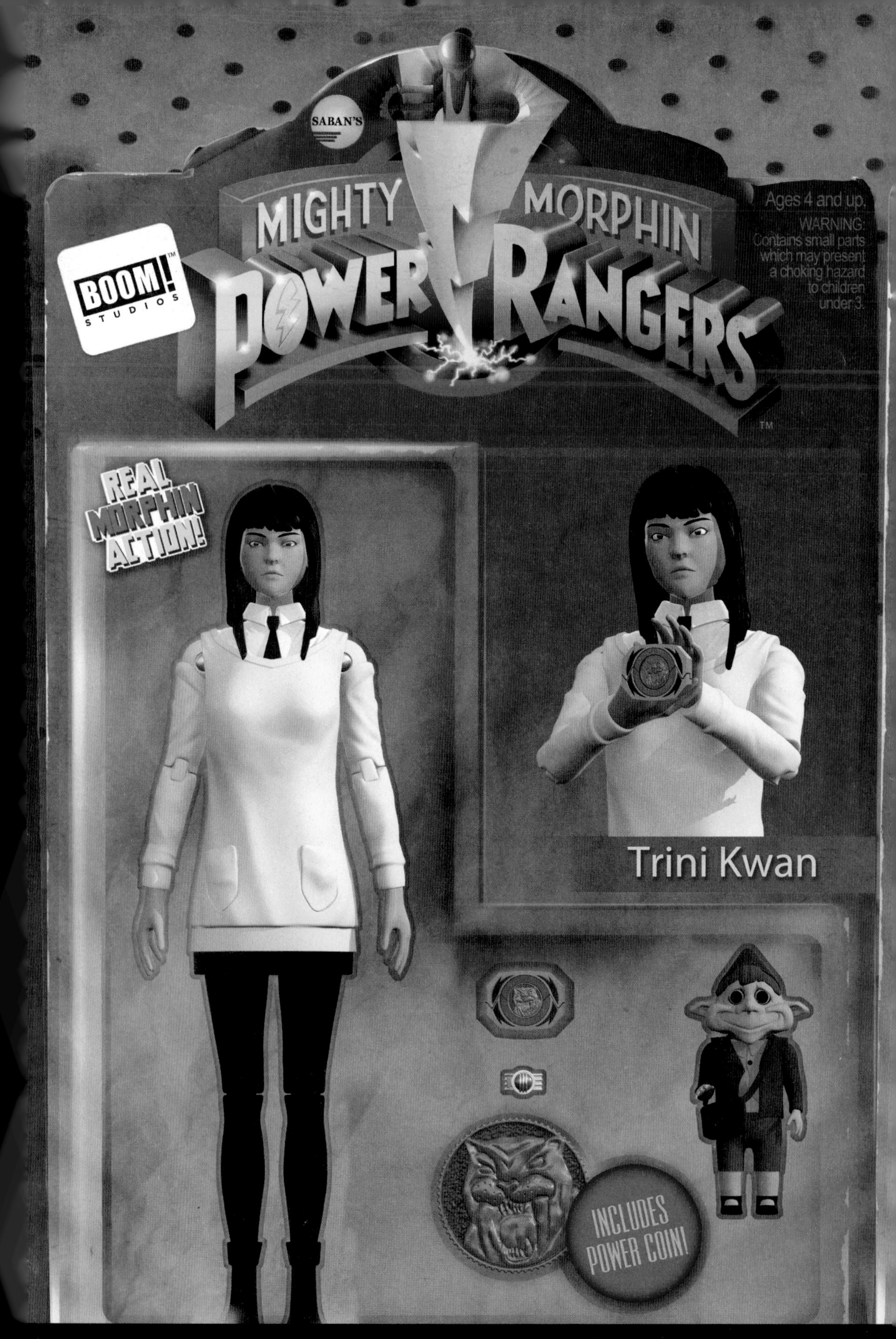
SABAN'S
MIGHTY MORPHIN
POWER RANGERS
TM
BOOM! STUDIOS
Ages 4 and up.
WARNING:
Contains small parts
which may present
a choking hazard
to children
under 3.
REAL MORPHIN ACTION!
Trini Kwan
INCLUDES POWER COIN!

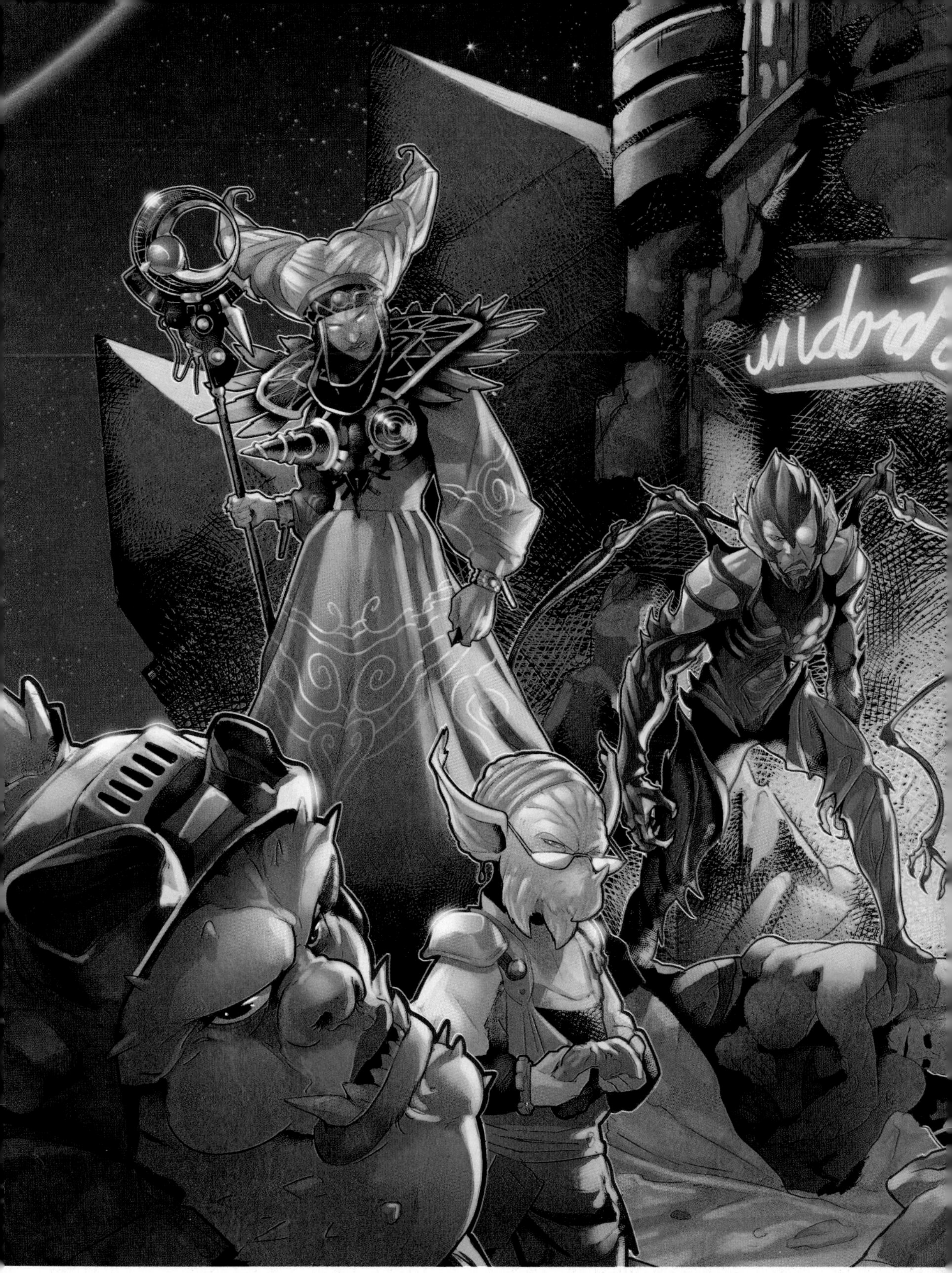

THE STORY CONTINUES IN

VOLUME SIX

DISCOVER
MORE POWER RANGERS!

HIGGINS · PRASETYA · HERMS
ORLANDO · HOWELL · LAWSON
MIGHTY MORPHIN POWER RANGERS
VOLUME ONE

MIGHTY MORPHIN POWER RANGERS
VOLUME TWO

FLETCHER
THOMPSON
HOWARD
DI NICUOLO
STERN
MIGHTY MORPHIN POWER RANGERS
PINK
INTRODUCTION BY AMY JO JOHNSON KIMBERLY HART, THE ORIGINAL PINK RANGER

SABAN'S
POWER RANGERS
AFTERSHOCK
RYAN PARROTT LUCAS WERNECK JOANA LAFUENTE

MIGHTY MORPHIN POWER RANGERS
POSTER BOOK
FEATURING 20 REMOVABLE POSTERS

MIGHTY MORPHIN POWER RANGERS
ADULT COLORING BOOK

Mighty Morphin Power Rangers
Kyle Higgins, Hendry Prasetya, Matt Herms
Volume 1
ISBN: 978-1-60886-893-3 | $19.99
Volume 2
ISBN: 978-1-60886-942-8 | $16.99
Volume 3
ISBN: 978-1-60886-977-0 | $16.99
Volume 4
ISBN: 978-1-68415-031-1 | $16.99

Mighty Morphin Power Rangers: Pink
Kelly Thompson, Brenden Fletcher, Tini Howard, Daniele Di Nicuolo
ISBN: 978-1-60886-952-7 | $19.99

Saban's Power Rangers: Aftershock
Ryan Parrott, Lucas Werneck
ISBN: 978-1-60886-937-4 | $14.99

Mighty Morphin Power Rangers Poster Book
Goñi Montes, Jamal Campbell, Joe Quinones
ISBN: 978-1-60886-966-4 | $19.99

Mighty Morphin Power Rangers Adult Coloring Book
Goni Montes, Jamal Campbell, Hendry Prasetya
ISBN: 978-1-60886-955-8 | $16.99

Mighty Morphin Power Rangers Year One: Deluxe HC
Kyle Higgins, Hendry Prasetya, Steve Orlando
ISBN: 978-1-68415-012-0 | $75.00

BOOM! STUDIOS

AVAILABLE AT YOUR LOCAL COMICS SHOP AND BOOKSTORE
To find a comics shop in your area, call 1-888-266-4226
WWW.**BOOM-STUDIOS**.COM

SABAN Brands

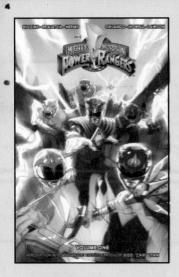

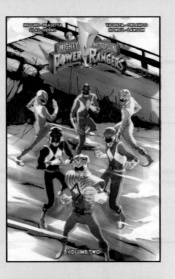

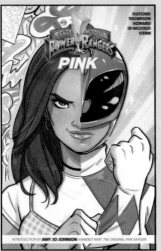

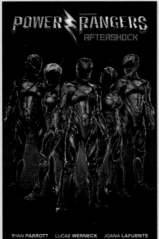

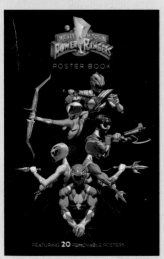

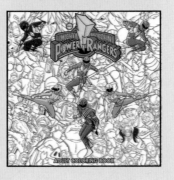

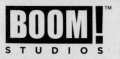

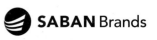